The National Alliance of Black Feminists

WOMEN, GENDER, AND SEXUALITY
IN AMERICAN HISTORY

For a list of books in the series, please see our website at www.press.uillinois.edu.

The National Alliance of Black Feminists

A History

ILEANA NACHESCU

UNIVERSITY OF ILLINOIS PRESS
Urbana, Chicago, and Springfield

This monograph quotes extensively from previously published articles and book chapters.

"'The Kind of World We Wanted to Be In': Protocol Feminism and Participatory Democracy in Intersectional Consciousness-Raising Groups." In *Feeling Democracy: Emotional Politics in the New Millennium*, edited by Arlene Stein and Sarah Tobias, 192–224. New Brunswick, NJ: Rutgers University Press, 2024.

"Censoring Anglogynophobia: Reconsidering the Disappearance of the National Alliance of Black Feminists." *Feminist Studies* 47, no. 1 (2021): 201–29.

"Intersectional Consciousness Raising, Black Women Political Intellectuals, and the National Alliance of Black Feminists." In *"Lifting as We Climb": Black Women Intellectuals in Modern U.S. History*, edited by Hettie V. Williams, 205–25. Santa Barbara, CA: Praeger (an imprint of Bloomsbury Publishing plc), 2017.

Manufactured in the United States of America
1 2 3 4 5 C P 5 4 3 2 1
∞ This book is printed on acid-free paper.

This publication was funded in part by the Office of the Executive Vice President for Academic Affairs at Rutgers University.

Cataloging-in-Publication Data available from the Library of Congress

ISBN 9780252046568 (cloth : alk.)
ISBN 9780252088674 (paper : alk.)
ISBN 9780252047879 (ebook)

Dedicated to Brenda Eichelberger,
Black feminist intellectual and activist

In Memoriam

Contents

Acknowledgments

The first debt of gratitude goes to the former NABF activists whom I interviewed for this project. They shared their memories and insights with me; invited me into their homes or to their favorite public places, thus teaching me their own geography of Chicago; and patiently answered my questions over multiple follow-up conversations, in person and by phone. I am grateful to Dr. Janie Nelson (1935–2023), Dr. Gayle Porter, C. A. Lofton, LaVerne Love, Elnora Washington, Barbara Baker, Helen Whigham, and Beryl Fitzpatrick. They are more than interviewees; they are interlocutors and mentors.

A small army of professionals helped me stay productive during many visits to Chicago-based archives, promptly answering questions and requests and going out of their way to help me in more ways than I can count. I would like to thank Kellee E. Warren and Matthew Clark at the University of Illinois at Chicago archives; Lesley Martin, Katie Levi, Sara Chapman, Angela Hoover, and Natalie Sinclair at the Chicago History Museum; and Elizabeth Loch, Cynthia Fife-Townsel, and the rest of the staff at the Vivian G. Harsh Collections. I very much appreciate the advice and assistance I received from Dr. W. Marvin Dulaney at the African American Museum in Dallas; Dr. Christina Kasman at the Esther Raushenbush Library at Sarah Lawrence College; Mary Ann Johnson, cofounder of the Chicago Women's History Center; and Kayo Denda at Rutgers University Libraries. I would also like to express my gratitude to Estelle Carol, former member of the Chicago Women's Graphics Collective, for licensing one of her posters for use in this book.

I wrote most of this book while working as a part-time lecturer (earning the name of the "highway flyer") at various institutions in New Jersey, without any kind of research or administrative support. This situation changed for the better once I joined the department of Women's, Gender, and Sexuality Studies at Rutgers University in 2018. At various times during the past five years, Kandi Berryman, Nimrah Saeed, Aretha Oliver-Crayton, Monique Gregory-McKinney, and Feronda Orders provided prompt and generous administrative assistance that made research and writing infinitely easier.

At Rutgers University, I was able to receive a benefit recently negotiated by my union: a sabbatical semester that allowed me to complete significant revisions to this manuscript. For that, I would like to thank the Rutgers AAUP–AFT New Brunswick chapter and the Department of Women's, Gender, and Sexuality Studies. More critical support came from the Rutgers University Research Council, which provided a Research Award in 2021–2022 for the completion of the manuscript and a Subvention Award in 2023–2024 for the publication of this book. I also received a Humanities Plus grant in the academic year 2019–2020 that afforded me one final trip to Chicago to consult, one more time, the archives that are so crucial for this project.

My dissertation advisor, Susan Cahn, believed in my scholarly future even during the long years when I was working as an adjunct. Mary Hawkesworth read and commented on an early draft of the entire manuscript, while Brittney Cooper read a near-final version of the book. I am thankful for their encouragements and suggestions. Both before and after finding an academic home, I received thoughtful and supportive feedback from moderators, panelists, and attendees at various conferences where, over the years, I presented different parts of this project. Being in conversation with these scholars enriched my work and nurtured my belief in the importance of this project, at a time when such sustenance was critical: Julie R. Enszer, Agatha Beins, Stephanie Gilmore, Alison Parker, Ashley Farmer (who suggested the term Black humanist feminism in a conversation after one of her talks at Rutgers University), Ula Taylor, Deborah Gray White, and Donna Murch (who gave me a crash course in Black Power history). I am also grateful to Naomi Extra, Victoria Fields, and Tiana Wilson for enlightening and energizing discussions about our research. At Rutgers University, the Institute for Research on Women (IRW), then under the directorship of Arlene Stein and associate directorship of Sarah Tobias, offered me an affiliate scholar position and an intellectually generative milieu through their Seminar in 2017–2018, where parts of this manuscript were discussed. In addition, a fragment was included in the conference program sponsored by IRW in 2020, Feeling Democracy, and in the subsequent edited volume, *Feeling Democracy: Emotional Politics in the New Millennium*.

Over the years, I published parts of this manuscript in various peer-reviewed outlets, whose editors urged me to refine my arguments and think more deeply about the relevance of this research. I am grateful to Hettie V. Williams, editor of *"Lifting as We Climb": Black Women Intellectuals in Modern U.S. History* (Santa Barbara, CA: Praeger, 2017); the editorial collective and anonymous reviewers of *Feminist Studies*; and to Arlene Stein and Sarah Tobias, editors of *Feeling Democracy: Emotional Politics in the New Millennium* (New Brunswick, NJ: Rutgers University Press, 2024).

Dominique Moore, UIP's acquisitions editor, made the manuscript acquisition process feel friendly and supportive. Two anonymous reviewers offered comprehensive suggestions for revision. I would like to thank Reviewer 2, whose aggregated recommendations amounted to a request to rewrite the manuscript. This ended up being a much better book, although all errors are, of course, my responsibility. I am grateful to visual artist and jazz historian Tierney Malone for creating the book cover artwork inspired by the NABF's history.

Family, friends, and writing group partners offered companionship and support over the almost fifteen years spent writing this book: Valeri Drach Weidmann and Jamie Shombert from the Highland Park writing group; Lei Yu, Ana Pairet Viñas, and Selin Bengi Gümrükçü from the Rutgers Transnational Scholar Network; Belinda Davis, a generous interlocutor on any topic from Marxism to writing and cats; and many other writers. My mother, Dorina Năchescu, who lives in Romania, prayed for me and sent me good writing energy every time I felt discouraged or exhausted; her image of me as hardworking, passionate about social change, and naturally gifted at learning foreign languages has energized me over the years. Charles Adair understands that writers and artists need time and resources to dedicate to their projects and did his best to make sure that I had access to both. My niece Andrada reminds me how urgent feminism is for younger women around the world. My brother Voicu and my sister-in-law Ozana read parts of my work and provided a home for me during my visits to Timișoara, Romania, and Barcelona, Spain.

But the utmost appreciation goes to the tireless activist and intellectual powerhouse that was Brenda Eichelberger (1939–2017). I first contacted Brenda Eichelberger almost fifteen years ago, hoping to write an article about intersectional consciousness-raising. As I consulted the archives and learned more about the NABF's rich history, I approached her about writing this book. She and her husband Calvin Holloway (to whom I would like to express my gratitude) welcomed me to their beautiful home in Silver Springs, Maryland. She helped me contact former NABF activists and read chapter drafts before her untimely passing in 2017. A Black feminist leader, activist, writer, theorist, archivist, teacher, and generous interlocutor—she will always be remembered with respect, admiration, and love by the many people who knew her. This book is a tribute to her memory.

The National Alliance of Black Feminists

Introduction

"Did you know . . . that a Black feminist movement is alive and well?" asks the National Alliance of Black Feminists (NABF)[1] in a mailing form sent to its constituents. The Chicago-based NABF, originally a local chapter of the National Black Feminist Organization (NBFO), was active from 1974 to 1983, part of a vibrant Black feminist movement. Under the leadership of Brenda Eichelberger (1937–2017), the NABF became one of the best-known Black women's organizations due to its activism, appearances on radio and television, and articles and essays published in African American and feminist venues. The NABF's 1977 conference, "A Meeting of the Minds," attracted more than two hundred Black women to Chicago. For two days, they discussed their experiences, listened to speakers, and developed a national agenda addressing the most pressing issues of the day. From 1976 to 1982, the NABF independently ran the Black Women's Center, located in downtown Chicago—a meeting place, archive, library, classroom, and job bulletin board. The NABF served numerous women beyond its immediate membership by providing referrals about topics ranging from job training to health care; running a rape crisis hotline, an Alternative School, and a Speaker's Bureau; and, as a multi-issue organization, fighting for a multiplicity of social justice causes concerning Black women, from reproductive rights to prison activism, in Chicago and the Midwest. And yet, the NABF is little known today beyond a small circle of feminist historians.

This erasure appears even more surprising given that NABF activists published a plethora of articles, position papers, doctoral dissertations, and academic publications both at the time of the NABF's existence and in its aftermath. Members of the NABF used consciousness-raising and rap sessions to generate knowledge about their experiences. Based on these sessions, Eichelberger and other NABF members published more than ten articles and essays about Black feminism, sprinkled throughout movement publications and popular magazines throughout the 1970s, but never collected in a volume. Together with organizational documents such as the NABF's platform, titled the Black Woman's Bill of Rights, the long list of resolutions passed at the 1977 "Meeting of the Minds" conference constitute the most comprehensive set of political, economic, and cultural demands collectively devised by African American women to this day.

This monograph excavates the history of a Midwestern Black feminist organization and contributes to the historiography of a vibrant 1970s Black women's liberation movement that was national in scope and continuous throughout the decade. The NABF's history connects the mid-to-late 1970s with the 1980s as years of Black feminist activism; Black women's liberation movement on the East Coast and the West Coast; and 1970s intellectual activism with Black academic feminism of the 1980s.

The 1970s Black women's liberation movement is one of the postwar iterations of Black feminism, whose continuous history started long before the twentieth century. Rooted in the histories and experiences of Black women, Black feminisms work toward a capacious ideal of justice that accounts for, in addition to race and gender, and sometimes embedded in these axes of oppression, class and cis-heteronormativity. Not all Black feminisms at all points in history balanced these axes of analysis perfectly well, nor are they entirely free of certain blind spots and exclusionary practices. After all, Black feminists, as historical actors, responded to circumstances not of their making, developing an affirmative politics out of questions of survival—physical or intellectual, immediate or strategic. Nor is Black feminism only or primarily a reaction to the exclusion and marginalization of Black women in the Black freedom struggle, predominantly white women's movements, or radical, communist, and anti-imperialist politics, although gender critique was foundational to Black women's engagements with these movements and their analytical frameworks. Affirmative of Black women's humanity, Black feminisms promote a political vision of liberation for all. Black feminisms (alongside other women of color feminisms) come closest to a truly comprehensive, and in fact universal, ideal of justice, as only they can say, with Anna Julia Cooper in Kimberle Crenshaw's reading: "when they enter, we all enter."[2]

In its 1970s incarnation, Black feminism has been documented in groundbreaking histories such as Benita Roth's *Separate Roads to Feminism*, Kimberly Springer's *Living for the Revolution*, and Duchess Harris's *Black Feminism from Kennedy to Obama*.[3] These histories have traced the genealogies of 1970s Black and women of color organizations in the

1960s Black freedom struggle; rectified the perception that women of color feminisms were late arrivals to the 1970s feminist scene, in reaction to white women's exclusionary practices; and finally, mapped and documented extensively the multifaceted activism of women of color, Black women especially, throughout the decade. Not all Black women active in the struggle for racial and gender justice embraced the feminist label, and other historians have widened the understanding of Black feminism as including Black women's radical organizing. They have documented extensively the leadership and activism of Black women within radical leftist, Civil Rights, Black Power, and anti-imperialist twentieth-century movements, extending the understanding of postwar Black feminism to include union organizing, electoral politics, and antipoverty activism.[4] The history of the NABF belongs to all these historical streams, as the NABF adamantly and explicitly identified as feminists, and were active, either as an organization or through their members, in all these arenas, thereby contributing directly to welfare rights, socialist, electoral, and anti-prison political activism.

In this monograph, I intentionally use the moniker of the Black women's liberation movement to refer to the iteration of Black feminism from the late 1960s to the early 1980s. The Black women's liberation movement (BWLM) had deep roots in the Civil Rights, Black Power, and anti-imperialist movements. The BWLM used consciousness-raising as an organizing strategy, which they theorized and traced back to the Black freedom struggle, the postwar therapeutic sensibility, and the decentered managerial practices of modern American corporations. The BWLM was profoundly intellectual and fought for (re)discovering Black women's traditions of thought and creative endeavors. It manifested in political activism, literature, arts, and music.[5] It fought for Black women's liberation as part of a larger agenda of racial freedom and liberation for humanity as a whole. The BWLM collaborated with and included other women of color, and was often in dialogue with the predominantly white movement.

The NABF was part of a larger number of Black feminist groups and organizations that were politically active in the BWLM. Among these, the Black Women's Liberation Caucus originated in 1968 in the Student Non-Violent Coordinating Committee, at the same time with emerging women's liberation organizing. It soon decided to open its membership to other women of color and renamed itself as the Third World Women's Alliance, published a newsletter titled *Triple Jeopardy* from 1971 to 1975, and had chapters on both the East and West Coast. In 1973, the Black Women Organized for Action formed in the Bay area, lasting until the middle of the decade.[6] The New York–based NBFO, starting in 1973, ignited the imagination and passion of Black feminists around the country, despite its short life span. It provided the fertile ground that fostered the emergence of the Combahee River Collective, whose visionary Black Feminist Statement remains the most widely read text of 1970s Black feminism,[7] and the NABF, in addition to shorter-lived or less well-documented local chapters whose history remains to be written.

The monograph of the NABF contributes to the history of the BWLM that was national in scope and continuous throughout the decade. A national organization based in Chicago, the NABF had several chapters and affiliates in the Midwest, whose history documents the geographic continuity of 1970s Black feminism nationwide, from the East Coast to the West Coast and from North to South. The NABF chapters and affiliates, the local chapters of its predecessor, the NBFO, and other Black women's groups whose history has been studied cohere in a national Black feminist movement concomitant with, yet independent of, mainstream women's liberation. The BWLM unfolded in cities and towns throughout the United States, where Black women, usually professional or educated, although for the most part coming from working-class backgrounds, met in consciousness-raising groups that discussed both race and gender, organized in their communities, collaborated with other women of color and occasionally white women, and presented a Black feminist point of view at the public debates and events of their time. In many cases, just like white women's groups, Black women's groups were small, and many were short lived. Some left archives, others organized a small number of events before dismantling, and others survive mostly in the memory of their participants. To overcome their spatial isolation, African American women tried to participate whenever possible in Black women's conferences, which occurred throughout the country during the 1970s.

This monograph extends the timeline of the 1970s Black feminist movement into the 1980s. In their foundational work on the Black feminist movement, Roth, Springer, and Harris convincingly refute the thesis of a delayed emergence of Black feminist activism as suggested by Wini Breines and other scholars.[8] The Black women's liberation movement emerged in 1968, simultaneously with the earliest white women's groups. Unlike white women, whose feminist commitments went through periods of abeyance,[9] Black women's struggle for gender justice, which they saw as inherent to racial justice, was continuous throughout the twentieth century.[10] At the other end of the period, Springer approximates the year 1980 as an end of a "formal and contemporary cycle" for the Black feminist movement.[11] In this monograph, I extend this timespan to the year 1983. In the early 1980s, the NABF organized for the passing of the Equal Rights Amendment and wrote a position paper on that topic after Ronald Reagan's electoral victory. Even after losing the space downtown that housed the Black Women's Center, a core group of NABF organizers continued to meet, participate in local events, file grant applications, and imagine ways to continue their work. In 1983, the NABF lost its tax-exempt status (the organization had not filed an end-of-year report the previous year) and was dissolved as a corporation by the state of Illinois. Former members continued working for racial and gender justice individually in their careers and political work, which extend to this day.

Extending the timeline of 1970s feminism until 1983 brings to the forefront another continuity: that between the social activism of Black feminists of the 1970s and the academic Black feminism of the 1980s. Postwar social movements, which mobilized youth and students, were adamant that academe had to reflect the histories, experiences, and perspectives of marginalized groups, be they women, people of color, or sexual minorities, although this process of academic institutionalization was never linear. Intellectual activism was the fertile ground that nourished, intellectually and politically, from a pedagogical and curricular point of view, the academic institutionalization of social justice movements.[12] In the case of Black feminism, the NABF fills this gap between social activism and extra-academic knowledge production[13] of the 1970s and academic Black feminism in the 1980s. The NABF organized community forums in Black communities and, through its Speaker's Bureau, was always ready to provide a Black feminist perspective on any topic or event. They participated in radio and television shows and had their own radio hour on a local station in Chicago. Although the NABF never secured a permanent foothold in academe, its members participated in conferences and answered invitations to lecture at universities, taught college courses on a part-time basis, and organized an Alternative School where they delivered a feminist anti-racist education. In addition, based on consciousness-raising sessions but always in dialogue with the few texts written by Black women that were available at the time, they published articles and position papers that became increasingly scholarly as the decade advanced. All these forms of activism nurtured the project of academic Black feminism throughout the decade, connecting personal experience, social and intellectual activism, knowledge production, and Black academic feminism in multiple, overlapping ways.

The simultaneity of the Black women's liberation movement with the predominantly white women's so-called Second Wave of feminist activism (starting in 1968, ending in 1982 with the failure of the ratification of the Equal Rights Amendment) raises the issue of the relationship between the

Black feminist movement, other women of color feminisms, and mainstream women's liberation. Some Black feminist organizations welcomed women of color among their members, and, of course, individual Black women and other women of color worked within predominantly white organizations. As Roth, Springer, Greene, and many others have argued, most Black feminists preferred to organize independently of white women.

Scholars have documented ways in which these independent groups and organizations built cross-racial coalitions during the movement years. Stephanie Gilmore, Anne Valk, Jennifer Nelson, and Christina Greene have documented coalition activism during the women's liberation movement years by focusing on welfare, housing, antiwar, antirape, women's health, and employment organizing. In Greene's words, these efforts resulted in "fragile bridges across racial, ethnic, class and political divides."[14] These important histories, however, tend to focus on coalition practices with few references to theoretical explorations of coalition work, especially by women of color. Liza Taylor excavates a vision of political-ethical coalition from the study of 1980s feminist writings by women of color such as Bernice Johnson Reagon, the Combahee River Collective, Barbara Smith, Gloria Anzaldúa, and others.[15] Taylor's analysis can be extended to account for the NABF's theoretical and practical coalition work in the 1970s. Coalition, I argue, was at the heart of the NABF's theorization and practice of Black humanist feminism—a term suggested by Ashley Farmer—as their humanist philosophy envisioned the transformation of all human beings. The NABF saw Black men as allies, collaborated often with other local women of color groups such as Mujeres Latinas en Acción, and were always willing to work together with white women. Sometimes coalitions with white women proved fruitful; other times the NABF organizers encountered marginalization and even censorship.

Although part of the same social movement, the vastly divergent histories of Black and white women guaranteed that every organizing practice or historical event would have different meanings. Black feminists engaged critically with feminist consciousness-raising as developed in the women's movement—a practice with roots in the Civil Rights movement and the therapeutic sensibility of the 1960s—to theorize it from an intersectional perspective and adapt it for Black women as well as men. The NABF even adapted consciousness-raising's less political successor, assertiveness training (a behavioral modification practice adapted from psychotherapy) for Black women. Eichelberger, especially, was attuned to the ways in which feminists harnessed psychotherapeutic knowledge for political practice, and used this information in her political organizing. Historians have excavated the roots of the practice of consciousness-raising, which

1970s feminists of all backgrounds used in their organizing, in the therapeutic establishment of the 1960s, and in new management practices such as training groups—decentered structures aimed at cultivating cooperative relationships between employees—yet their studies have centered the experiences of white women.[16] Cellestine Ware, the author of an early history of the women's movement (1970), whose work discusses in detail both the 1960s therapeutic sensibility and the influence of training groups on postwar political organizing,[17] influenced Eichelberger's understanding of consciousness-raising. Rather than seeing psychological discourses as enemies of political organizing, Eichelberger felt that they could be harnessed for Black women's liberation. By documenting Black feminism's engagements with the therapeutic sensibility of the 1970s, this monograph highlights the variety of theoretical orientations within 1970s Black feminism.

Finally, this monograph paints a more complex picture of the contributions of lesbians to the Black feminist movement. While the history of Black lesbian groups such as the Combahee River Collective has been well documented, other groups such as the poetry collective Jemima have received less attention. The NABF struggled with the twin pressures of respectability politics and lesbian baiting (a tactic of invoking the cliché of the "manhating lesbian" to disqualify feminist critiques). The NABF's policy toward its lesbian members was to support them in private while publicly maintaining silence on the topic. Lesbianism was publicly debated at the NABF only in a handful of instances, and while some of the organization's documents state its support for Black women's freedom to enjoy their sexuality, the NABF never developed a critique of heteronormativity. Yet in private, NABF lesbians socialized, participated in consciousness-raising sessions, and were a vibrant part of the organization.

Finally, this monograph of the NABF documents the systematic erasure of 1970s Black feminism, a process that I argue did not originate in movement histories published after the 1970s, but was integral to women's liberation narratives. Whether through marginalization, tokenism, or direct censorship, many 1970s feminists refused to center the voices of women of color and rejected their leadership, solidifying colorblind feminism in the second half of the 1970s. There were numerous exceptions to this rule, especially among socialist women, who fought for better lives for all women and centered race and class in their analysis.[18] As a result, an enduring image of the "feminist" crystallized in the public imagination as a woman fighting for gender equality only, as in Roxane Gay's memorable portrait. (In contrast, the "bad feminist," a woman of color, appears as a corruption of this normative ideal.) Documenting the Black women's liberation movement as a national movement continuous throughout the decade, multi-issue, theoretically diverse, and rooted in Black women's experiences, represents an alternative version of 1970s feminism, more generative and responsive to today's anticolonial and intersectional commitments.

"I was interested in meeting Black women like myself . . . ": African American women in the 1970s

"All I knew was I was interested in meeting Black women like myself," Brenda Eichelberger recalls about her interest in feminism. "I was looking for women who weren't male defined, who didn't seek definitions of themselves through a male."[19] Brenda Daniels Eichelberger (1939–2017) grew up in a Black middle-class family in Washington, DC, and enjoyed a comfortable childhood. She graduated from the University of the District of Columbia in 1963, with a major in English and a minor in Business Education. After living briefly in New York and Iowa, where she followed her first husband, whose name she retained after their divorce, she enrolled in the master's program at Chicago State University and graduated with an MS degree in Guidance and Counseling. At the time of her first contact with the NBFO, she was working in the Chicago public school system.

Eichelberger's claim that she was seeking Black women who did not identify themselves through a male might seem surprising, especially given Black women's historical experience of working outside their homes, being heads of their families, and enjoying sexual independence—demands that the 1970s women's liberation movement was making for white women. In fact, the infamous Moynihan report even blamed Black women's independence for the social and economic woes of their communities, conveniently forgetting that Black women had also been ruthlessly exploited throughout their centuries-long history in the Western hemisphere. We might interpret Eichelberger's claim as resistance to her middle-class upbringing, as African American families of her social class often adopted the values of respectability and heterosexual marriage. Yet her statement goes further than that: by looking for self-definition together with other Black women, she was searching for a collective imagining of a future different from the past. She was looking for a Black feminist community. In 1974, she discovered it: the newly formed National Black Feminist Organization, headquartered in New York. Soon she would become the President of the NBFO's Chicago chapter and, after the NBFO ended, the Executive Director of the National Alliance of Black Feminists, which lasted until 1983.

Eichelberger was very excited to discover the existence of a Black feminist organization because she was already familiar with both the Black freedom struggle and the women's liberation movement. She had worked as a Civil Rights organizer, and she recalls enjoying the feelings of camaraderie and sisterhood with other women. She was an avid reader of *Ms. Magazine* and a member of the National Organization for Women, Chicago Women's Liberation Union, Chicago Legal Action for Women, Coalition of Labor Union Women, and other similar organizations, and had started a Women's Liberation Club at the high school where she worked as a counselor.[20] In these organizations, some led by Black women, she had been exposed to a wide range of ideas about gender, race, and class, in addition to activist practices and organizing strategies. After attending the NBFO's conference in New York in the spring of 1974, she offered to start a chapter in her city, Chicago, thus planting the seed of a future organization, the National Alliance of Black Feminists.

Eichelberger was part of a generation of Black women who, benefitting from the gains of the Civil Rights movement and especially antidiscrimination legislation, attended colleges and universities in unprecedented numbers and, for the first time in history, were able to convey their education into professional careers and middle-class lifestyles. Given school desegregation and affirmative action, by the mid-1970s, the percentage of African American high school graduates who went on to college became almost similar to that of their white counterparts. In the aftermath of the Civil Rights movement, Black women had made tremendous gains in predominantly women's occupations: in 1960, more than 60 percent of all Black women worked in service jobs, out of which nearly 63 percent worked in private households; by 1970, only 42 percent of employed Black women held service positions, the majority, almost two thirds, in non-household settings.[21] African American women's share of employment in white collar jobs increased from 5 percent in 1950 to 21 percent in 1970,[22] a trend that continued in the next decade. At the national level, by 1980, Black women approached parity with white women in terms of wages and concentration in clerical service, although their incomes lagged behind both white and Black men's. However, not all Black women experienced this progress, and its nature was rather contradictory. As the 1970s advanced, poor and working-class women witnessed a gradual diminishing of their prospects, and the gap between middle- and working-class Blacks would continue to expand during the next decade.[23]

Historians refer to "the long 1970s" to underline the fact that many of the decade's landmark events and historical turns had their roots in the 1960s and continued in the early 1980s. Given its longevity, the NABF evolved with the decade, as its organizers responded to circumstances not of their making. The NABF worked in dialogue with leftist social movements such as women's liberation, the Black freedom struggle, gay liberation, and the New Left. Yet the NABF's long existence overlaps with a period when the country gradually turned toward conservativism, moving from upholding Civil Rights to colorblindness, from the belief in government's ability to redress historical harms suffered collectively to individualism, and from expanding the New Deal toward neoliberalism. The NABF's history allows us to read the longer historical trends originating in the 1970s from the perspective of a community of Black feminists who organized, analyzed their personal experiences, debated, researched, wrote articles, and empowered each other to pursue individual careers during and after the women's liberation movement.

The NABF's historical narrative is placed in the historical context of the women's movement, which, by the mid-1970s, had already scored important victories. The most prominent organization, the National Organization for Women, had grown from one hundred and fifty chapters and less than ten thousand members in 1971 to about thirty thousand members in 1973, and almost doubled its membership again by the middle of the decade.[24] Within a year of its founding, by October 1973, *Ms. Magazine* had "a monthly circulation of 350,000 and a renewal rate of 70 percent."[25] In 1973, the Supreme Court had passed its landmark Roe v. Wade decision, ruling that laws restricting a woman's right to abortion prior to viability are unconstitutional. Only two years earlier, Title IX had become law, prohibiting sex discrimination in federally funded education programs. The Equal Rights Amendment seemed to be well on its path to ratification, although Phyllis Schlafly had already launched her career as an ERA opponent by providing commentaries on the Chicago news radio station WBBM, and was about to move on to CBS Morning News.[26]

Activism for lesbian and gay rights continued throughout the decade, after the 1969 Stonewall rebellion and the first gay rights marches starting in the early 1970s. In 1973, the American Psychiatric Association removed homosexuality from its *Diagnostic and Statistical Manual*, and in 1975, the US Civil Service Commission removed its ban on the employment of gays and lesbians. Often, such successes were met with swift resistance from conservative groups. When, in 1977, an ordinance prohibiting discrimination against gays and lesbians passed in Dade County, Florida, religious conservatives led by popular singer Anita Bryant soon organized against it by adding a referendum on the ballot of a special election. Despite activists' intense organizing, the ordinance was overturned. Religious conservatives soon put similar measures on the ballot in Saint Paul, Minnesota; Eugene,

Oregon; and California.[27] However, the organizing efforts to resist these initiatives created a more visible gay and lesbian rights movement. In 1979, more than one hundred thousand people participated in the first March on Washington for Lesbian and Gay Rights, although the movement remained predominantly white, focused on the needs of gay men and occasionally lesbians, and marginalized trans and nonbinary people and people of color.[28]

The 1970s were a period of energetic participation in activism for African Americans. As a direct consequence of the 1965 Voting Rights Act, Black participation in electoral politics increased, energized by the Black freedom struggle, which championed social changes ranging from cultural to economic to political. Their voting power led to a dramatic increase in the number of elected Black office holders—over 6,600 at all levels of government in 1987[29]—with the Democratic Party serving as a vehicle toward securing political power.[30] According to historian Peniel E. Joseph, Black Power "remained a formidable presence during the mid-1970s," featuring "alliances between grassroots activists and politicians, burgeoning of independent black political and cultural institutions, and the flowering of a contemporary black feminism."[31] Black feminists such as Toni Cade, Gwen Patton, Frances Beal, Florynce Kennedy, and Shirley Chisholm had started their political work in the Black Power movement.[32] Radical organizations such as the Black Panthers, despite brutal repression such as the political assassination of Fred Hampton, had active chapters in many major cities. In addition to Oakland, New York, and Chicago, there were chapters in Atlanta, Boston, Dallas, and Washington, DC.[33] Under the leadership of Fred Hampton, Chicago's Black Panther Party (BPP) built an inclusive coalition—the "original" Rainbow coalition—that united poor African Americans living on the South and West Sides of Chicago with socially conscious gangs such as the Young Lords (Puerto Rican), the Young Patriots (Appalachian whites who had recently migrated to the city) and Rising Up Angry (working class youth, mostly white). These groups shared the experience of poverty, substandard living conditions, and police brutality. The idea of a Rainbow coalition spread to other BPP chapters on the West Coast, in Houston, and in New York. After the political assassination of Fred Hampton, the Chicago coalition was instrumental to the election of Harold Washington, the first Black mayor of Chicago, in 1983. After Washington's victory, Reverend Jesse Jackson used the concept and the name in his 1984 and 1988 presidential campaigns.[34] In addition, Black Power ideas influenced the radical activism of Latinos, Asians, and Native Americans, who attempted to emulate them throughout the 1970s and in the process engendered new versions of identity-based activisms:

the Brown Berets, the Young Lords, the Red Guard, the American Indian Movement[35] and others.[36]

White Americans developed several different responses to racial minorities' organizing around their identities. On the one hand, whites appropriated identitarian discourses by appealing to their own ethnic heritage. Italian and Polish Americans, for example, recently included into whiteness, reclaimed their past histories of exclusion from mainstream American society and reconstructed their identities based on nationally specific cultural values.[37] Sociologists have named these identities "optional ethnicities," as unlike African Americans or Native Americans, being Polish or Italian did not result in unwanted consequences for their bearers, who could shift in and out of these identities at will. Yet white privilege did not prevent a group of Italian American faculty at the City University of New York from petitioning that they be considered for affirmative action for hiring and promotion in 1976.[38]

The second white response to Black and ethnic advancement consisted in developing the ideology of colorblindness. Historically, colorblindness appeared at a certain moment in the Black freedom struggle, in Martin Luther King Jr.'s "I Have a Dream" speech, where he stated his belief in the equality of all races, whose members he hoped would one day be judged "not by the color of their skin but by the content of their character." Yet by the mid-1970s, politicians reinterpreted colorblindness and used it as a means used toward dismantling welfare provisions going back to the New Deal era, as historian Justin Gomer argues.[39] Beginning in the mid-1970s and continuing throughout the 1980s, colorblindness coalesced as "a politically expedient 'race-neutral' ideology that cherry picks and coopts language from the civil rights era . . . in order to reinvent and reinforce white supremacy in the post-civil rights era."[40] The ideology of colorblindness evolved during the mid-1970s, at a time when the successes of the Civil Rights movement made explicit displays of racism unacceptable. Whites used the ideology of colorblindness to resist school integration and affirmative action, which were reframed as "forced busing" or attacks on neighborhood schools and, respectively, "forced discrimination" in universities and workplaces.

Beyond appropriating the language of the Civil Rights movement to reverse its accomplishments, colorblindness ideology intersected with neoliberalism, which gained momentum in the 1970s as it seemed to offer an answer to the economic problems of the decade. For the first time after World War II, the United States experienced a period of economic downturns, as inflation caused by Vietnam War spending combined with a dramatic increase in oil prices and a slowing economy created the phenomenon of stagflation, undermining public confidence in the American economy.[41] Of course, these economic woes were not experienced in the same way across race and class lines, as social programs such as the War on Poverty, which had one-tenth of the budget of the Vietnam War, were simply eliminated. In fact, the second half of the decade witnessed dramatic cuts in social services and austerity measures that curtailed and even reverted many of the gains made by African Americans in the aftermath of the Civil Rights movement.[42]

Politically, the nation was in turmoil as well. In 1974, following impeachment hearings that started in May and lasted three months, Richard Nixon became the first US president forced to resign. After being appointed president, Gerald Ford failed to win election, while his successor, Democratic President Jimmy Carter, was unable to win reelection. Loss of faith in government and political processes motivated a turn toward antistatist individualism and a belief in market solutions to all problems, both hallmarks of neoliberalism. Gomer insists that colorblindness played a pivotal role in the neoliberal turn, as between 1974 and 1978 this racial ideology crystallized "in order to handcuff the government's ability to intervene in matters of race." Beginning in the mid-1970s, colorblindness solidified as neoliberalism's racial politics.[43]

The mainstream women's liberation movement embraced colorblindness through their focus on gender politics to the detriment of racial critiques, and thereby aligned itself with the turn toward neoliberalism. Nancy Fraser, in an oft-quoted essay, suggests that "second-wave feminism has unwittingly provided a key ingredient of the new spirit of neoliberalism,"[44] via feminist critiques of the family wage, emphasis on culture to the detriment of economic critique, promoting an antihierarchical and participatory ethos, and envisioning a global, as opposed to a national political project ("sisterhood is global"). It is worth noting that in her article, Fraser refers to "second-wave feminism whole," and "not this or that sociological stratum of women," after which she proceeds to trace the genealogy of this feminism in the New Left—without mentioning the Black freedom struggle. Fraser's "feminism whole" in fact refers strictly to the white stream of the movement. Women of color had few reasons to be critical of the family wage and never lost sight of the economic dimensions of their oppression. In the 1970s, feminists of color in fact resisted the turn toward neoliberalism, yet they were marginalized in the movement, as whiteness remained the norm of feminism despite critiques. While not all segments of the white women's movement embraced colorblindness—socialist feminists, most notably, continued to develop their race and class analysis and to support Black feminists, as the NABF experience shows—colorblind feminism, defined as white women's pursuit of gender justice without questioning race or often even class privilege, remained the dominant orientation throughout the 1970s.

Reading the NABF Archive

The NABF archive includes tens of linear feet of documents and more than a hundred hours of tape recordings, carefully preserved at three different repositories in Chicago: Brenda Eichelberger / National Alliance of Black Feminists Papers, Vivian G. Harsh Research Collection of Afro-American History and Literature, Chicago Public Library; Brenda Eichelberger/ National Alliance of Black Feminists Papers, 1974–1997, Chicago History Museum Research Center; and National Black Feminist Organization collection, Special Collections and University Archives, University of Illinois at Chicago. I read these archives with several commitments. The first one is to name as many participants as possible and document the full extent of the NABF's activism. In this, I am engaged in the process of listing, as named by Brittney Cooper, an antidote to the intellectual erasure of African American women's work.[45] But as Laura Ann Stoler reminds us in her work on colonial archival sites, archives are best conceptualized not as "sites of knowledge retrieval," but as sites of knowledge production. The NABF archive is the result of Eichelberger's efforts; she tirelessly documented Black women's lives and intellectual production, both past and of her time. Eichelberger created archival sources by taping consciousness-raising group sessions, public events, and speaking engagements, a process made possible by the availability of inexpensive means of sound recording in the 1970s. These tapes document the NABF as an intellectual community and as a counter-public sphere. In using these sources, I attempt to map out the coordinates of these conversations and the positionalities of various speakers. Reading the archive created by Eichelberger as a site of intellectual production shows how Black feminists actively created their own narratives about their lives, theorized, shared their insights, and saw themselves as intellectuals and activists at the same time.[46] Lastly, archives of activist organizations are also repositories of social justice dreams that never came to be. The neoliberal turn occurring in the late 1970s and early 1980s made state funding available for nonprofit organizations, while cutting back social services. NABF activists wrote several major grants, which in my reading document the NABF's vision on how to practically implement their social justice goals. However, despite its tremendous expertise, stellar reputation, and rootedness in the local community, the NABF was never able to secure significant funding from such sources.

In addition to archival work, I conducted oral history interviews with nine former NABF members, most of whom occupied leadership positions in the organization. In many cases, I had multiple follow-up phone conversations and in-person meetings with the former NABF activists. I am incredibly grateful to my interviewees, who invited me to their homes and shared their memories with me. The questions I asked in my interviews were open-ended. I asked former members about their experiences with political activism before, during, and after the NABF, the kind of work they did in the NABF, and their memories of the organization, both positive and negative. I also asked to what extent Black feminism influenced their lives and careers. Most initial interviews lasted about an hour. I started by interviewing Brenda Eichelberger, who supported my research by suggesting other former members to contact and encouraging the ones she had stayed in touch with to support this book. I also placed an ad in the *Chicago Defender*, and one former member answered the ad. Another former NABF activist declined to participate in this research.

Oral history interviews with former activists show aspects of the organization that, by their nature, go beyond archived documents. I learned from my interviewees that the NABF provided referrals to Black women who needed assistance, helping them, in the pre-internet time, locate resources and allies. I also paid attention in my interviews to the affective dimension of political work, for the way activists contextualized Black feminism in their own personal circumstances, and for the activists' narratives of their lives before and after their participation in the NABF.

Feminist practitioners of oral history have been critical of the field's original promises to access an unmediated record, as well as of its tendency to privilege gender at the expense of race or class or sexuality.[47] Race, especially, is likely to shape interviewer-interviewee relationships. Even oral interviews where both interviewer and interviewee identify as feminists are produced within existing hierarchies shaped by race and sexuality, nationality, and class.

As a recent immigrant from Eastern Europe (Romania) in a Western settler society, my American identity is best described as the "new immigrant whiteness," in the words of Claudia Sadowski-Smith. Like millions of others, I experienced the shock therapy of neoliberalism applied to Eastern European economies in the 1990s; as a result of these disastrous policies, nowadays one in four Romanians live abroad. While Sadowski-Smith circumscribes her narrative to immigrants from the former Soviet Union, I recognize my experiences in her book, as an immigrant who benefits from white privilege, even though the conditions that helped advance the inclusion of earlier generations of immigrants from my part of the world into middle-class whiteness do not exist anymore: legislation such as the GI Bill or industrial jobs paying a "family wage."[48] Yet, as I argue elsewhere, the fact of our white privilege remains.[49]

I am convinced that the way I am racialized in the United States influenced my communication with NABF activists, who in their long and successful careers have had multiple opportunities to work with white feminists. I would guess that they found feminism and our political commitment as a common ground, that perhaps they muted to a certain extent their critiques of white women in our interactions to make me feel more comfortable. At the same time, given my noticeable position as an immigrant—foreign name, audible accent—it is possible that my interviewees occasionally saw me as an outsider, did their best to educate me, and in the process articulated their own assumptions about Black women's realities.

There are other ways in which my background shapes this narrative of the NABF, and I can easily identify among them my long-term interest in censorship, which I experienced in Romania under the dictatorship of Nicolae Ceaușescu. Censorship, of course, functions differently in a society that prides itself on defending freedom of speech at great lengths. The (re)production of whiteness in women's liberation was the result of censorship, both direct and indirect, of Black women's words—and Black feminists painfully experienced it as such. However, as much as I would like to be self-reflective in my writing, I can accept, together with Edouard Glissant, that "there are places where my identity is obscure to me," and that feeling in solidarity with others means accepting their opacity to me.[50] This is, after all, a project of a situated knowledge, from the perspective of a Romanian American (read white) cis-heterosexual researcher, whose whiteness translates into having a theoretical—as opposed to lived—understanding of Blackness. It is my hope that soon another narrator, differently positioned, will come along and tell a different and perhaps better story about the NABF.

In the first chapter, I revisit the energizing moment of the NBFO's formation, which inspired Black women to form local chapters around the country within weeks. The Chicago NBFO chapter developed an original vision of social change that blended intellectual and social activism by theorizing intersectional consciousness-raising and organizing feminist forums in the Black community. Once the NBFO gradually ended, by mid-1975, Chicago Black feminists decided to form their own national organization, the NABF.

Activists for the NABF collectively created the philosophy of the new organization, blending Black nationalism, humanistic psychology, decolonial thought, and feminist ideas in an original synthesis that I call, in chapter 2, Black humanist feminism. A vanguard philosophy that maintained that the liberation of Black women would mean the liberation of all, Black humanist feminism was strictly rooted in the experiences of African American women, but envisioned coalition work as paramount for liberation. While the NABF did not identify as socialist, class, poverty, and dispossession were implied in the NABF's analysis of race. Faithful to its principles, the NABF sought collaborations across gender and racial lines, worked together with socialist organizations and publications, and engaged in anti-prison activism.

Chapters 3 and 4 explore the geographies of the Black feminist movement in the 1970s. The NABF managed to achieve its ambitious plans due to its headquarters, the Black Women's Center—a meeting space, classroom, library, archive, and open office, among others. As I show in chapter 3, the Center intervened in the gender and racial geography of downtown Chicago (a de facto segregated city). This Black feminist space enacted exclusions of its own and created a financial burden that ended up influencing the NABF's activism, as the organization needed to attract professional Black women to its membership.

In its efforts to create a national movement, the NABF organized a Black women's conference that adopted a comprehensive list of resolutions demanding improvements in all areas of Black women's lives, from health care to cultural representation, which I explore in chapter 4. Although the NABF was regional rather than national in its reach, mapping its affiliates and chapters and adding these groups to already documented NBFO chapters, other local entities, and larger Black women's organizations shows that Black feminism in the 1970s was a national movement, unfolding in all the regions of the United States.

In chapter 5, I interrogate the relationship between the independent Black feminist movement, other women of color groups, and white women, who represented the majority among feminists. The NABF adapted the therapeutic practices used in the women's movement, such as assertiveness training, for Black women. Faithful to its coalition ethos, the NABF attempted to work and publish together with white women, yet in response they experienced tokenism, censorship, and erasure.

Faced with relentless homophobia, the NABF offered its lesbian members private support, but was reluctant to challenge heteronormativity in a public way, as I demonstrate in chapter 6. As more lesbians joined and demanded more visibility, the organization experienced tensions related to sexuality, which affected the NABF's prospects toward the end of the decade. Respectability politics played an outsized role in the lesbian-straight split that affected the NABF.

Although by the 1980s the organization confronted difficulties, NABF activists fought hard to continue their work, as I show in chapter 7. In the aftermath of Ronald Reagan's electoral victory, they self-published a position paper on the Equal Rights Amendment, advocating coalition activism as a path toward ratification. The NABF applied for several state grants. These applications show the NABF's organizing vision in the absence of financial constraints. While the organization fought very hard to continue its work, rising rents and dwindling membership brough it to an end in 1983, although individual members carried on the NABF's insights in their professional and activist lives.

In "Conclusion: Toward a History of the Black Women's Liberation Movement," I argue that the long history of the NABF completes the picture of a Black women's liberation movement that was national in scope and continuous throughout the decade. Black women's liberation manifested and evolved separately from, yet simultaneous with, the predominantly white segment of the women's movement. Beyond challenging the narrative that centers whiteness in histories of the women's liberation movement, *The National Alliance of Black Feminists: A History* shows the theoretical diversity, political creativity, and commitment to coalition work of 1970s Midwestern Black feminists, enriching the lessons that women's liberation history can teach us today.

CHAPTER 1

The Growing Dynamo

Black Women's Liberation

> First of all, allow me to thank you for embracing me into the National Black Feminist Organization, even though the Chicago Chapter is, at this point, but a germ of our imagination. I appreciate the vote of confidence and augur that at our first chapter meeting that germ will sprout and from there . . . why, there's just no harnessing of the growing dynamo.
>
> —Brenda Eichelberger to Margaret Sloan, NBFO President

Introduction

The fragment above is from a letter that Brenda Eichelberger, a school counselor at the William Cullen Bryant Elementary School in Chicago, wrote to Margaret Sloan, president of the National Black Feminist Organization (NBFO). Eichelberger was very excited to join a women's liberation organization created and controlled by Black women. Many others shared her excitement and started ten local chapters around the country in a matter of days after the NBFO became public. They believed that they could use feminist ideas and tactics to uplift their own communities and were convinced that their experiences, interpreted through a feminist lens, could lend more credence to the women's movement. They anticipated resistance to feminist ideas within their own communities—Eichelberger confessed her disappointment whenever she encountered Black women "who miss the whole issue and equate Black feminism with Black male castration"—yet nonetheless were ready to volunteer their time, resources, and energy to build a Black women's liberation movement.[1] While the NBFO lasted less than two years, its impact on the Black women's liberation movement was indelible. The NBFO created a national framework that proved fertile ground for activist groups as different as the NABF (the successor of the Chicago chapter) and the Combahee River Collective (the offshoot of NBFO Boston), in addition to other chapters, to continue their work throughout the decade.

The Chicago chapter had its own identity and organizing philosophy from the very beginning. At the root of this philosophy was intersectional consciousness-raising, an original adaptation by Brenda Eichelberger and other Black feminists. Eichelberger initiated the process of adapting feminist consciousness-raising to Black women's needs in an unpublished paper describing and advocating the process for both Black women and men. Written for a conference of the Association of Black Psychologists, the paper discusses feminist consciousness-raising in the context of the therapeutic culture, history of Black feminism, and with an eye to the liberation of Black communities. Its originality lies in creating guidelines for consciousness-raising specifically for Black women, taking into account their experiences, and just as importantly, in trying to raise the consciousness of Black men. The Chicago NBFO chapter was adamant that Black feminism could transform Black communities, liberating both Black women and men.

Inspired by insights gained during consciousness-raising sessions, the Chicago chapter engaged in intellectual activism in places ranging from universities to Black communities, and promoted a racially conscious alternative to a variety of feminist issues, from rape and sexual assault to labor and political representation. In their local work, they demonstrated the vision of a national organization. The Chicago chapter received an enthusiastic reception, both from white dominated institutions and women's liberation groups, and, most importantly, from Black women themselves. These insights encouraged the group of Black feminists at the core of the Chicago chapter to believe they could create a new national Black women's organization when the NBFO ended.

By sending her letter to Margaret Sloan, Eichelberger was about to start a new chapter in her life, as leader of the Chicago chapter of the NBFO and later founder of the National Alliance of Black Feminists (NABF). Over the next nine years, she would meet hundreds of people, write for national publications, go on television shows, and become recognizable as one of the faces of Black feminism in the Midwest, if not nationally. In her letter, a certain anticipation and intuition of the magnitude of her project is present in the metaphors that describe Black feminism in Chicago as the irrepressible growth of a seed, or as a dynamo, a generator that would be impossible to stop, once started.

Black Women and Feminism in the 1970s

Chicago-based Black feminists started meeting in the summer of 1974. An undated list, probably from 1974, includes nineteen women, out of which eleven are identified as dedicated supporters: LaVerne Bennett, Michele Gautreaux, Carolyn Gioia, Vernita Gray, Carolyn Hall, Linda Johnston, Pamela Miller, Diane Nash, Sharon Page Ritchie, Regina Taylor, and Patricia Yates.[2] Some of the women who joined the Chicago chapter had a background similar to Brenda Eichelberger's, who had worked as an organizer in the Civil Rights movement. Diane Nash was a distinguished Civil Rights organizer who had been among the founding members of the Student Non-Violent Coordinating Committee.[3] Others would continue their activity in other movement arenas, such as Sharon Page Ritchie, who after meeting Margaret Sloan, the president of the NBFO, would move to Boston and become part of the Combahee River Collective, authors of the famous "Black Feminist Statement,"[4] another offshoot of the NBFO. Vernita Gray, already involved with the Chicago gay liberation scene (she had created a hotline for Chicago members of the LGBT community and cofounded the Chicago lesbian publication *Lavender Woman*), would continue her activism in Chicago's lesbian movement.[5] Chicago chapter members were active in multiple organizations and many found ways to continue their social justice work in their careers as well, long after the untimely demise of the NBFO.

Founded in 1973 in New York, the NBFO quickly achieved national fame. Its official history as a national feminist organization is rather brief; however, its local successors continued its efforts for years to come. Officially announced through a press conference in August 1973,[6] the NBFO included among its members luminaries like Shirley Chisholm, Alice Walker, Eleanor Holmes Norton, Florynce Kennedy, Doris Wright, and Margaret Sloan, the organization's first and only president. Other well-known African American women associated with the NBFO were Faith Ringgold, Michele Wallace, and Barbara Smith. The organization was able to mobilize a large audience very early in its life. Four hundred women attended its first conference in New York, on November 30, 1973. By 1974, the NBFO had more than one thousand members on its mailing list,[7] most of them African American women. According to Deborah Gray White, the NBFO, "more than any organization in the century . . . launched a frontal attack on sexism and racism."[8] This attack unfolded nationally and continued throughout the decade. In addition to the impetus to organize, the New York–based NBFO gave Black women around the country the outlines of a Black feminist philosophy, a name that included the word feminist in its title, and the framework of a nonprofit organization. Like other local chapters, the Chicago-based NBFO, under Eichelberger's leadership, easily identified projects that responded to the needs of the local community, and, inspired by NBFO's philosophy, members of the Chicago chapter developed their own Black feminist thought.

The NBFO's Statement of Purpose outlined an ideal of self-determination for Black women:

> It has been hard for Black women to emerge from the myriad of distorted images that have portrayed us as grinning Beulahs, castrating Sapphires, and pancake box Jemimahs. As Black Feminists, we realized the need to establish ourselves as an independent Black Feminist organization. Our above ground presence will lend enormous credibility to the current Women's Liberation Movement, which unfortunately is not seen as the serious political and economic revolutionary force that it is. We will strengthen the current efforts of the Black Liberation struggle in this country by encouraging *all* of the talents and creativities of Black women to emerge, strong and beautiful, not to feel guilty or divisive, and assume positions of leadership and honor in the Black community.[9]

The statement also articulates a liberatory vision: critical of a long history of dehumanization and stereotyping, Black feminists assert that they could now emerge, establishing themselves as independent and visible, "above ground." Instead of being buried by stereotypes that limited them to serving the needs of others, Black women could now assert their talent and creativity as full human beings.

Throughout the country, Black women debated the possibilities of this synergy between the Black freedom movement and feminism, a movement they perceived as predominantly white. On June 19, 1974, at the budding Chicago chapter's first meeting, participants discussed NBFO's goals and strategies and envisioned a wide range of activism in the fields of "employment, health care, sexuality, drug abuse, alcoholism, women prisoners, ex-offenders, childcare, rape, consciousness-raising." A "heated discussion ensued" when the attendants discussed the organization's name, as some feared that the term "feminist" would alienate the Black community and Black men. Others stated that the name was "pro-female," rather than "antimale" and that any name change would signify a break from the national organization. Some participants suggested that the group should in fact be independent of the NBFO, adopt its own name, and work together with Black men.[10]

Other planning meetings held over the summer of 1974 focused on locating an office space and forming committees and task groups, such as consciousness-raising, rape crisis intervention, and education, as the organization planned to offer courses ranging "from auto mechanics and karate to women's history . . . typing, and G.E.D." The new group invited speakers to talk about federal laws prohibiting sex discrimination (Valeska Hinton, Community Relations Specialist for the US Commission for Civil Rights) and rape and crisis intervention (Michele Gautreaux).[11] The women elected temporary officers of the new chapter: Brenda Eichelberger as president, Michele Gautreaux as secretary, and Pat Yates as treasurer; and decided to attend a consciousness-raising workshop held at the Chicago Women's Liberation Union to learn more about the process.[12] At the last meeting, in July 1974, the Steering Committee, composed of LaVerne Bennett, Brenda Eichelberger, Michele Gautreaux, Vernita Gray, Carolyn Hall, Pamela Miller, Diane Nash, Sharon Ritchie, and Patricia Yates, decided to take a break from general meetings until September in order to organize informal consciousness-raising groups and to learn as much as possible about the national office in New York.[13]

Following the guidelines provided by the NBFO New York, the Chicago chapter was highly structured and followed Robert's Rules. Unlike other Second Wave feminist organizations, including the Chicago Women's Liberation Union, which had started as a nonhierarchical organization, the local chapter of the NBFO, as a nonprofit corporation, had members, committees, an elected president, and solved disagreements by a majority vote rather than by consensus.[14] The organization resembled NOW rather than the more egalitarian and oftentimes fleeting women's liberation groups.

Through its multiple chapters located around the country, the NBFO created a network of feminist organizers who often communicated among themselves, supported each other's initiatives, and exchanged ideas about how best to work together. In Chicago, Brenda Eichelberger initiated contacts with other local chapters, hoping to create a "meaningful dialogue with one another."[15] Yet most importantly, the Black feminists from Chicago used consciousness-raising, which they theorized in order to discuss race and class in addition to gender, to identify their local concerns.

Consciousness-Raising and the Intersections of Race and Class

The political and intellectual identity of Black feminism in Chicago was rooted in consciousness-raising. Eichelberger theorized the process in an unpublished conference paper where she adopted consciousness-raising groups, the preferred organizing method of women's liberation, as an intersectional strategy for both African American women and men. Her original understanding of consciousness-raising shaped the activism of the NABF.

The consciousness-raising groups of Second Wave feminism were a highly successful organizing strategy that helped thousands of women interpret their experiences in a political way, search for personal liberation, and often become activists as a result of this process. Dubbed as the "most widespread organizational unit of the [Women's Liberation] movement,"[16] "the heart and soul of the woman's movement,"[17] and "the strength of our movement,"[18] by 1974 consciousness-raising groups, for mostly white women, took place in a variety of settings around the country and helped spread the ideas of women's liberation. They were organized by "many organizations, by women in neighborhoods, churches, places of employment, YWCAs, and clubs."[19] The small groups followed a simple set of rules: only women could participate, who had to speak from experience, maintain confidentiality, and avoid dominating group sessions.[20] Several guidelines circulated in the movement; they included lists of topics for analysis, sets of questions, and potential problems that might arise in the group. With rare exceptions,[21] women's liberation literature was enthusiastic about consciousness-raising. In these texts, white feminists decried the absence of Black women from their groups, but rarely examined the reasons for that absence. Eichelberger avidly collected such guidelines and adapted the process for Black women.

The guidelines generated by women's liberation focused on gendered experiences, did not acknowledge that the participants might enjoy racial privilege, and tended to assume a middle-class background. How could consciousness-raising groups work for women whose lives were shaped not only by sex, but by race and implicitly class as well? Brenda Eichelberger, who was elected president of the Chicago chapter at the third meeting,[22] presented a paper titled "Black Feminism—A New Directive: Consciousness Raising Guidelines for Black Men and Women" at the Association of Black Psychologists National Convention in August 1974. Never published, the paper explores the entanglements of feminist consciousness-raising and 1970s therapeutic culture and reconfigures consciousness-raising groups to simultaneously discuss sexism and racism and to organize together with Black men.[23]

Eichelberger begins her paper by rejecting the myth of the Black matriarchy propagated by Daniel Patrick Moynihan in his infamous 1965 report, which claimed that the key problem preventing African Americans' advancement after the (recent) passing of the Civil Rights Acts lies in the Black family, which had been forced into a "matriarchal structure." Moynihan supported his claim by documenting the large number of Black women heading single-parent households. In a society where patriarchal values are dominant, this family structure, a "tangle of pathology," negatively affects Black people from a social, economic, and political point of view.[24] The report argues that economic and social differences between African Americans and whites could be eliminated by promoting a patriarchal family structure among the former and not by addressing structural obstacles to their advancement. In addition, by portraying Black women as domineering and powerful, the report blamed Black women for circumstances not of their making and stereotyped them as "strong," regardless of their economic position.[25]

Eichelberger strongly reacted by pointing out Black women's dire economic situation. She cited national statistics showing Black women's income as being lower than white women's and Black men's, and less than a third of white men's earnings. Compared with other ethnicities, Black women had the highest percentage of heads of families living in poverty, of women raising children alone, and of working in service occupations. In addition to this dire economic situation, sexism in the Black community adds to the burden experienced by Black women: "There is a *definite* [emphasis in original] problem between Black men and women."[26] Eichelberger quotes other Black women who had expressed their discontent, including Gwen Patton, Abbey Lincoln, Angela Davis, and, finally the NBFO Statement of Purpose.

Eichelberger chooses to define Black feminists rather than feminism in itself: "A Black feminist is autonomous, self-initiating, assertive, independent, and freethinking. Moreover, she is a humanist. Therefore she cannot be, as many suggest, antimale . . . What the feminist is, however, is pro-female. She does not seek definition of herself through a man but realizes she is a person in her own right." Eichelberger is outlining a new model of Black womanhood, and the complex issue of the relationship with Black men, as one of independence and solidarity ("she does not seek definition of herself through a man" and "she cannot be antimale"). By choosing to define Black feminists rather than Black feminism itself, Eichelberger focuses on a process of transformation and liberation rather than a political ideology.

Eichelberger articulates an intersectional analysis by insisting on Black women's independence from both white women and Black men: "Just as Black men can't fully identify with our problems because they don't experience sexism, white women can't fully identify with our problems because they don't experience racism. If we are to disallow Black men admission, we must be consistent and exclude white women in like manner." Free from the white and male gaze, the Black woman could reject demeaning societal expectations and elaborate new understandings of herself, as she "must *divest* [emphasis in original] herself of her role and become a person free to express herself without the bounds of her 'place' as Black and woman."[27] In theorizing Black women's efforts to liberate themselves from the "double bind of sexism and racism" Eichelberger articulates a vision of feminism as a process of transformation of individuals and communities, rooted in the experiences of Black women but reverberating across the whole of society.

Eichelberger carefully differentiates between feminist consciousness-raising groups and encounter groups, at the time very popular among educated middle-class professionals. The two types of groups are comparable in that they involve discussing personal experiences, and that participation in the group can be at times "emotionally heavy." Moreover, both types of groups can help members change their behavior if they wish to do so. Yet the similarities end there, as in the encounter group, the final purpose is adjustment to social conditions, while in consciousness-raising, the direction is "to move away from seeing pain as a personal problem to perceiving the social issue."[28]

To adapt consciousness-raising for Black women, Eichelberger suggests a list of discussion topics derived from Black women's experiences: "Childhood, Job discrimination, Image of the Black family, Mothers, Sexism in education, Fathers, Racism in education, Interracial courtship, Menstruation, Experience in therapy, Sexual experiences, Abortions, Marriage, Lesbians, Politics of the Women's Movement, Politics of the Black Movement, Divorce, Rape, Violence, Soul food, Menopause, Image of the Black woman."[29] For certain topics, Eichelberger provides a series of questions, some of them inspired by women's liberation pamphlets like Jane Freeman and Marge Piercy's "Getting Together: How to Start a Consciousness-Raising Group"[30]: "Childhood: In what ways, if any, was my childhood different from that of my brother's or other boys my age? Was I limited to certain activities because I was a girl? Was I limited to only certain games or activities because I was a girl? Was I considered to be a tomboy? If so, how did my family react? . . . Puberty: What was I told about puberty from my family and friends?"[31] Eichelberger adds several lists of questions for Black women, beginning with the complex issue of relationships between African American women and men:

> Because of today's societal treatment of Black people, do I feel I should support my Black man? Do I feel comfortable with the new Black male

> image in the movies? How does it make me feel as a Black woman? Do I get respect from Black men? Has the image of the Black male made me feel like I should cater to his manhood? Who gives me support as a Black woman? Does the history of Black women reflect the way I view my role in society today? How does the history of the Black man relate to the decisions I have made about my role in society today?

While some of the questions designed by white feminists seemed generic enough for all women, they most likely would have elicited racially specific answers. Eichelberger adds further questions that pinpoint Black women's different experiences and concerns, such as gender roles within the Black community and widespread lack of awareness of Black women's history. Eichelberger invites group members to situate personal experience in a larger cultural and historical context.

Another set of questions explores the women liberation movement's relevance for Black women.

> Do I feel that the Women's Movement thus far has met my needs? To meet the needs of Black women, what suggestions do I have for the Women's Movement? Do I feel the need to belong to an all-Black group within the movement? How effective do I think the separation would be? Do I find that within the Women's Movement there is still racism or is sexism a priority to me?[32]

Rather than rejecting, outright, feminism as a white women's concern, Eichelberger considers it an opportunity to discuss Black women's needs. By bringing up the issue of organizing independently within women's liberation, Eichelberger articulates the need for an African American women's separate space, while inviting Black women to examine possible connections with the movement.

Perhaps Eichelberger's most original contribution consists in attempting to create consciousness-raising groups for Black men, whom she saw as potential allies in Black women's struggles for liberation.[33] Black men's groups, the writer thought, could be modeled after women's groups and thus create a space where Black men could interrogate the assumptions of Black masculinity and engage seriously in a process of reexamining their relationships with women. For men's groups, Eichelberger suggests several topics, such as sports, business, finance, and politics:

> *Sports*. When did I first have an interest in sports? Was I ever as good in athletics as the other guys? Did I ever fantasize myself to be a sports hero? Have I ever felt people would like me and appreciate me more if I excelled in sports? How much time do I spend watching football,

> baseball and other sports events on television? Do I identify with the players on the screen? If so, why?[34]

Given African American men's stereotypical image of physical prowess and athletic ability, the questions weave together starting points for an analysis of racial clichés with insights into the dynamic process through which men acquire their masculinity. Eichelberger considers this discussion of socialization practices only the beginning of a more vulnerable conversation among men that would address rape, the image of the Black woman, the image of the Black man, prostitution, and Black-white relationships. On the issue of rape, for example, after pointing out the worrisome statistic that out of all rape cases, 70 percent were of Black women raped by Black men, she suggests the following questions:

> What is my definition of rape? Have I ever used physical force in order to have sex with a woman? . . . Do I feel that men have the right to rape a woman if they can get away with it? To my knowledge, has my mother, sister, daughter, or other close female family member been raped? Do I feel certain women—such as prostitutes, "loose" women and those I dislike—deserve to be raped?[35]

Eichelberger's uncomfortable questions are meant to encourage men to connect their definitions of rape with their assumptions about gender roles and thus understand rape as an act of power. In addition, by asking men to consider the experiences of women who had been raped, Eichelberger invites them to articulate a critique of male privilege while acknowledging the suffering of rape victims.

Written for a professional audience, Eichelberger's paper invites the Black male psychologists attending the conference to participate in a consciousness-raising exercise of their own, by reflecting upon the following questions:

> Do I dismiss as unimportant the concerns of my female clients, especially in those areas which are peculiar to women, such as: menstruation, rape, pregnancy, abortion, childbirth, miscarriage, menopause? Do I expect my female clients to adjust to "woman's role"? If so, what does woman's role mean to me? Do I feel compelled to flirt with all my female clients, even though I may not feel a physical attraction? Do I tend to perceive the problems of my male clients as being more "mature," more important than my female clients? Do I take a paternalistic posture in my therapy sessions?[36]

These pointed, specific questions are meant to raise the consciousness of Black male therapists regarding their own gendered assumptions and to question the therapeutic establishment's view about gender roles. In her conclusion, Eichelberger recommends that the handful of Black women psychologists present at the conference study feminist psychology and pay particular attention to issues such as rape and health care in order to better serve their Black women clients.

Although never published, Eichelberger's paper belongs to the canon of 1970s Black feminist theory, beginning with Toni Cade's edited anthology *The Black Woman.*[37] Eichelberger's theory of intersectional consciousness-raising groups anticipates arguments about the importance of addressing race, class, and gender in consciousness-raising. A few years later, in 1979, Barbara Smith, Tia Cross, Freada Klein, and Beverly Smith wrote a set of guidelines for anti-racist feminist consciousness-raising. These guidelines were circulated in the movement and included in *But Some of Us Are Brave: Black Women's Studies.*[38] The guidelines weave an examination of women's awareness of race into the discussion of gendered experiences in childhood, adolescence, adulthood, and both heterosexual and same-sex relationships. Yet, unlike the Chicago NBFO's vision of small consciousness-raising groups exclusively for Black women, the guidelines for anti-racist consciousness-raising by Barbara Smith and others were specifically intended for white women who hoped to "unlearn" their racism. Eichelberger theorized consciousness raising as a process for Black women, rather than attempting to teach antiracism to white women. Written in 1974, Eichelberger's theorizing of intersectional consciousness-raising groups makes the connection between early writings collected in Toni Cade's anthology and 1980s anti-racist work.

Indeed, in consciousness-raising groups, when Black women revealed their experiences, the "talk" was "different," as Carol Kleiman writes in an article about the NABF for the *Chicago Tribune* in June 1975. Class and race inflected gender in Black women's experiences as narrated small groups. Black women did not need empowerment to pursue careers; they knew that full-time employment, often in less than desirable jobs, had always been a necessity. The sexual double standard labeled Black women as "promiscuous" far more often than their white counterparts. In housing opportunities, Black women's options were far more limited, and it was known that some stores offered lower credit ceilings for Black women. In terms of self-image, many Black women felt that even within the Black community, light complexions and straight hair counted as more desirable and darker-skinned Black women often felt discriminated against by their own sisters. Other topics discussed referred to the popularity of soul food, the myth of Black matriarchy, and relationships between black men and white women, of which the participants generally disapproved.[39] Black women's groups gave participants a way to name their experiences and analyze how racism and sexism, sometimes together, intertwined in their lives.

For former participants, consciousness-raising group sessions proved transformative. Gayle Porter, former chairperson of the NABF, recalls:

> Some of it was information sharing, not knowing that Black women earned less money than any other group in this country . . . At that time, what you would often hear about was how Black women can always find work but the reality was the work they found was domestic work. And then just the bonding, what did you think and feel when you heard this kind of information, especially if you had sons and brothers or husbands? It was a wonderful time.

In the pre-internet era, basic information about Black women's economic and political status was not readily available, and thus consciousness-raising groups generated knowledge that was often lifesaving for Black women. In small groups, they could reflect on the personal side of various forms of discrimination and build a supportive community:

> Another area that we talked about a lot was appearance. Why is it that Black women spend more on cosmetics than any other group of women? What is that about? We spend more on clothes. We are far more apt to wind up in bankruptcy and 33% of all fur coats were bought by Black women. I don't know if this statistic has changed, but again, this need to try to prove that we are beautiful.[40]

These in-depth conversations about beauty, personal life, and resistance to racism, occurring within an all-Black female group, offered both understanding and support for Black feminists willing to look critically at social norms. The fact that, more than forty years later, Gayle Porter remembers particular conversations held in that group testifies to the long-lasting impact of intersectional consciousness-raising.

Yet the most immediate effect of Black women's consciousness-raising groups was to articulate a collective vision of liberation and a black feminist perspective on various topics. Chicago NBFO organizers seized that energy and immediately started to promote their work as speakers on a variety of issues. Mass media outlets, universities, and women's liberation organizations quickly embraced the opportunity to hear Black feminists.

"The Most Qualified Person to Speak on the Topic of Black Women . . . "

The Chicago chapter of the NBFO soon started recruiting new members, looking for an office, doing consciousness-raising, and corresponding with other feminists from the NBFO's national network. In August 1974, Eichelberger wrote that "so far 65 women have attended our meetings and we have over 200 on our mailing list. Although we have not gone public, we plan to make some press releases soon."[41] Eichelberger and other Black feminists carefully prepared their public presence and wisely use media outlets to generate publicity for their cause. As the end of August approached, they sent letters to various Chicago institutions and national and organizations, such as the American Association of University Women, Illinois Women Political Caucus, National Association of Black Social Workers, and various universities and media outlets, inviting Black women who were "interested in women's liberation" to contact them. "The local chapter is in the process of developing programs which are relevant to Black women's needs and invites all Black women to join them in implementing the programs. Business meetings are held regularly and consciousness-raising sessions are held weekly."[42] Eichelberger's savvy use of media and intellectual activism were instrumental in creating a highly visible Black feminist organization, one that worked "within the system" to address the problems faced by Black women from all walks of life.

A Black feminist group in Chicago meant that Black women were ready to take control of public discourses and define themselves: "The women in our organization feel that the most qualified person to speak on the topic of black women in Africa is an African woman," wrote Brenda Eichelberger in response to an invitation from the Chicago Women's Liberation Union at an International Women's Day program.[43] NBFO Chicago reached out to media outlets, participated in feminist conferences, pressured university officials to provide courses on Black women, and created their own newsletter to reach out to their constituency.

Media outlets, both local and national, gladly offered Black feminists opportunities to spread their message. Within the first few months of its existence, the NBFO had been mentioned in *Essence*, *Ms. Magazine*, *Sepia*, *Encore*, *Off Our Backs*, *Jet*, the Chicago Women's Directory, *The New York Times*, *The New Yorker*, and *Esquire*.[44] The Chicago NBFO was met with similar interest ("We get deluged with speaking engagements," stated the chapter's second newsletter). To answer the constant stream of requests for public speakers, the Chicago NBFO set up a Speaker's Bureau. Members were invited to craft a Black feminist perspective on a wide range of topics, including health care, rape, women prisoners, women drug abusers, welfare reforms, consciousness-raising, sexism in education, self-image and media image, sex work, the relationship of Black feminism to the Black movement and women's movement, and racism and sexism in employment, thus documenting the breadth of the chapter's concerns.[45]

Local media outlets were always glad to cover NBFO events. At the NBFO political forum organized with state, council, and city candidates, with the express purpose of motivating them to address issues of poverty, exploitation, and economic opportunities for Black women, local politicians and the television network WBBM–TV[46] attended, although few voters were present.[47] In addition, Chicago Black feminists were often invited to speak on various radio and television stations. Their mass media appearances during January 1975 included four sessions aired on various radio stations in Chicago (WBBM, WFYR, and WVON—an hour-long live show) and two live appearances on television, on Channel 32.

Aware of the possibilities of media activism, the Chicago NBFO collaborated with other chapters in a nationwide campaign against the TV show *That's My Mama*, broadcast on the television network ABC. The Atlanta chapter of the NBFO, with the support of the Washington, DC, Detroit, and Chicago chapters, led a letter-writing campaign that criticized the show as racist and depicting Black women in stereotypical ways.[48] The campaign resulted in a meeting between activists and the show's producer, which, according to Kimberly Springer, allowed Black feminists a "direct, unprecedented impact on the portrayal of African American women."[49]

Feminist conferences sponsored by universities and professional associations often sought to include a Black feminist perspective. In October 1974, Brenda Eichelberger and Patricia Yates participated in a conference at Sangamon State University, titled "Women's Worlds: Roles and Realities,"[50] and taught a workshop titled "Perspectives on Black Feminism" at a conference titled "Racism, Sexism, and Ageism in Social Work."[51] Chicago Black feminists demanded that universities offer courses on African American women, taught from a Black feminist perspective. When Mary Lenox, African Americanist scholar, who was completing her doctorate in urban education at the University of Massachusetts–Amherst, taught a course in the winter of 1975 at Governors State University,[52] the Chicago chapter encouraged members to enjoy this opportunity to enroll in the class,[53] and insisted that such courses on Black women should become part of the general curriculum.

By 1974, women's studies programs were functioning at 78 institutions, and about two thousand courses were being offered on another five hundred campuses.[54] Chicago Black feminists were convinced that such women's studies courses needed to diversify in terms of race, and in February 1975, the NBFO chapter sponsored an event titled "Collegiate Course on the Black Woman," in which they invited faculty members and administrators from local universities, such as the Illinois Institute of Technology, DePaul University, Northwestern University, Chicago State University, and Northeastern University, to discuss the possibility of offering courses on African American women, although the results of the meeting are not documented in the archives.[55]

With or without institutional support from universities, members of NBFO Chicago used their own expertise in articulating a feminist and anti-racist view of Black women, offered their services as speakers, researchers, and consultants,[56] and planned to develop a resource center and a collection of materials on women in general and Black women in particular.[57] To further this Black feminist educational project, the NBFO chapter planned to create an anthology on Black feminism similar to the one published in 1970 by Toni Cade Bambara, *The Black Woman*, a collection of essays, personal narratives, and poetry by well-known figures such as Nikki Giovanni, Audre Lorde, Alice Walker, Frances Beal, and Verta Mae Grosvenor, in addition to pieces inspired by consciousness-raising sessions, and signed collectively.[58] Ten Chicago Black feminists attended a meeting on April 25, 1975, in order to discuss the possibility of such an anthology, and the meetings continued throughout the year.[59] In June 1975, NBFO members participated in a panel at the Black Writers' Conference.[60] Although the anthology was never published, Brenda Eichelberger and a few other women wrote many articles, position papers, essays, doctoral theses, and books on African American women.

Yet their intellectual activism was not limited to academic institutions. Faithful to their ethos of organizing together with Black men, the Chicago NBFO organized community forums in African American neighborhoods. These forums were among the chapter's most successful events, where prominent members of the local Black community, both men and women, were invited to speak on a panel, after which a "rap session" offered space for the audience to engage with the speakers.

The first such forum, Black Women United, took place in March 1975.[61] The guests were Black women professionals working for state and government institutions, organizers for Black women's civil rights organizations, and other women working for welfare, prison reform, and anti-racist organizations. The panelists were invited to discuss their lives as Black women, an exercise that attendees found exhilarating. "For many women it was the first time they had gotten together to discuss issues which so profoundly affect our lives," reported the chapter's *Newsletter*. "It was such a dynamic session and there was so much feedback that two of the panelists did not have a chance to speak."[62] It was a successful consciousness-raising session, where Black women came together to speak publicly about their experiences from a feminist perspective.

Given the success of the first forum, the NBFO chapter decided to organize another forum, this time including men, focused on African American male/female relationships. While "relationships" were defined widely, the forum announcement made it clear that the particular focus of the event was on heterosexual love relationships.

> The Chicago chapter of the NBFO is very much concerned about building black unity and we are especially concerned about strengthening the ties between black men and women. We feel that any relationship between the black male and the black female (e.g. mother to son, father to daughter, employer to employee, colleague to colleague, friend to friend) can be enhanced, but we are particularly concerned about the black male/female relationship—husband to wife and lover to lover—which seems to be weakening. Thus we make an appeal to all black men and women to make concerted efforts to bridge any schism that may separate.[63]

Intended as open spaces for dialogue, the forums were consciousness-raising sessions for both Black men and women. In focusing on heterosexual relationships between Black men and women, the Chicago NBFO was departing from the ethos of the predominantly white Women's Liberation Movement, which rarely prioritized educating men. However, this heteronormative focus came at the expense of Black lesbians, who ended up being marginalized and erased. If the NBFO's New York chapter, the headquarters of the organization, included lesbians among its founding members,[64] the Chicago chapter, although it numbered Black lesbians among its members, preferred to focus on heterosexual relationships when organizing in the Black community. The Chicago chapter's successor organization, the NABF, would provide more support and recognition for lesbians within the organization, although rarely in a public way.

Unlike regular meetings of Chicago Black feminists, which provided a space for Black women only, this forum allowed African American men to participate both as panelists and as attendees. As Eichelberger recalls, such forums were enthusiastically received: "[The forums] . . . were very popular. Any time we had a forum on that, we had a packed house."[65] In advance of the meeting, on April 13, 1975, conveners LaVerne Bennett and Edwin C. Washington participated in a talk show aired live on radio station WFYR.[66] The forum enlisted the participation of African American men from a variety of institutions, businesses, and political organizations,[67] and was so successful that the organizers felt that it should be followed by future opportunities to allow Black men to reflect more deeply on sex roles in the African American community. As a result of this forum, the Chicago NBFO established a committee for Authentic Black Male / Female Relationships, including LaVerne Bennett and Pamela Miller of the NBFO and Edwin C. Washington of Operation PUSH / Black Men Pushing, who volunteered to develop consciousness-raising guidelines for black men.[68]

Consciousness-raising groups, in addition to building support and gathering knowledge, were meant to engender activism. Based on the early meetings that always doubled as consciousness-raising sessions and the group sessions held over the summer of 1974, two topics of activism emerged: rape and employment. Without hesitation, the Chicago chapter started collaborating with local organizations and creating its own activist projects to address local needs, using a Black feminist lens and an activist approach rooted in the historical experiences of Black women.

Race and Class in Black Feminists Organizing against Rape

At the fourth meeting of the Chicago chapter, Michele Gautreaux gave a detailed report on rape, crisis intervention, and counseling.[69] Members learned that, while the media focused on white women as victims of rape by Black men, from a statistical perspective, such situations were actually rare, as 70 percent of rape victims were Black women.[70] This racialized, sexualized violence against Black women was usually marginalized in public narratives, as the media preferred to reiterate information that confirmed racist tropes of the Black male as rapist and, up until the 1970s, rarely considered Black women's bodily integrity as worthy of defense, despite activism and resistance from the Black community.[71] In response, the NBFO chapter developed a multipronged approach to antirape organizing, focusing on raising members' consciousness, educating law enforcement agencies, and collaborating across racial lines with other women's groups.

The 1970s witnessed a dramatic shift in the way state institutions responded to rape, a response that was shaped by myths about rape in addition to gender and racial stereotypes. According to historian Dawn Rae Flood's study of rape cases in Chicago from the midcentury on, between the mid-1950s and the 1970s, women who reported sexual attacks had to answer questions about their past sexual history, as judicial decisions focused on protecting the rights of the accused and scrutinized the behavior of victimized women.[72] Racial power differences ensured that Black women victims rarely were successful in their search for justice, but the number of cases brought to court gradually increased throughout the 1950s, thus showing that the state saw these cases as potential wins. However, "racial privilege shaped the majority of the successful prosecutions, as African American women almost never appeared in court testifying against white men, and white women testified against black men far more often than they did against white rape defendants."[73] With the advent of the women's movement, activists helped create victim advocacy programs and provided support for the women who chose to come forward with accusations of rape, but judicial procedures became more difficult for victims, as their narrative needed to be corroborated by expert testimony. The creation of the standardized rape kit, for example, was extremely helpful for the victims as it provided evidence to the courts.[74]

The women's movement managed to implement significant changes by offering services to victims outside of the legal system. Medical reforms included providing rape counseling, a female nurse to accompany the patient or victim at all times at medical examinations, or even a victim's advocate, and they were in fact implemented in Chicago hospitals by the 1970s.[75] Yet the medical system did not address Black women's needs in a racially sensitive manner.[76]

The NBFO's Chicago-based Anti-Rape Committee, already active by November 1974, planned to offer services to Black women rape victims. They provided counseling, escorted victims to the police station, the hospital, and the courts, and they trained advocates.[77] Noting that the police often revictimized Black women who tried to file complaints about rape,[78] Chicago Black feminists reached out to the Afro-American Patrolmen's League, the Coalition of Concerned Women in the War on Crime, and other similar groups, and met with State Attorney General Bernard Carey in order to discuss the issue and give him guidelines regarding the treatment of rape victims. Although initially unresponsive to the suggestions provided by Black feminists,[79] the attorney general's office soon invited the organization to participate in an event on the issue, the Citizens' Advisory Panel on Rape.[80] Although the meeting's proceedings have not been documented, the NBFO chapter continued to raise awareness about African American women's rape experiences by reaching out to local citizens.

One such action was the Community Meeting on Rape, organized by the NBFO in collaboration with the Northside Rape Crisis Line and Chicago Legal Action for Women (CLAW) on November 2, 1974, and at an Action Fair Conference at Northwestern University, where the NBFO participated in two antirape workshops. The collaboration with CLAW, of whom Eichelberger was a member, continued through 1975. In addition, the NBFO organized a series of community actions that brought together representatives of law enforcement (the District Commander of the 21st Police District) with feminist organizations such as the Northside Rape Crisis Line, CLAW, Black women's groups such as the League of Black Women, local agencies such as the Hyde Park-Kenwood Community Conference, and the public at large.[81]

Like other women's organizations, the NBFO offered self-defense seminars and rape prevention courses. In April 1975, the Chicago chapter offered such a seminar taught by Taya Sun, a policewoman with nine years' experience in the Preventive Program of the Chicago Police Department.[82]

While the consequences of the Chicago Black feminists' antirape activism are hard to quantify, the year 1975 marked a legal victory that gave many women liberationists and prison activists hope that the tide had turned, and that American society was ready to recognize Black women's rights to their own bodies. That year, Joan Little, a twenty-year old Black woman imprisoned in county jail in Washington, North Carolina, was accused of killing a white officer who was raping her. Given the context of the Civil Rights and women's liberation movements, the story soon acquired national prominence. Movement magazines spread Little's story; Angela Davis wrote an essay about her in *Ms. Magazine*, while Ron Maulana Karenga, a prominent Black Power advocate and the founder of Kwanzaa, expressed his support in *The Black Scholar*. Bernice Johnson Reagon, of the group Sweet Honey in the Rock, wrote a song titled "Joan Little," which became known nationally.[83] The NBFO's Chicago members rallied in solidarity with other chapters around the country, the National Organization for Women, the Southern Poverty Law Center, and a host of other groups, and helped fundraise for Little's defense.[84] These many actors projected an image of Joan Little as Everywoman, in spite of her very specific class and race identity. Because her supporters could identify with her from a variety of perspectives, her defense was able to both turn her case into a national cause and build a large defense fund, which was instrumental in her acquittal.[85] In addition to these national allies, poor Black women from North Carolina rallied to her defense. They formed the organization Concerned Women for Justice and Fairness to Joan Little, which formulated an early critique of what would later be called the "prison industrial system."[86]

The antirape activism of the Chicago chapter deepens the anti-racist dimension that they brought to feminist approaches to rape. Their strategy was multipronged, ranging from working at the institutional level (educating law enforcement agencies) to the movement level (working together with other groups) to educating individual members. In addition to antirape activism, another topic that emerged at the earliest NBFO meetings was Black women's experiences in the workforce. NBFO members attempted several approaches that addressed class differences among African American women and offered help to professional workers, working class Black women, and poor women who needed government support.

Supporting Black Women in the Workforce

Many NBFO Chicago members were college educated or in the process of acquiring their degrees, although most came from working-class backgrounds. They were aware that, although Black women as a group were situated at the bottom of the economic ladder, class differences created different needs. Chicago Black feminists reached out to poor Black women through the NBFO newsletter, which regularly published information about government programs, and through referral services offered by NBFO professionals. In addition, NBFO members educated themselves about employment discrimination and took a public stand for Black professionals, both men and women.

The Chicago chapter reached out to welfare recipients, and provided information about government programs. The January 1975 *Newsletter* offered details of the Work Incentive Program (WIN), a Department of Welfare program that paid for childcare for parents who were working or in training, and offered opportunities to parents looking for employment as well. The same *Newsletter* announced that Sheila Griffie, a member of the NBFO and also of Women's, Inc., provided, through the latter organization, consulting services to professional Black women working in areas such as engineering and business administration and placement services to more than five hundred companies throughout the Midwest.[87] In April that same year, Griffie became Task Force Coordinator for the Chicago chapter.[88] The Chicago Black feminists thus started their referral program, which would later on become a feature of the National Alliance of Black Feminists.

In addition to providing information about employment opportunities, the Chicago NBFO started educating members on filing sex discrimination complaints. Members discussed a report written by Elsie Bradberry of Los Angeles, California, who had charged her employer with sex discrimination regarding her retirement plan,[89] and participated in a series of five workshops on unionism offered by the Coalition of Labor Union Women. The Chicago NBFO may have envisioned a more activist role for itself, hoping to file lawsuits on behalf of individual members; for example, they were planning to sue downtown businesses that hired white women and systematically excluded Black women.[90] However, the organization simply did not have the necessary resources, both financial and professional, to achieve that.

The NBFO Chicago chapter could nevertheless publicly support African American professionals, both men and women. In January 1975, members started a letter-writing campaign in support of Edwina Moore, the only Black female anchor in the larger Chicago metro area, who had been demoted to street reporter the previous year.[91] In April 1975, the NBFO *Newsletter* encouraged members to fundraise and send letters in support of Kenneth Edelin, the first Black obstetrician to serve as chief resident at Boston Hospital, who in February of the same year had been convicted of manslaughter for performing a legal abortion.[92] Like many of Edelin's supporters around the country, the NBFO felt that he had been unfairly targeted, especially given that the Supreme Court decision to legalize abortion, on January 22, 1973, was very recent. Edelin had been sentenced to a year's probation; in 1976, the Massachusetts Supreme Court overturned his conviction.[93]

NBFO Chicago established itself as willing to address any issues faced by their constituents, regardless of class. Black feminists were adamant that their movement had to serve poor and working-class Black women, and constantly looked for ways of serving this constituency. The organization grew very fast in its first year, attracting both new members and the attention of mass media institutions. However, financial resources often lagged behind the NBFO chapter's increased visibility and diversified activism.

Mobilizing Black Women

While the interest in Black feminism grew exponentially, evoking the image of the growing dynamo that Eichelberger had used in her letter from April 1974, the organization's resources developed at a much slower pace. Initially, member dues were on a sliding scale (one particular member set hers at $23),[94] then set at $5 annually in January 1975. The adoption of a membership fee did not occur without disagreement among members. In a letter to Jane Galvin-Lewis, president of the Atlanta NBFO chapter, Eichelberger complained: "Jane, it was not until January that I finally had to put my foot down and insist that women pay the astronomical sum of $5 annually in order to have official NBFO membership. Can you believe, I was met with great criticism after I had been—and still am—subsidizing the organization for months!"[95] Like other Black women's organizations, where one woman's efforts were crucial for the organization's survival, Eichelberger's labor and contributions were crucial for the organization's growth. In another letter to Galvin-Lewis, Eichelberger complains: "It takes money for NBFO or any organization to be viable. I have poured over $1,000 of my own funds into the Chicago chapter to help build it . . . Founders such as A. LaVerne Bennett and Michele Gautreaux periodically donate money to help get Chicago NBFO out of the red."[96]

Inspired by Eichelberger, other Black women professionals, who could afford to donate money to the organization, joined in her efforts. The newsletter mentioned larger donations, such as $50 from LaVerne Bennett, and smaller ones of $5. "Heaven knows we need all the money we can get," stated the newsletter from January 1975, and then continued, "We are in the red." In fact, steering committee members had to cover the monthly expenses, such as postage ($40), telephone ($50), stationery, post office box rental, incorporation fee, and transportation and parking ($40). Potential members were also invited to donate their resources and expertise. A registration form from 1974 inquires about access to office equipment for xeroxing, typing, or mimeographing; bookkeeping, clerical, or other skills; an office or home that could be used for fundraising; and areas of expertise, from public speaking and fundraising to writing and photography. These questions further the sense that the Chicago NBFO assumed and perhaps even looked for a professional, educated, or upwardly mobile membership.

Although initially the Chicago NBFO mailed announcements to anybody who requested information about the NABF, the steering committee decided to send just one informational package to potential members, followed by a request to pay the membership fee.[97] The $5 yearly membership fee was an obstacle for poor women who wanted to join the NBFO, and the Steering Committee's decision not to send any announcements to nonmembers probably prevented poor Black women from finding out about events organized by NBFO, especially at a time when the chapter did not have a stable headquarters. Chicago Black feminists found a compromise by organizing open meetings where everyone could participate, regardless of membership status, but full membership and thus access to decision-making power remained elusive for poor Black women.

While in the mid-1970s, African American women still represented the lowest paid category compared to both white women and Black men (they earned 55.6% of white men's median income, while white women and Black men earned 58.9% and 74.5%, respectively),[98] a small number of Chicago Black feminists did the arduous work of starting a new organization. They had to make pragmatic decisions about how to balance efforts directed at growing the organization with attempts to help as many women as possible.

Within less than a year after Eichelberger's first letter to Margaret Sloan, the Chicago chapter was busy doing consciousness-raising, organizing against rape, doing prison activism, supporting Black professionals, distributing a newsletter, speaking out in the media and at various venues, and organizing community forums. However, while maintaining a busy public agenda, the Chicago chapter encountered its own share of conflict. As a result of these tense circumstances—by no means rare in the women's movement—a new organization was born.

The Beginning of a New Organization

While the membership of the Chicago chapter was growing, NBFO's headquarters in New York was struggling to overcome a series of crises that shortened the organization's life. The first crisis occurred in July 1974, when Margaret Sloan, NBFO's president, resigned and was replaced by Jane Galvin-Lewis as a coordinator, a change that was not communicated to the local chapters until later.[99] In the fall of 1974, the national office held elections for the Coordinating Council, whose new members (Elizabeth Bell, Dorothy King, Diane Lacey, Jane Galvin-Lewis, Doreen McGill, Deborah Singletary, and Inez Turner) sent out information to the local chapters. NBFO members around the country received the financial statement for 1973 and a list of organizational goals, activities, and committees, proposed ways to improve communication with the general membership, and the appointment of a Secretary and a Treasurer.[100] Yet the local chapters did not receive the NBFO's bylaws and constitution, documents they needed to adopt in order to become full-fledged chapters, and their attempts to contact the headquarters often went unanswered.[101] In April 1975, the National Black Feminist Organization held a conference in Detroit, Michigan, which was attended by representatives of the NBFO from places such as Houston, Kansas City, Philadelphia, Detroit, Chicago, Los Angeles, Oakland, Cleveland, and Boston. "It was a beautiful experience to meet black women from all over the country with such a high feminist consciousness," stated the Chicago NBFO newsletter.[102] The New York–based NBFO did not survive very long after the conference, and NBFO members found out about the organization's demise only years later and in an indirect fashion.[103]

In the meantime, the Chicago chapter itself suffered from factionalism and infighting. A group of Black women—who, according to Eichelberger's correspondence with Jane Galvin-Lewis, were neither founding members of the chapter nor elected officials—mailed a letter to the members calling for a general meeting, started collecting membership dues, and overall alienated potential members through "repeated attempts at sabotage."[104] Ten days later, Eichelberger ended another letter to Galvin-Lewis on a positive note, expressing her hope that both the troubles of the Chicago chapter and the crisis of the national New York–based headquarters would end soon: "Hopefully, the Chicago chapter will not have internal problems of this magnitude and I hope the same holds for the National Office and the other chapters."[105] However, it seems that the disagreements continued, which prompted Eichelberger to find a permanent solution to the local and national crisis by starting a new organization. In a letter dated September 10, 1975, written on NBFO letterhead, but with the underlined title of the National Alliance of Black Feminists, Eichelberger announced a new "national organization which will be headquartered in Illinois," which had recently received nonprofit status.[106]

If, during the summer of 1975, there were conflicts among Chicago chapter members, who, in addition, lacked information about the NBFO's New York–based headquarters and plans, this was not apparent to the general public. Florynce Kennedy appeared as a guest on the *Phil Donahue Show* on June 5, 1975, and, in response to the show, a wave of letters from viewers started arriving at the Chicago chapter. In these letters, viewers expressed their delight in hearing a Black feminist point of view presented on national television, and often stated their wish to create or join a local chapter. "I just finished watching Florynce Kennedy," wrote a student at the University of Michigan. "She was fantastic!"[107] "If there's any organization worth knowing about, I feel yours is the one," wrote a viewer from Highland Park, Michigan.[108] Cynthia Wilson from Detroit, Michigan, expressed her desire to join a "constructive organization that deals with oppressive sexual practices" and start a chapter in Detroit.[109]

The television show appealed to Black women of various ages and social statuses, from teenagers to middle-aged women. "I feel that as an 18-year-old Black woman I should be finding out what other sisters are doing all over the U.S.," wrote a viewer from Detroit, who declared herself "overwhelmed."[110] A fifteen-year-old Black woman wrote that "although I am very young, I have seen, heard, and felt discrimination, and I am able to deal with it fairly."[111] Another letter writer, who contacted the Chicago chapter before the TV show, mentioned that she had six children, aged seventeen to ten, and stated: "I am hoping to get in the movement, to see if I can find myself."[112]

Some of the Black women who wrote letters to the NBFO were already participating, or at least were familiar with the women's movement, yet felt dissatisfied with its lack of diversity; others wanted to start Black women's groups on their own. "Being a Black woman in white America's society . . . I would like to become active in some organization I could identify with,"[113] wrote Barbara McCants from Port Huron, Michigan. A history major at Indiana University wrote that she had tried to join the women's movement, but was disappointed to discover its lack of diversity: "I am a member of the Lake County women's group and believe it or not I was one of two black women in the organization."[114] Some writers from Wilmington, Ohio, requested materials about how to start their own consciousness-raising group.[115]

While many letters were brief and expressed the writers' support for or wish to learn more about the organization, others were longer, more intimate, and explored the writers' personal feelings. "My feminism suddenly thrust itself on the scene," wrote Diana Pughsley, a senior at Denison University in Granville, Ohio. "It's just things I feel, emotions I would like to express, but find it hard to totally relate it to the white sisters in the struggle. I went through periods of being afraid that my feelings were nothing but latent lesbian feelings." The writer rejects conflating feminism with latent lesbianism, a view that was often expressed at the time by critics of the movement, and chooses to assume her feelings and look instead for other women with similar interests:

> I realize now that the feelings I have (that of the mere fact that I should be able to do what I feel I am capable of doing and not doing what is expected of me due to the "peculiarities of womanhood") are my own and have been within me for as long as I can remember. Anyway, I would like to now hear how other Black women feel towards liberation so I don't feel like I'm alone or wrong to have these feelings.[116]

This writer echoes the same feelings Eichelberger expressed in her first letter to Sloan, her amazement at the discovery of others who were passionate about feminism. Other writers shared Pughsley's belief that Black feminism would help her find empowerment and autonomy. From Detroit, Michigan, another woman expressed her wish to become a member of the NBFO "because it is a growing concern and offers a lot of fulfillment for an individual."[117] For reasons ranging from the deeply personal to the heartfelt political, Black women around the country were ready to answer the call of a Black feminist movement.

Conclusion

The NBFO's impact on the women's liberation movement and especially Black women's liberation is indelible. The NBFO encouraged African American women to organize as feminists, created a national network, and made evident Black women's desire to participate in women's liberation on their own terms. Over the following years, although many of the local chapters would dismantle, Black feminists would find ways to start new groups, join bigger organizations as affiliates, and attend national and regional Black women's conferences. Local NBFO chapters had endless opportunities to shape their local activism in ways that responded to local needs and their own understandings of Black feminism. The NBFO provided fertile ground for the emergence of entities as different as the Combahee River Collective (radical, collective, anti-imperialist) and the National Alliance of Black Feminists (committed to working within the system, hierarchical, and in dialogue with Black nationalism).

The NBFO gave Eichelberger and a group of other Chicago-based Black feminists the impetus to start a local organization, the general outlines of a philosophy, and a nationally recognized name that included the words "Black" and "feminist." They would reappear in the name of the new organization created in Chicago, the National Alliance of Black Feminists (NABF).[118] Most importantly, the NBFO's legacy included the vision of a national Black women's liberation movement, which the NABF would continue to develop.

The NABF built on the NBFO's foundation by elaborating their own philosophy, Black humanist feminism, and creating a feminist practice derived from its principles. The NABF's version of humanism included demands for economic justice, given that social class represented a key dimension of their racial analysis. In addition, NABF members were active in leftist organizations, and socialist publications were eager to learn from the perspectives of Black feminists. Lastly, the NABF's vision for social justice was capacious enough to include prison activism alongside their work on behalf of poor and working-class Black women. Black humanist feminism was the NABF's original synthesis situated at the intersection of Black nationalism, decolonial thought, humanistic psychology, and the historical experience of Black women.

CHAPTER 2

The Theory and Practice of Black Humanist Feminism

> Our organizing principle is feminism which we view as a dimension of humanism. We are pro Black women, yet anti no one. Therefore, we are willing to work with any person or group of persons dedicated to the establishment of a more humane world. In such a world certain rights are basic to the development of all people. As Black women in a hostile world we therefore feel compelled to establish the following Bill of Rights.
>
> —NABF, "The Black Woman's Bill of Rights"

Introduction

The NABF's motto, printed on all of its documents, briefly states the basis for the organization's philosophy: "Where feminism is a dimension of humanism . . . " The use of the adverb "where" allows us to interpret the NABF as a communal intellectual space, a physical location, and a point of view. In this space, Black feminism affirms the value of all human beings and works to liberate all who are oppressed. The motto sits right under the organization's logo, a drawing of two hands in the process of breaking a rope that used to tie them together. "Racism," reads the rope fragment on the left side; "sexism," the one on the right. Together, the drawing and the motto appear on all the organization's mailing items, publicity materials, flyers, posters, and brochures, and are as defining for the NABF's identity as the Black Women's Center address, always printed in the visual vicinity of the logo. The NABF understood Black women as the agents of their own liberation and in the middle of a process of transformation, of freeing themselves from the twin chains of racism and sexism. Following the NABF's own documents and historian Ashley Farmer's suggestion, I call its philosophy Black humanist feminism.

A political doctrine rooted in the experiences of Black women, Black humanist feminism emerges from an intersectional analysis that accounts for gender, race, and class. It is a specific form of vanguard feminism—in Benita Roth's words, the belief that the liberation of women on the bottom of society would lead to the liberation of all. A capacious philosophy that can accommodate multiple points of view and theoretical frameworks, Black humanist feminism sees Black women as primary agents of their own liberation, yet it posits coalition as a core organizing strategy, while maintaining political control for Black women. Black humanist feminism envisions intersectional consciousness-raising as the primary vehicle for gathering knowledge, community building, organizing, and upholding Black women's position at the center of the Black feminist discourse. By emphasizing unity and similarity of experience due to gender and race, Black humanist feminism tends to minimize possible fracture lines across other axes of identity, such as sexuality. Given Black women's experiences of dispossession, class is deeply intertwined with the Black humanist feminist analysis of race. In the way it derives collective politics out of Black women's experiences, Black humanist feminism is rooted in two intellectual traditions, Black nationalism and humanist thought.

As philosopher Tommie Shelby defines it, Black nationalism, one of the oldest and most generative traditions in American political philosophy, advocates for "Black self-determination, racial solidarity and group self-reliance, various forms of voluntary racial separation, pride in the historic achievements of those of African descent, a concerted effort to overcome racial self-hate and to instill Black self-love, militant resistance to anti-Black racism, and the recognition of Africa as the true homeland of those who are racially Black."[1] He differentiates between two types of nationalism: strong, or classical Black nationalism, and weak, or pragmatic. Strong nationalism might aim to establish an independent state or a national identity and considers separatism and Black self-reliance not only as paths toward social justice, but as the "political destiny" of African Americans. In contrast, weak, or pragmatic nationalism, "urges Black solidarity and concerted action as a political strategy to lift or resist oppression." Pragmatic nationalism's final goals can range from forming separate communities, including nation-states, to racial integration or even the emergence of a post-racial world.[2] The NABF, of course, belongs to the pragmatic Black nationalist tradition.

From the perspective of gender politics, historians have explored the complex relationships between Black feminism and Black nationalism. Deborah Gray White and Benita Roth emphasize the feminist critique of

Black nationalism's emphasis on masculinity and traditional gender roles for women. Other scholars have envisioned Black feminism as emerging in dialogue with Black nationalist ideas, adopting some and rejecting others, but influenced by it nonetheless. E. Frances White examines the potential of Black nationalism for feminist liberation, seeing it as "an oppositional strategy that both counters racism and constructs conservative utopian images of African American life"; she further suggests that it is possible to create a "black feminist discourse that attempts to combine nationalist and feminist insights in a way that counters racism but tries to avoid [nationalism's] sexist pitfalls."[3]

Another major influence on the NABF's political philosophy, humanism had historically emerged during the Renaissance and Enlightenment, about the same time as the global slave trade was being established, and promoted a vision of liberation limited to white European males, while excluding women and nonwestern people. Yet the basic tenets of humanism—in Erich Fromm's formulation, "the belief in the unity of human race and man's potential to perfect himself by his own efforts"—widely circulated in the 1970s, in various manifestations including humanistic psychology, postcolonial Black humanism, and the more academic socialist humanism.

The Black Woman's Bill of Rights articulated Black humanist feminism in the most direct and elaborate way, yet activists elaborated on their philosophy in other position papers, organizational documents, essays, and articles. The result of a collective process, a synthesis of a variety of points of view, the Black Woman's Bill of Rights promotes a comprehensive philosophy of liberation and a political agenda that the NABF worked to achieve through its organizing work.

Both Black nationalism and humanism converged in the NABF's coalition politics. Black nationalism's influence on NABF coalition philosophy and work translated into the organization's commitment to working together with Black men. As a humanist revolution would liberate everybody, the NABF was willing to work with other women of color, white women and men, and Black men, and offered them affiliate membership in the organization, thus allowing allies to contribute to the struggle, yet maintaining Black women's control of these spaces. Just as importantly, through its practice of offering honorary memberships to Black women organizers whose work was already known in the Black community, the NABF placed itself in a tradition of Black women's political work and united different generations of activists under the banner of Black feminism.

Black Feminism's Dialogues with Black Nationalism

It is difficult to overestimate the impact of the Black Power movement as an intellectual and political influence on the social movements of the 1970s.[4] Its relationship with Black nationalism was a complex one. As Jeffrey Ogbar argues,

> [BlackPower's] thrust was "black nationalism," though Black Power was not necessarily nationalist. Black Power employed—even coopted—the activism typified in civil rights struggles and operated on basic assumptions of rights and privileges. In essence, it demanded inclusion while advocating autonomy and self-determination. It asserted black access to full citizenship rights while conspicuously cultivating pride in much that was not American. . . . Two fundamental themes, however, were widely celebrated among proponents: black pride and black self-determination.[5]

For African American women, the Black freedom struggle represented the primary catalyst to their political awakening. The gender politics of the Black Power movement was complex, and Black women participated in roles ranging from supportive organizers to charismatic leaders and everything in between. For the NABF, the Black Power movement signified a generative force that grounded the NABF's philosophy, a formidable opponent against whom they had to define their project, a source of potential collaborators, and a fierce competitor for the allegiances of Black women whom the NABF tried to recruit.

As Ashley Farmer and Kimberly Springer demonstrate, Black Power organizations had a direct generative effect on the emergence of 1970s Black feminism. The history of the Third World Women's Alliance shows this direct connection. Frances Beal and other members of the Student Non-Violent Coordinating Committee (SNCC), including Gwendolyn Patton, formed the Black Women's Liberation Caucus (BWLC) in 1969, which soon expanded its political goals and renamed itself as the Black Women's Alliance (BWA) by the fall of that same year. The BWLC and BWA both assumed an anti-imperialist agenda and built solidarity with women of color around the world, thus continuing the antiwar and anti-imperialist politics of the SNCC.[6]

A few years later, the NABF's founding principles and statement of purpose, the Black Woman's Bill of Rights, echoed Black Power ideas. If Stokely Carmichael insisted that "Black people must redefine themselves, and only they can do that," accordingly, in the NABF, full membership was restricted to "women of African descent." Carmichael's vision of new models for Black people, who should view themselves, he argued, as "energetic, determined, intelligent, beautiful, and peace-loving,"[7] reverberates in the NABF's statement of purpose: "we do encourage [Black] women to be themselves and not their notions of what others think they should be . . . to be autonomous, self-initiating, assertive, and free thinking."[8] The NABF's political activism was fueled by a transformative vision of Black womanhood based on shared experiences.

In fact, the NABF's political project aligns with the emphasis on reimagined gender roles occurring within Black Power organizing. According to Ashley Farmer, while different activists and groups espoused varying understandings of Black Power, "they were united in their declaration of a new militant racial consciousness and driven by the collective goal of creating a new Black identity." Redefining gender roles was, in fact, a consistent feature of Black Power—that "new ideas about Black manhood and womanhood were the scaffolding on which they [Black Americans] could erect new ideas about Black Power and empowerment." The ongoing conversation about gender roles, unfolding during and in the aftermath of the Black Power years,[9] was thus not a marginal conversation, but a foundational one for the process of liberation from white dominance, for the individual and for collective reimagining of Blackness.[10] These passionate debates about gender roles provided a fertile ground for the emergence of Black feminist radicalism, as Stephen Ward and Sherie Randolph argue.[11]

The influence of Black Power ideas on the NABF's organizing practice was apparent not only in the restriction of membership to African American women but also in the articulation of racial separatism rooted in the different histories of Black and white women. In 1971, Kathleen Cleaver stated that "The problems of Black women and the problems of white women are so completely diverse they cannot be possibly be solved in the same type of organization nor met by the same type of activity."[12] Less than four years later, in "Voices on Black Feminism," an article based on interviews with eight Black feminists, Eichelberger quoted Cozetta Milton, stating that Black feminists "are not appendages of the white feminist movement but . . . we are very separate and different."[13] The NABF's stance on independent organizing did not prevent them from repeatedly reaching out to white women and attempting to build coalitions with them.

Other Black Power influences are evident in the double emphasis on cultural and social activism[14] that was inherent to the NABF's political philosophy. While many white women's liberation organizations focused on either social activism or theorizing and publishing, the NABF saw intellectual activism and community work as profoundly connected aspects of the liberation of Black women. The Black Woman's Bill of Rights emphasizes the right to appropriate representation in the media, nonracist and nonsexist education, and cultural production, alongside social and economic demands.

In addition, the NABF wholeheartedly supported Black economic nationalism—the idea that African Americans needed to control the economies of their own communities, including businesses and employment[15]—and insisted that Black women's empowerment to pursue professional careers would benefit Black families: "the Black woman, for example, who is no longer unemployed or underemployed, can help lift some of the financial burden strain off her husband and thus help the Black family realize greater financial independence."[16] Far from dividing the African American community, Black feminism could strengthen the family, hailed as a pillar of the community, and bring about economic empowerment for all. The push toward autonomy and independence for women inherent to feminism was thus coterminous with a focus on uplifting the Black community.

The NABF reiterated many times their support for Black men because they had to repeatedly answer a question that often read as an accusation: was Black feminism dividing the Black freedom struggle and was it exclusionary related to Black men? The NABF argues that a reexamination of gender roles would gain "total freedom for ALL Blacks." The NABF fought the perception that feminism encouraged Black women to act in an individualistic way, and instead suggested that the liberation brought about by feminism could benefit their families or relationships (always imagined as heterosexual). In the NABF's philosophy, Black women's liberation could have both tangible, material effects on the well-being of Black communities, and more indirect ones.

In this vein, the NABF addressed the issue of "competition" between Black women and men, albeit in terms that challenged Black nationalist views. Contesting Huey Newton's claim that the Black man feels "less than a man. Often his wife (who is able to secure a job as a maid, cleaning for White people) is the breadwinner," the NABF rejected the association between Black women's backbreaking labor and the emasculation of Black men.[17] Rather than accepting the allegation that Black feminism is divisive because it excludes Black men, the NABF emphasized their outreach to and support for Black men, whose raised consciousness was essential to Black feminism, and they encouraged both Black men and women "to examine society's sex role stereotypes."[18] Indeed, the NABF suggested that feminist liberation, if it occurred for both genders, could benefit the entire African American community.

Yet, often, NABF activists could not avoid disagreeing with more conservative accounts of gender roles within Black nationalism, and the rejection of such views sometimes took the rhetorical shape of a written dialogue. In founding documents, such as the organization's brochure, a section titled "More about the NABF!" presents arguments for the existence of an independent Black feminist organization in the question-and-answer format used by many women's liberation publications. The section begins by asking whether Black women needed a feminist movement at all, as they had "*always* [italics in original] been liberated." In response, feminists ironically present a list of "freedoms" that the Black woman had historically enjoyed, going back to slavery: backbreaking plantation work, sexual abuse, having to nurture white children before her own, witnessing the breaking up of her family, and many others. Post-slavery, Black women had to experience exploitation as domestic workers and as sole providers for their families, while being expected to come home after a long day and then work a second shift in their own homes. Yet the most unfair aspect of this prejudiced account of Black women as "liberated," in the NABF's view, refers to being "considered a Black matriarch by white racists and Black nationalists." The NABF protests this point of convergence between Black nationalism and white racism, as some Black men tended to agree with the infamous Moynihan report, which argued that Black families were too "matriarchal" for Black men to fulfill their proper masculine roles, and that female-headed households were responsible for the "tangle of pathology" affecting the Black community.[19] In contrast, the NABF points out the bitter irony that the so-called liberated Black woman was only "free" to be considered "the major cause, if not the sole cause, of Black juvenile delinquency."

The NABF's critiques of the Black Power movement stemmed from what Black feminists saw as its failure to extend its liberation potential to Black women. Yet the NABF's perspective was limited in other ways, especially when we compare it with the anti-imperialist, internationalist agenda of Black Power. The NABF's emphasis on consciousness-raising and organizing against the issues experienced by its members came to the detriment of an anticolonial and international analysis: the Black woman whose rights the NABF defended was a Black American woman. This stance set the NABF apart from the Combahee River Collective, for example, who did not see themselves as isolated within the United States, but rather as part of a larger movement of people of color against imperialism and colonialism.[20] The Third World Women's Alliance was similarly committed to internationalism, celebrating International Women's Day and, in their organizing practice, welcoming other women of color as full members.[21] Only for a short time, after receiving the visit of the London-based Organization of Women of African and Asian Descent, did the NABF temporarily adopt the moniker of women of color, yet in a way that did not alter the NABF's political outlook in the long term.

Humanism, Psychology, and the Feminist Movement

The NABF's intersectional feminism was rooted in humanist ideas, as it envisioned the liberation and transformation of all human beings, leading to a humanist revolution. The most easily accessible channel through which humanist ideas permeated the cultural atmosphere of the 1970s was through humanistic psychology, which by the middle of the decade had become one of its most generative mainstream intellectual trends. Abraham Maslow, widely considered the father of humanistic psychology, thought that psychology, and science in general, had to "move toward a centering upon human needs and fulfillment and aspirations."[22] Rejecting Freudian theory, Maslow insisted that rebellion against oppressive conditions was nothing more than the sign of a healthy psyche, which did not need therapy as a form of adjustment. In fact, Maslow saw psychological health as a form of resistance to conformity, and human nature (human potential) as essentially positive, preceding socialization, and unrelenting in its drive to actualize itself. Maslow's concepts, such as human potential and the hierarchy of needs, influenced the social movements of the 1960s and 1970s, although Maslow himself was rather ambivalent about their political use.[23] Founding documents and statements of the New Left, the Civil Rights movement, and the radical feminist movement freely invoked the idea of human potential.[24]

According to historian Ellen Herman, a fruitful interaction between psychotherapeutic knowledge and feminist politics was formative for the movement's early years. Feminists were adamant that psychotherapeutic discourses that touted adjustment for women, rather than social change, served the patriarchal status quo, yet they creatively used the vocabulary of humanistic psychology, among other psychotherapeutic discourses. As Herman reminds us, Betty Friedan, who had taken graduate courses in psychology at Berkeley, used Maslow's theories in her best-selling book *The Feminine Mystique* to refute Freudian understandings of the female psyche centered on achieving a traditional version of femininity as the key to life satisfaction for women.[25] The 1966 Statement of Purpose of the National Organization for Women included humanistic language, stating that women must have "the chance to develop their fullest human potential."[26] Pamela Allen, in her influential book *Free Space*, similarly argued that "we maintain and deepen our contact with our feelings" and used Maslow's vocabulary when she stated that in consciousness-raising groups "we begin to build a vision of our human potential."[27]

Key concepts of humanistic psychology, such as the idea of human potential, appeared in countless books and movement publications, and Black feminists were among those who used them creatively to advance their political goals. In *Woman Power*, one of the earliest accounts of the women's liberation movement (1970), Black feminist Cellestine Ware made a parallel between the Human Potential Movement, with its emphasis on self-disclosure and emotional honesty, and consciousness-raising, women's liberation preferred organizing strategy, which relied on theorizing personal experience. Ware agreed with other women liberationists that there was a difference between the two, as the Human Potential Movement was apolitical, while the goal of consciousness-raising was "to relate fragmented and seemingly unrelated problems in the lives of individual women and to construct a politic from the issues discovered in the process."[28] Like other early historians of the women's liberation movement, Ware saw individual and collective liberation as occurring simultaneously; indeed, without a collective of women, individual liberation was impossible.

Ware's book undoubtedly influenced Eichelberger's thinking on feminism and African American women's place in the feminist movement, as over the years Eichelberger wrote many articles attempting to answer questions raised in *Woman Power*. Members of the NABF assiduously read Ware's book, and in 1979, nine years after its publication date, Eichelberger complained that *Woman Power* was impossible to find in bookstores, although similar writings by white feminists were largely available.[29]

If Eichelberger was very familiar with humanistic psychology, given her master's degree in counseling, she could have derived her concept of humanism from other sources as well, including philosophical debates that attempted to address humanism's limitations in terms of gender and race. Historically, humanism's tenets had mostly applied to white European males, generally considered human beings upon birth; endowed with the right to freedom; recognized as thinking, feelings creatures; and considered independent moral actors.[30] Yet postcolonial writers such as Frantz Fanon, Aimé Césaire, René Maran, and Léopold Senghor engaged with humanism by trying to widen its scope. In his famous *Discourse on Colonialism*, Aimé Césaire criticizes Western humanism, claiming that "at the very time when it most often mouths the word, the West has never been further from being able to live a true humanism—a humanism made to the measure of the world."[31] And yet, the idea of humanism had appeared as a possibility to be reclaimed in the intellectual work of the négritude movement in France in the 1930s and, later on, after the Second World War, in which Césaire, René Maran, and Léopold Senghor played predominant roles. In this movement for cultural and political liberation, the term "humanism" occasionally appeared as a possible synthesis between Western philosophy and African culture. In the early years of the movement, Léopold Senghor had defined Black humanism as a cultural synthesis that "aimed to explore the Black man's identity using Western reason and the Negro soul as investigative tools, since both reason and intuition are required."[32] For Senghor, a synthesis between African values and Western technologies could be instrumental to human liberation.

Academic philosophers sometimes sought to create a synthesis between humanism and socialism, in the 1960s. An international symposium, followed by *Socialist Humanism*, a volume edited by Erich Fromm and published in 1966, brought together authors from the United States, postcolonial nations, and socialist countries. Among the more notable contributions were those of Herbert Marcuse, Ernst Bloch, Erich Fromm, and Léopold Senghor, who by that time had become president of the Republic of Senegal. In the introduction to the volume, Fromm distinguishes socialist humanism from Enlightenment and Renaissance humanism, which had sought to achieve human betterment through education, and from classical Marxism, which envisioned the socialist revolution as a full transformation of the individual, yet never considered the possibility that working classes in affluent societies might "prosper materially and share in the capitalist spirit."[33] The papers in the volume endeavor to build on the conceptual overlaps and cross-fertilizations between socialism and humanism from various theoretical angles. Léopold Senghor, for example, writing from a postcolonial perspective, unhesitatingly answered yes to the question of whether "Negro-African values, especially religious values"[34] could be integrated into socialism. Nevertheless, debates such as the ones published in this volume likely appealed to a rather narrow segment of the left-leaning reading public, as George Lichtheim noted in his review for *The New York Review of Books*, opining that *Socialist Humanism* was "more suited to the academy than to the organization of a mass movement."[35]

Originally blending concepts that circulated in political circles at the time, the NABF articulated its philosophy in a consistent manner in various documents that are now part of the organization's archive, including official papers, public statements and publicity materials, and articles published by the organization's executive director, Brenda Eichelberger. The NABF's articles of incorporation define the purpose of the new organization as to "help educate Black women in developing to their fullest potential by pursuing the ideals of feminism herein defined as the political, economic, and social equality of the sexes." To achieve its goals, the NABF planned to "create positive self-concepts for Black women," organize programs that would fight "sex, race, and age discrimination," encourage "Black woman's economic potential," and work to eliminate "sex and race role stereotyping."[36] Although these articles of incorporation were not intended for a public reading, they clearly state the new organization's philosophy, one rooted in the tenets of humanistic psychology, intersectional feminism, and Black economic nationalism. The Black Woman's Bill of Rights, the NABF's platform, most comprehensively articulated Black humanist feminism.

Black Women's Rights as Universal Rights

"Historically Black women from all walks of life have suffered from the negative effects of racism and sexism," begins the NABF's platform, the Black Woman's Bill of Rights. "Such sufferings have heightened our awareness of the plight of others in their multifold oppressions." The Black Woman's Bill of Rights articulates an intersectional framework for thinking about social justice ("racism and sexism"), and narrates a history of solidarity with others. Organizing "around our priorities as Black women against both racism and sexism" is positioned as a new stage of the same history of solidarity, yet this time as coalition politics.

> Our organizing principle is feminism which we view as a dimension of humanism. We are pro Black women, yet anti no one. Therefore, we are willing to work with any person or group of persons dedicated to the establishment of a more humane world. In such a world certain rights are basic to the development of all people.[37]

Rather than dedicating their energies to other groups' struggles, the NABF decided to organize around Black women's priorities, a commitment that emphatically does not exclude others, not even those who might stand to benefit from Black women's oppression. Both in the Black Woman's Bill of Rights and in other documents, the NABF articulates a vision of coalition politics that would lead to a more humane world, where all can thrive.

This understanding of coalition politics appears similar to politico-ethical coalition, a concept developed by political theorist Liza Taylor, based on the writings of 1970s and 1980s women of color: Bernice Johnson Reagon, the Combahee River Collective, Barbara Smith, Audre Lorde, Gloria Anzaldúa and others. For these writers and activists, coalition politics is rooted in their organizing experiences and builds on concepts such as intersectionality, identity politics, and border thinking. Black humanist feminism, I argue, provides another example of politico-ethical coalition.

Liza Taylor defines politico-ethical coalitions, based on Bernice Johnson Reagon's famous discourse, as having three characteristics: "an emphasis on coalition as dangerous and even life-threatening *struggle*; an understanding that coalition is generated out of a shared *self-reflexive* political commitment to undermining oppression; and an emphasis on *existential transformation* as inherent to the very process of coalescing [emphasis in original]."[38] The Black Woman's Bill of Rights alludes to the possibility of danger within coalition politics when the authors refer to their experiences "as Black Women in a hostile world." Furthermore, the document emphasizes the need for a shared commitment to undermining oppression. In the NABF's theory and practice, existential transformation is paramount, both for Black men, who needed to raise their consciousness about sexism, as I show in chapter 1, and for white women, with whom the NABF often collaborated. The series Anglogynophobia, as I show in chapter 5, is one long plea for white women to reject white supremacy, a process that amounted to undergoing an existential transformation. Affiliate memberships translate the NABF's commitment to working together with anybody supporting their agenda, while centering the project of liberation on the needs, experiences, and history of Black women.

The Black Woman's Bill of Rights not only anticipates, by two decades, Hilary Clinton's reclamation of women's rights as human rights in her famous 1997 discourse, but grounds this reclamation of "basic" rights for "all people" (universal rights[39]) in the experience of interlocking oppressions. The Black Woman's Bill of Rights codifies experiences that crisscross the public and the private, the cultural and the economic, to articulate a holistic vision of justice.

The Black Woman's Bill of Rights is the result of a collective process, coalescing the insights of a group of organizers led by Eichelberger: "Presently we are formulating our bylaws, statement of purpose, and platform," wrote Brenda Eichelberger to Myrtlene Clark, from Denver, Colorado. "Tentatively the statement of purpose is entitled 'womanifesto' and the platform is entitled 'Woman's Bill of Rights' or 'Black Woman's Bill of Rights'. We would like to have your ideas on the enclosures."[40] While the Bill of Rights was created collectively and the bottom of the document only bears the inscription "National Alliance of Black Feminists 1976," without listing specific names, in the following I will do my best to name as many authors as possible, thus attempting to engage in the process of "listing," as outlined by Brittney Cooper, meant to resist the "intellectual erasure"[41] of African American women's intellectual work.

The process of creating the Black Woman's Bill of Rights was collaborative. In her letter to Myrtlene Clark, Eichelberger mentions having written drafts of the bylaws, a statement of purpose, and a platform (the Bill of Rights), stating that "other women are going to submit their drafts and hopefully we'll come up with a winner." However, attempting to identify specifically which members, in addition to Eichelberger and possibly Clark, participated in the creation of the Bill of Rights, proves difficult for the contemporary historian. The NABF had an extraordinary appeal, yet often struggled with the fact that member participation was intermittent. In June 1975, in an article about Black feminists and consciousness raising, author Carol Kleiman quotes, in addition to Brenda Eichelberger, Patricia Yates, Marion Fisher, Lillian Jefferson, and LaVerne Bennett.[42] A list of paid members of the Chicago chapter of the NBFO (the NABF's predecessor), dated June 1975, a few months before the formation of the NABF, includes eighty-five names, but it is unclear to what extent the women who had paid the membership fee chose to be active in the organization.[43] Less than a year later, only two names are included in the first NABF press release, Brenda Eichelberger as Executive Director and Laverne Bennett as Secretary. Obviously, even during its transition from local NBFO chapter to a new, independent organization, the NABF must have had several members, but specific lists that detail the names of the women who participated in writing the Black Woman's Bill of Rights are not available in the archives, and perhaps never existed. An article published in the *Chicago Defender* about the NABF on June 26, 1976, mentions, in addition to Eichelberger and Bennett, Betty Smith, Evelyn Tolliver, and Louisa Hunt as members.[44] The names of Monica Stewart, Marta White, and Brenda Hunt also appear in mid-1976 minutes of the Board of Directors meetings.[45] As these women had been active in the Chicago chapter of the NBFO and held leadership positions in the successor organization, it is possible that they participated in writing the Black Woman's Bill of Rights. In addition, other women whose names do not appear in the archives could have participated in writing and revising the Bill of Rights.

"Accurate media portrayal" is the first right listed in the Bill of Rights, as the organizers protest both Black women's invisibility and their hypervisibility: "The right to a nonracist, nonsexist media image . . . to media coverage proportionate to her number in the population."[46] Other cultural demands refer to "quality education," an education free of sexual and racial bias and based on "her own history (herstory)," and the right to cultural participation and equal subsidies for cultural activities, a means of taking control of their own representation. Cultural activities for Black women would also include participation in sports and the "hierarchy of organized religion," as well as the promotion of cultural practices "free of race, sex, age, and marital status bias."

Rather than being critical of the family, seen as oppressive by white feminists, or defending it as a pillar of the community, as seen by Black nationalists, the NABF demands for Black women "a stable home life." This comprehensive demand allows Black women control over their relationships, as the Bill of Rights supports various types of families and living arrangements (single woman, couple, single parent, nuclear, and extended families) and demands laws for the protection of all. Other demands include equal sharing of household and child-rearing duties, legal protection for displaced homemakers, and an end to housing discrimination. By focusing on home life instead of the family, the NABF can simultaneously demand fair housing, equal partnership in marriage, and Black women's freedom to choose a wide variety of living arrangements. The Bill of Rights additionally lists the right to "quality childcare" a demand that encompasses both economic demands, such as childcare facilities and the inclusion of childcare as a tax-deductible expense, and cultural ones, such as freedom from sex-role stereotypes in education. In an attempt to protect Black children, the Bill of Rights demands legislation against child abuse, for adequate child support payments, and support for Black families who adopt Black children.

The right to quality health care is rooted in African American women's experiences as victims and unwilling subjects of medical experiments and involuntary sterilization. The Bill of Rights demands the expansion of health insurance and research "without exploitation" into the health disparities (including mental health) among Black women. The Bill further demands protection from unnecessary surgeries, support for victims of domestic violence, and the right to informed consent, anticipating by several years the demands made by coalitions of feminist activists in the late 1970s for health and reproductive justice.

In a similar way, the NABF's platform addresses civil and criminal justice, demanding "justice in the courts, penal institutions, and work release programs free of discrimination based on race, sex, and socioeconomic status." The statement also insists that Black women needed "freedom from unwarranted search and seizure" and "freedom from police harassment," a far-reaching analysis of sexism and racism in the criminal justice system.

The Bill of Rights outlines an expansive list of economic and political rights. The rubric "economic/consumer development," demands the right to equal employment opportunity and meaningful work, in addition to "the right to adequate standard of living" and equitable laws governing social security, insurance, pension, and retirement. This comprehensive list sees Black women as participating in the economy as producers and consumers, demanding meaningful work and equal opportunities alongside consumer rights such as availability of credit, participation in the entrepreneurial system, and availability of goods and services designed for diverse bodies, skin tones, and hair textures. Rather than advocate overthrowing capitalism, the NABF demands an equal place for Black women within this system. In a similar vein, the NABF demands political rights, such as proportional representation, the right to unionize, parental benefits, and legal protection for household workers, among which Black women were still disproportionally represented in the late 1970s.

The Bill of Rights also establishes the NABF's stance about lesbians. While it demands "decriminalization of laws against private, sexual, consensual behavior among adults," and, for the Black woman, "total freedom to express her sexuality in private with any consenting adult of her choosing," this statement in support of nonheteronormative sexualities is contingent upon privacy. The NABF offered its Black lesbian members private support at the price of public silence.

The language of rights, a hallmark of humanist thought, was particularly appealing to a generation of Black women and men who had recently experienced the Civil Rights movement.[47] When NABF speakers gave talks about Black feminism at universities, organizations, community forums, and all sorts of media outlets, the language of rights allowed them to connect with their audience. In an oral history interview, Eichelberger recalls:

> When I had a speaking engagement, they realized that basically I was just talking about having rights, like everybody wanted to have rights. And the Black people could identify with wanting to have some basic rights, so explaining to them, well, the women's movement is no different, we're just talking about people having rights. And I would make analogies with other movements.[48]

The NABF mailed the Black Woman's Bill of Rights to any letter writer who requested information about the organization. A woman from Saint Louis, Missouri, expressed her desire to read it, stating that "The only way we can put an end to our double oppression as women and as black is through our militant combativeness."[49] Other correspondents expressed their intention to use the document as a political manifesto for their organizing efforts. From the State Correctional Institution at Huntingdon, Pennsylvania, a letter arrived requesting the Black Woman's Bill of Rights and other documents concerning rights, as she planned to share them with "all the women prisoners in this state in order to bring about prison reform."[50] Another writer interested in the Bill of Rights was Margaret Anderson, who was involved in preparing the report of the National Commission on the Observance of the International Women's Year. She intended to include the Bill of Rights in the Commission's report, and was interested in starting an NABF chapter in Washington, DC.[51]

The Black Woman's Bill of Rights encapsulates the political program of Black humanist feminism by listing a comprehensive list of political goals rooted in the experiences of Black women. Although these demands were revolutionary compared to the state of Black women's experiences at the time, the NABF's philosophy was reformist. By using the language of rights and demanding concrete improvements of Black women's lives, the NABF hoped to attract Black women from all walks of life. As the organization started growing, its Black humanist feminist philosophy translated into the organization's structure and practices, hierarchies and labor, membership and inclusion.

Organizing Black Humanist Feminism

Organizers for the NABF proved savvy users of mass media. On May 17, 1976, a press conference followed by an open house at the Black Women's Center introduced the new organization and a new feminist movement: "Who says Women's Lib is only for white women? A new movement has begun!" According to the press release, the organization emerged in response to African American women's need "to have more control over the social, political, and economic aspects of their lives." The NABF intended to function as a multi-issue organization working in all the areas outlined in the Bill of Rights, in collaboration with other Black women's clubs and professional organizations.[52] The NABF would be a "cohesive unit—apart from social clubs or exclusive professional societies . . . an individual and collective forum,"[53] an organization where every Black woman was welcome. NABF organizers saw themselves as building a political and national movement by and for Black women.

In practice, Black humanist feminism meant that the NABF offered full membership to Black women only, but hoped to build coalitions with Black men; feminists of all races, including white; and socialist organizations. Supporters of Black women's liberation could join the NABF as affiliate members. The NABF recognized few hierarchies among Black women, although as a nonprofit organization, it had to define certain leadership functions. The only hierarchy NABF willfully embraced was that of activist experience. The organization offered honorary memberships to well-known Black women activists, thus connecting different generations of African American women. In its organizing practice, the NABF centered consciousness-raising, which allowed it to maintain a laser focus on Black women's experiences. Despite sustained attempts to the contrary, the NABF's politics often ended up centering the experiences of the professional Black women who could join as paid members and access leadership positions.

In its administrative structure, the NABF followed the model of its predecessor, the NBFO. Unlike the myriad of ad hoc feminist groups that formed and dissolved throughout the country, the NABF registered as a nonprofit 501(c)(4) organization with the State of Illinois, and had to identify its executive director, secretary, and treasurer, and clearly define their roles.[54] The NABF further formalized its structure by creating a steering committee, which made general recommendations, and a board of directors, who made routine decisions. Any paid member could join the steering committee, provided she attended the general business meetings, held monthly,[55] and members in good standing could join the board of directors if they submitted a statement detailing their understanding of Black feminism, their experience, and their objectives for the organization. In addition, the NABF established committees to address specific aspects of the organization's work: the Membership Committee, Program / Publicity Committee, an Education Committee, and a Fund-Raising Committee.[56] Other committees such as Consciousness Raising, the Program Committee, Peer Counseling, and so on, were added at a later date.[57] The NABF's organizing practice shows its commitment to multi-issue organizing, addressing every aspect of Black women's lives and every topic that came out of consciousness-raising sessions.

Although the NABF's formal structure seems like a far cry from the nonhierarchical, consciousness-raising based, communal groups of women's liberation, in everyday practice, as former members recall, the division of labor was much more fluid and decentered. When asked what type of work she did in the organization, former treasurer Helen Whigham recalls, "At the time, the organization was just getting started. Myself, and Brenda, and Marta, and a few other ladies, we kind of did whatever was necessary. Whatever was needed, that's what we did."[58] Given that board members had to juggle full-time jobs or school, family responsibilities, and volunteering for the NABF, in the end everyone had to do the work required by the organization.

The NABF reserved the position of honorary members for Black women, usually of an older generation, who were known and respected for their activist work in the African American community. In that capacity, while not participating in the NABF's everyday work, they offered their expertise, participated in specific events or projects, and connected the NABF and its members to other similar organizations in Chicago. For example, Reverend Willie Barrow, founder of Operation PUSH, was involved in the early work of organizing consciousness-raising groups for Black men and participated in many panels that debated the role of feminism in the African American community. (A veteran for the Civil Rights movement, she had started out as a field organizer for the Southern Christian Leadership Conference, and in the 1970s worked together with Reverend Jesse Jackson to organize Operation Breadbasket, which was later followed by Operation PUSH.)[59] Reverend Willie Barrow's longtime friend, Addie Wyatt, Civil Rights and labor organizer, one of the founders of the Coalition of Labor Union Women (CLUW) and of the National Organization for Women (NOW),[60] was also an honorary member of the NABF, in which capacity she advised the organization on issues related to working women's rights. Ethel Payne,[61] a pioneering Black journalist who by the mid-1970s enjoyed a national reputation, worked as an editor and wrote a column for the *Chicago Defender*, the African American newspaper in Chicago, helping connect NABF with media outlets. Other honorary members included Congresswoman Yvonne Braithwaite Burke; Connie Seals, Executive Director of the Illinois Commission on Human Relations; Nezzie Willis, Director of Programs, Chicago Welfare Rights;[62] and Dr. Arnita Y. Boswell, the founder of Chicago's League of Black Women, who attended the April 16, 1976, press conference announcing the formation of the NABF, thus lending her credibility to the new organization.

Beyond the honorary members, the NABF did its best to attract African American women from all ages, social classes, and geographic locations. "Just what *kinds* of Black women are in NABF anyway?" asks the questions and answer section of the brochure. "ALL kinds. We range from minors to senior citizens, from grade school educations to postdoctoral degrees, from East Coast to West Coast and from North to South, from single to married, to separated, to divorced, to widowed, from poverty level to 'modestly' affluent." The answer suggests NABF's national ambition, as the organization tried to position itself as the successor to the NBFO and hoped to reach a similarly wide audience.

Over time, the NABF managed to attract a group of dedicated organizers, who occupied and rotated various functions within the organization. An undated document lists the "organization's governing body" as consisting of Brenda Eichelberger as Executive Director, Gayle Porter as Chairperson, Marva Jolly as Co-Chairperson, C. A. Lofton as Recording Secretary, Lilliard Lofton Thomas as Corresponding Secretary, Beti Ellerson as Membership Secretary, and Cheryl Bruce Kumlager as Financial

Secretary.[63] Another undated document lists the NABF's board members as Brenda Eichelberger, Beti Ellerson, Janie Nelson, Beryl Fitzpatrick, and Gayle K. Porter.[64] These members contributed to the organization in multiple ways, from volunteering their work, expertise, and resources, to sometimes even supporting the organization financially. They were also able to accumulate knowledge about the organization's strengths and weaknesses, as well as develop a personal philosophy inspired by Black feminism, an experience that influenced their careers after the organization ended.

Black Humanist Feminism and the Politics of Class

Both the leadership and general membership of the NABF consisted largely of educated, professional Black women, although the majority came from working-class backgrounds. Their class status was rather fluid, and many experienced poverty, both at the time of the organization and later on in their lives. While the NABF's founding documents did not analyze class from a Marxist perspective, Black women's economic position as the poorest Americans grounded their racial analysis. This approach limited the organization's ability to deal with tensions and differences among Black women based on class and educational status. The NABF celebrated Black women's advancement in professional careers and their intellectual labor while trying to support Black women who were working class, on welfare, and incarcerated.

One of the key arguments for Black women's liberation rested on their position at the bottom of the economic hierarchy. For example, the sarcastic answer to the statement "after all, the Black woman has always been liberated," which opens the question-and-answer section of the NABF brochure, counts among the supposed "freedoms" that Black women have always enjoyed the ability to "Earn less income (as documented by the Census Bureau, Labor Department, and Women's Bureau) than white males, black males, and white females" as well as the capacity to "Be, as a result of circumstance, the sole provider for her family much more often than her 'pedestaled' white counterpart." Another one of Black women's so-called freedoms was to "Discover, after decades of mindless day work, that she's not entitled to social security or other benefits."[65] By pointing out economic woes, the NABF formulated a gender and race theory contingent upon a class analysis and rooted in a specific historic experience.

Black women's lowest position in the economic hierarchy created financial difficulties for activists who were trying to build an organization entirely controlled by Black women: "The financial situation of our organization is reflective of our membership,"[66] the leadership stated in an undated membership letter. The NABF had to increase the yearly membership fee from $5 per year at the time of the Chicago chapter of the NBFO to $15 per year, an amount needed because of postage and phone expenses and the rent for the NABF's headquarters. The membership fee made joining the NABF more difficult. Nancy Lewers, who wanted to start a chapter in Detroit, wrote: "I had not been able to remit the $15 before, but it is enclosed now."[67] Rosemary Bray, who was attending Yale University, also found that she had to postpone joining the organization: "Before leaving Chicago, I had every intention of joining your organization, but time and finances were against me." Bray's letter documents the difficulties that Black female students, even if they were attending prestigious universities, encountered when they intended to join the NABF. Nevertheless, Bray was determined to start a chapter in New London, Connecticut: "There is a women's center here that is currently in its formative stages, but their politics seem more in line with the Federation of Women's Clubs than with any real feminism."[68] Perhaps it was this perception that the NABF promoted "real feminism" that encouraged women like Bray to do their best to support it. For example, one Black woman asked that her wedding present consist in a contribution to the National Alliance of Black Feminists: "I offered to give her either a present or a check to a good cause, and she wanted a check to you,"[69] wrote the woman's friend, in her letter attached to the donation.

In the absence of sustained sources of income, the NABF had practiced community fundraising, which creates ties with marginalized groups and generates "grassroots income," which is defined as any income generated from individual donations, fee-for-service, publications, and membership fees, and which "can increase and strengthen . . . accountability to the communities most affected by injustice."[70] Stephanie Guilloud and William Cordery claim that community fundraising can be understood as a form of activism, rather than as an activity that is separate from activism and precedes or enables it: "Grassroots fundraising is a strategy to maintain a firm connection to our base and to initiate community-based economic structures. We define organizing as building relationships and institutions to sustain community power, and it follows that fundraising is organizing."[71] The strategies of community fundraising that the NABF used in order to generate grassroots income—membership fees, community forums, and so on—allowed the NABF to expand its base, gain visibility, and spread its ideas, while staying accountable only to the community it served. In its fundraising efforts, the NABF appealed first and foremost to the Black community, urging memberships upon both women, who could be full members, and men, who could join the organization as affiliates and support the organization in other ways. There are no records of the NABF appealing to white women for support.

The NABF used community action workers for office tasks, through the Community Action Agencies established in 1964 by the Economic Opportunity Act.[72] Nevertheless, members did all the leadership work, which was uncompensated. Therefore, the women who had more time to dedicate to the NABF, mostly professional women, often ended up as leaders of the organization's various committees, thus making decisions and influencing its policy. According to Kimberly Springer, middle-class Black women were "more available to assert their needs within the NABF than working-class women with less discretionary time and income."[73]

However, even Black women who held professional positions felt that poverty was never remote from their experience. Members expressed their own analyses about how the trifecta of race, gender, and class shaped their worlds. Board members' applications, for example, document their thoughtful self-assessment and political analysis of Black women's needs.[74] Marta White, who was working on a degree in Public Administration, insisted on Black women's specific difference in terms of race and class: "Black women, for too long, have had to accept the lowest wages in this country. We have had to choose between poverty and a low paying job because of inadequate, or nonexistent childcare facilities. We have had the joys and burdens of raising our children by themselves [*sic*]. We have continued to rationalize ourselves into dependency on our men because we have been brainwashed into believing that actively seeking liberation for ourselves will result in a polarization of the Black race." For White, Black women experienced racial and gender differences through economic hardship and devalued work: "the lowest wages in this country." Yet she is equally critical of a Black freedom struggle that would prioritize the demand for unity and see women's needs as secondary. She hopes that the NABF would develop a special membership fee and outreach program for high school women, "to make them develop a strong self-image and make them aware of the resources that are available to them."[75]

Despite members' busy lives as professionals and active participants in their communities, many were, in fact, active in multiple organizations, including socialist ones. The NABF's collaborations with socialist and New Left organizations continued throughout its existence. Barbara Williams, a board member who defines feminism in her application as "a theory of political and economic equality of the sexes,"[76] was also working for feminist issues with the Black Workers' Congress, a socialist organization.

Other NABF members were active in the Socialist Workers' Party (SWP), most notably Willie Mae Reid, who had joined the Black feminist movement in Chicago from its start in 1974.[77] The SWP consistently reached out to African Americans and considered the Black nationalist movement as an essential part of the revolutionary struggle. In its "Transitional Program for Black Liberation," adopted at the twenty-third National Convention held in New York City in 1969, SWP formulated a list of preliminary demands inspired by the Black freedom struggle, including Black control of the police force, government funds, and public institutions such as hospitals and libraries in the Black community. The SWP also envisioned the formation of a Black political party, and demanded jobs, free medical care, enforced housing codes, and a Black-controlled education system, as well as a review of all cases of Black prisoners, given that "they had not received a fair trial." For the SWP, the Black freedom struggle was essentially an anti-capitalist movement: "The Black liberation movement . . . is at one and the same time a nationalist movement for self determination and a proletarian struggle against the capitalist possessors of wealth."[78]

Willie Mae Reid, an NABF member, held leadership positions in the SWP. She was their candidate in the 1975 Chicago mayoral race, coming in third with almost 17,000 votes against Richard Daley. In 1976, Reid was SWP's vice-presidential candidate (with Peter Camejo as presidential candidate), and in 1992 she ran again, in the same position, this time with James "Mac" Warren running for presidency. As a prominent member, Reid invited representatives of the SWP to NABF forums on Black women's experiences and Black women and men's relationships, and she reported on the NABF's 1977 conference, "A Meeting of the Minds," for *The Militant*, a leftist publication.

The NABF collaborated with other New Left organizations such as the New American Movement (NAM), who invited Eichelberger to speak at their 1979 conference, "Socialist Feminist Theory of Sexuality." That same year, Eichelberger published an article on Black feminism in *Women Organizing: A Socialist Feminist Bulletin*, a NAM publication.[79] In this article, Eichelberger examines the causes of Black women's apparently limited participation in the women's movement, stating that class differences create one large obstacle preventing Black women's mass participation in women's liberation. She identifies the racism of the women's liberation movement as another reason for Black women's distrust of white feminists. White women, argues Eichelberger, have been unable to recognize the experiences of involuntary sterilization suffered by women of color and reframe the abortion debate as reproductive rights. Black and white women's experiences further diverged in their attitude toward the nuclear family, seen as desirable by Black women, for whom it was an institution under constant threat, while white women saw it as the locus of their oppression. In contrast to white feminists, the NABF saw as its mission to reach out to Black men and provide them with a feminist education: "to many black feminists, fostering relationships between black women and black men is a feminist issue," Eichelberger states. Finally, according to Eichelberger, Black and white women's priorities diverged in the area of sexuality: although for white women, lesbianism is an important issue, it is still "not yet a predominant theme among black women";[80] thus, the NABF engaged in the secondary marginalization of lesbians.

There were other forms of exclusion that the NABF unwittingly perpetrated. The language used in the organization's publications studiously avoided the Black vernacular. Eichelberger's constant use of mainstream English sometimes alienated potential members, who perceived her professional demeanor and middle-class background (her father had graduated from Howard University and had held a government job during the Depression era, which allowed Eichelberger and her siblings a comfortable childhood and adolescence) as too removed from most Black women's experiences. To what extent could a light-skinned, highly educated, middle-class woman represent African American women from Chicago? Janie Nelson recalls, "This is what Brenda was up against. [People said that] She's from out of town, she's speaking perfect English, she didn't grow up in a poor neighborhood."[81] If Eichelberger's middle-class manners attracted the admiration of many of her followers, her avoidance of the Black vernacular reinforced the perception that the NABF was, indeed, a professional Black women's organization, in spite of its efforts to reach beyond that group.

Still, the NABF constantly tried to reach out to poor African American women who had neither the resources nor the time or energy to participate more fully in Black feminist activism. Through the Black Women's Center, the NABF made its resources available to everyone. The bulletin board, for example, was usually filled with announcements for employment opportunities, some of which were republished in the newsletter.[82] When a woman from Chicago wrote to the organization and mentioned that she was in danger of losing her job, the reply from the NABF encouraged her to come to the Black Women's Center and consult the employment opportunities published on the bulletin board.[83] While requests for monthly pledges and the membership fee did limit the ability of many Black women to join the NABF as paid members, in reality many more women used the services provided by the organization. According to poet C. A. Lofton, in the pre-internet era, the referral services offered by the NABF helped many poor

Black women navigate the system of government institutions in order to access the resources they needed. In her recollections, the NABF never refused services to someone who couldn't afford the membership fee.

INTERVIEWER: Didn't they have to pay a fee?

C. A. LOFTON: Sometimes, but most of the time we'd overlook it. They requested it, but if somebody didn't pay, they just didn't pay. That doesn't mean you're going to put them out. A lot of the women that were being battered, they came from the streets. How are you going to tell a woman that is homeless, or a woman that is suffering from mental illness—and we had some of those too, because they would gravitate to any new organization, you know—that we weren't going to support them. I don't remember any instance where anybody was put out for not paying dues.

INTERVIEWER: How did the NABF support them?

C. A. LOFTON: They would take them to different groups. We developed a resource list. At that time, there were no resources that were collected in one group. It looked like one book. We would go through it and see what categories they might fit into. We would use our own personal experiences. Like my mother was a case worker, so that meant that I had a lot of information about public aid. Dr. Porter did a lot of stuff with different school age kids and knew how you could get help for them.

Eichelberger kept a list of places that she would refer people to. She could gather up this information and . . . we all knew where it was. Check inside on the desk and you go down the list and you check this off and check that off. That's it. You didn't have human resource centers like you have now.[84]

In the pre-internet era, the Women's Center and the NABF provided information about a variety of resources available in Chicago, and could help Black women who needed assistance to locate them. In addition, by visiting the Women's Center, any Black woman could have access to both the expertise and the network of a group of young, educated, upwardly mobile Black women, who worked for various city agencies and were familiar with various resources, both in the nonprofit sector and provided by the government. Thus, the referral services offered by the NABF were both formal and informal, consisting in the lists of agencies compiled by NABF members, in addition to providing supportive contacts within certain agencies.

The referrals went beyond issues of employment and interacting with social agencies, as they included education about health and sexuality, making available to African American women the information about women's bodies that was already circulating in the white women's liberation movement. C. A. Lofton remembers:

> We referred people to the hospitals for mammograms and for pap smears. This was very forward thinking. We also referred people so that they would know how to deal with their own sexuality too. There was no such thing as Howard Brown. This was way back in the day, right?
>
> Even if sometimes white women would have access to this kind of information because they were, like, in the movement and there was this kind of stuff and they were educated, things were easier. But for a lot of women of color and African American women, it was harder for them to access this sort of information. Plus, there was a lot of taboo.[85]

These types of interactions are rarely documented in the archives, which record only certain types of events through newsletters, correspondence, and membership receipts. According to the NABF July/August 1979 membership letter, the career and job opportunities received by the NABF were "much too numerous to include in our membership letter." However, these opportunities were posted on the bulletin board at the Black Women's Center; C. A. Lofton, Social Service director, was available to help women search for materials and assist applicants in filling out forms for Workmen's Compensation and Public Aid.[86] If, indeed, more poor and working-class Black women received help through the Women's Center than are documented in the archives, then the claim that middle-class Black women benefitted the most from the NABF can be nuanced by noting the NABF's tireless attempts to reach out to poor and working-class women, as well as their activism on behalf of incarcerated women.

Black Feminism and the Prison Industrial Complex

In the NABF's practice, Black humanist feminism signified a commitment to working with working-class women and incarcerated women. Aware that Black women were criminalized at a higher rate than their white peers, the NABF, from its very inception as the Chicago chapter of the NBFO, and throughout its long life, extended its support to Black female prisoners, as its founding documents show. The Bill of Rights mentions as one of Black women's fundamental rights "justice in the courts, penal institutions, and work release programs free of discrimination based on race, sex, and socioeconomic status," in addition to freedom from police harassment. The NABF's guidelines for local chapters similarly list working with

Black female prisoners among the possible projects Black women's groups could undertake.[87] The national Black women's conference "A Meeting of the Minds" included a panel on civil / criminal justice, with the purpose of exploring the "inequities in the judiciary system," addressing the position of Black women as offenders and ex-offenders and as victims of street crime.[88]

The NABF's activism was rooted in the experiences of professional Black women delivering services to incarcerated African Americans, and to a lesser extent in the experiences of formerly incarcerated Black women. Prior to joining the NBFO, Eichelberger had done her practicum for her master's degree in counseling at the House of Corrections for Women in 1972, and recalled the struggles of Black women prisoners who were mothers. Other members had taught workshops in prisons and were aware of the appalling conditions that Black women prisoners experienced.[89]

Faithful to the principles of Black humanist feminism, NABF activism extended not only on behalf of incarcerated women, but addressed the needs of male inmates as well. In 1977, Eichelberger delivered a two-day workshop to the inmates of Sheridan Correctional Center in Lasalle, Illinois. The program centered on discussing sexuality as a form of communication, and it included feature films like *Sexuality and Communication*, *Dynamite Willie*, and *Diary of a Mad Housewife*. The program included film discussions followed by discussions of participants' expectations in relationships, power struggles and traditional gender roles, and their experiences relating to Black women and white women.[90]

In 1975, Eichelberger and her collaborators had organized on behalf of Joan Little, participating in coalition work with a host of progressive entities around the country.[91] Less than a year later, the NABF led a coalition of local groups and organizations to support Cassandra Peten. An African American woman from California, Peten had suffered years of abuse at the hands of her husband, who attacked her in a public space, at a bank. She attempted to defend herself by firing a single shot, and as a result, she was accused of assault with a deadly weapon and was facing ten years in prison. The NABF insisted that Peten had "responded . . . with an instinctive and justified action for her own survival." For several feverish weeks before Cassandra Peten's October 23, 1978, trial date, the NABF and a host of feminist organizations around the country created fundraisers for Peten's defense fund (which, as estimated, could have cost as much as $10,000) and collected signatures on petitions demanding justice for her. Eichelberger and C. A. Lofton were the most active NABF members in the Chicago Coalition for Cassandra Peten's Defense Fund,[92] participating in meetings, contacting other local groups such as Mujeres Latinas en Acción,[93] and co-organizing a benefit disco.[94] In the end, the judge decided to sentence Peten for the time she had already spent in prison (ninety days).[95] After returning home to Oakland, California, Cassandra Peten became a member of the NABF.[96]

Conclusion

Black humanist feminism, an original version of intersectional feminist theory, adopted a humanist perspective and the use of the language of rights, anticipating by decades the 1990s discourse of women's rights as human rights, to devise a highly comprehensive agenda that accounted for a variety of Black women's experiences. Their race / gender analysis was grounded in a discussion of Black women's economic position, thereby obscuring tensions and differences between Black women of different social and professional status, although the class status even of educated Black women was very much in flux in the 1970s, and many experienced poverty. Other distinctive features of Black humanist feminism lie in its unabashed support for Black communities, who, as the NABF argued, would benefit the most from Black women's liberation, including economically.

Black humanist feminism was deeply rooted in the experiences of NABF members, collected via consciousness-raising and translated into founding organizational documents and articles and essays. This collective process of creating both Black feminist theory and activism ensured their seamless integration, as the NABF's activism was as diverse and multipronged as its program. This focus on African American women's experiences ensured the authenticity of their work, yet limited their political vision. The NABF did not express any critique of imperialism or apartheid and did not connect Black women's experiences with the experiences of other women of color, as other Black feminist organizations did.

The NABF reserved full membership for Black women, and only full members could participate in decision-making or leadership positions. Like other groups, they maintained organizational independence, while ready to work in coalition with others. Yet the NABF took their commitment to building alliances one step further, as they offered affiliate memberships to anybody who supported their mission.

The central location of the Black Women's Center in downtown Chicago both enabled and circumscribed the NABF's ability to turn their vision into reality. The expenses of keeping the Center open created an economic burden on the organization. Nevertheless, the Center's location and the NABF's continued presence there allowed organizers to serve their community. From a rented space in a downtown Chicago office building, Black feminist ideas were disseminated to local African American communities, the white-dominated feminist movement, and around the country.

CHAPTER 3

202 South State Street

Did you know . . . that a Black feminist movement is alive and well?
—The NABF, undated mailing form

Introduction

On May 23, 1976, the NABF announced by press release the opening of the Black Women's Center at 202 South State Street, Suite 1024: "the only women's center presently known . . . completely organized, financed, and controlled by black women."[1] For six years, at the height of the women's liberation movement, the NABF's Black Women's Center functioned as a physical location of Black feminism in Chicago. Its central position allowed any Black woman to simply walk in, meet other feminists, and enjoy access to a wealth of resources that were unavailable elsewhere, from reading materials to referrals to government services. The Center's archive nurtured intellectual activist efforts, such as writing and study groups. Finally, its permanence as a Black feminist space enabled the formation of a political community whose collective narratives the NABF worked to disseminate in the Black community in Chicago, in the women's liberation movement, and to the general public.

Activists for the NABF were convinced that their organization needed a dedicated space, a room of their own, and spent hours debating the best location. They were initially offered a room, free of rent, at a local YMCA, an offer Eichelberger regretfully rejected: "The members said, why would a women's organization be at the YMCA? And I agreed with that, but the point was this was free! So I was very conflicted about that . . . and there was no money coming in, or no resources." Fortunately, they were able to locate a more suitable space, a large room in an office building in downtown Chicago, available for rent for $100 a month. Eichelberger relives the excitement she felt: "Even back then in the 1970s, that was a very low rent for a big room downtown. It was a big room, it was super big! . . . At the time, that was ideal. So the women just put the money together to pay for the rent."[2] Although the expenses related to rent, electricity, and phone created a long-term financial burden, having a dedicated space meant that Black women were the only ones defining its agenda and that they could be creative in imagining its possible uses. A meeting space, a library, an announcement board, an archive, and a classroom, the Center would stay open for the next six years, an extraordinary feat for an independent women's center, especially one run by women of color.

Given its central location downtown, the Center altered the geography of the business district, infusing it with a Black feminist presence. "Racism and sexism are also spatial acts and illustrate Black women's geographic experiences and knowledges as they are made possible through domination," writes Katherine McKittrick. "If practices of subjugation are also spatial acts, then the ways in which Black women think, write, and negotiate their surroundings are intermingled with space-based critiques, or respatializations."[3] The Center disrupted the continuity of Chicago downtown as a space of white control and male domination. In a de facto segregated city, it was accessible to any Black woman, who could visit it, spend time there, use the Center's resources, and simply relax and meet other Black women. Given its multiple uses, the Center offered the material basis for a Black feminist counter-public sphere. In that space, NABF organizers developed a multiplicity of narratives and political arguments rooted in Black women's experiences, and worked to disseminate their insights via media to the general public, thus creating other, more fleeting counter-public spaces. NABF activists tailored their message to the multiple audiences they were addressing, creating feminist counter-publics in African American communities and bringing their perspective to predominantly white feminist spaces while building a national Black feminist movement.

The Location of Black Feminism

Where was the Black women's movement? Gayle Porter asked, as she realized that Black female students from the middle school where she worked as a counselor were not recommended for transfer to Chicago Vocational School (CVS). At the time, CVS was a competitive high school that sent its most deserving students to elite universities, such as the Massachusetts Institute of Technology, thus opening a path toward upward social mobility for high-achieving youth from underprivileged backgrounds. The school principal, Porter discovered, did not submit the files of female students she had recommended for admission to CVS. Instead, he had sent the files of male student-athletes, even when their grade averages were lower. Incensed by what she rightly saw as gender discrimination, she threatened the school principal with a class action lawsuit on behalf of the girls and their parents. She started looking for a feminist organization: "There was no Google, there was none of that then because this is back in 1976, and so I looked in the phone book and I found the National Alliance for Black Feminists. I called, and Brenda answered the phone, and I joined that Saturday. Eventually, I became the chairperson of the National Alliance for Black Feminists."[4] Porter was able to find the NABF because the Black Women's Center was listed in the phone book and because, already committed to fighting for Black girls' rights, she was searching for it. Other Black women, whether they were or were not interested in feminism, easily found the Women's Center because of its central location. At a time when the Chicago downtown district, the Loop, was rapidly gentrifying, the location of the Black Women's Center, at 202 South State Street, in an office building that housed predominantly white institutions and businesses, signified both resistance to gentrification and a claim to equality for Black women.

According to Finn Enke's influential study, during the women's liberation movement, women of various races, sexualities, and classes "created a massive groundswell of feminist activism by directly intervening in the built environment"—feminist centers, coffee shops, bookstores and lending organizations—and intervened in the public landscape by taking over marketplaces, civic spaces, and public institutions. Most women's liberation groups met either in public places made available by local institutions or in the homes of their members, yet a number of institutions that managed to secure their own space created an alternative, feminist geography of the city. In Chicago, one of the most visible feminist groups was the Chicago Women's Liberation Union, an umbrella organization that started in 1969 and continued, while generating many working groups, chapters, and projects, until 1976.[5] One of these subgroups, the Chicago Women's Graphics Collective, designed many posters and flyers for women's movement events. It used the second floor of CLUW's office at 852 W. Belmont Ave.[6] The Midwest Women's Center opened in 1975 in the South Loop and provided services such as job training and literacy education. Artemisia, a women artists' cooperative started by graduates of the Chicago Arts Institute in 1973, housed exhibitions by women artists and offered a space downtown to discuss feminist political issues. Another gallery run by women, ARC, opened its doors that same year. More traditional institutions, such as universities, offered stable locations to women's groups, especially at the University of Illinois at Chicago, where the Women's

Studies program started in the early 1970s.[7] On the North Side, the Mountain Moving Coffeehouse, founded in 1975, was a women-owned feminist coffeehouse, which operated until 2005. The suburb of Evaston, Illinois, had its own feminist space, the Evanston Women's Liberation Center, open in the 1970s.

The many progressive movements unfolding in the Midwest created an energizing environment for all kinds of radical and progressive activism, and women were an integral part of that. The National Coalition of Labor Union Women started in Chicago in 1973.[8] Latina women started Mujeres Latinas en Acción around 1973, an organization that still exists today,[9] and some women who were active in the Chicano movement started formulating feminist ideas in the 1970s.[10] In addition, most national women's organizations had a Chicago chapter, including NOW, which had several chapters in the city and surrounding suburbs; the American Association of University Women; the National Council of Negro Women; the Democratic Socialists of America Feminist Commission; the Coalition of Labor Union Women, founded in Chicago in 1974; the National Welfare Rights Organization; and many others. Chicago had several feminist periodicals such as *Womankind*, published in the early 1970s by CLUW; *Mountain Moving*, run by the Mountain Moving Collective in Evanston, Illinois; *Women's News . . . for a Change*, which published some of Eichelberger's writings; and, in the 1980s, the short-lived *Sister Source* (subtitled "a midwestern lesbian / feminist newspaper") and *Catalyst: Chicago Womyn's Paper*. These organizations created multiple spaces where feminist ideas were debated, spaces that could be permanent or fleeting. As Enke states, "Feminist activism, then, was not just 'everywhere' and 'in the air'; rather, it was known and practiced on the ground of everyday life."[11]

This feminist geography overlaps with an older one, which, given Chicago's long history of segregation, marked certain spaces in the city as welcoming or unwelcoming to African American women. Black feminists living in Chicago moved through and around the various spaces, temporary or more permanent, of the women's movement; they also lived, worked, and spent their free time in a de facto segregated city. Historians have demonstrated that Northern segregation operated differently from its Southern counterpart: while public spaces were not legally divided between whites and Blacks, "schools, housing, and jobs operated on a strict racial hierarchy," and many public spaces in fact practiced racial segregation.[12] African Americans were concentrated on the south and west sides of the city, a historical pattern of exclusion by whites, whose resistance to integration was both stubborn and creative,[13] and enjoyed the support of powerful local politicians. Mayor Richard J. Daley, despite federal and state laws, resisted school desegregation until his death in 1976.[14] By the mid-1970s, Chicago's Black population, which had increased by a third in the 1960s, from 812,637 to 1,102,620, was expanding into new areas of the city, although old patterns of segregation and resegregation continued, contributing to housing discrimination for Black Chicagoans. On the West Side, for example, an increase in the number of Black residents triggered processes both formal and informal that contributed to the devaluation of housing, an increase in mortgage rates, a decrease in garbage pickup, and a high number of police abuse cases, as officers were assigned to these communities as a punishment for misconduct.[15] A 1978 report of the Chicago Urban League estimated that for segregation to end, 93 percent of Black Chicagoans would have to relocate.[16]

The Loop, the business district downtown, was experiencing urban decay by the 1970s, but this situation was changing fast in the 1970s. In 1960, about 10 percent of the district's 4,337 inhabitants were Black.[17] They were disproportionately affected by Chicago's postindustrial economic downturn. Chicago's 1970s white flight led to a decrease in urban employment by 14 percent (in the suburbs, hiring increased by 45%), which exacerbated employment difficulties for people of color,[18] who had had to contend with employment discrimination going back to the 1950s.[19] One of the first actions of Chicago's Black feminists was to create an employment committee that would fight discrimination against Black women in employment and file complaints against "those Loop and near North business establishments which hire white women and systematically exclude Black women."[20]

By the end of the 1970s, the neighborhood was experiencing dramatic changes, as downtown investment between 1979 and 1987 exceeded $6 billion, and office towers, upscale restaurants and shops, and luxury housing reshaped the urban landscape. As C. A. Lofton recalls, gentrification had turned South State Street into a predominantly white and professional space, and the office building housing the Black Women's Center was no exception: "There was a lot of gentrification [going on] and a lot of the people downtown worked for the city. There were restaurants down that road, and you were not that far from Lake Shore Drive either . . . cabs would stop and would pick you up and stuff like that." The office building at 202 South State Street was part of the same landscape: "There was a restaurant and bar on the first floor. You saw people of color coming in, but most of the people were people who worked in offices." The Black Women's Center occupied one of the few offices rented by tenants of color: "I think there might have been two others, but they had what you'd call middle-class clients. One was in real estate or something like that." By renting the space at 202 South State Street, the NABF infused a gentrifying area with a Black feminist presence and reclaimed equal rights to occupying space for Black women.

Choosing a space located inside the Loop, in the business district, instead of the South Side, where many Black women lived, might feel surprising, especially as there were vibrant Black organizations, such as the DuSable Museum (originally the Ebony Museum) located there.[21] Chicago had emerged as one of the main destinations during the Great Migration, although housing for African Americans was limited to a narrow strip on the South Side, where, as historian Davarian Baldwin states, "landlords could extract the highest rents for the worst housing from the most economically disenfranchised population."[22] In spite of these prohibitive circumstances, the first half of the twentieth century witnessed a thriving cultural scene during Chicago's Black Renaissance, where women had played an active role both as cultural producers and as organizers who worked to support cultural institutions, schools, and public housing projects, often through the network of women's clubs that flourished in the city.[23] Chicago was an important site of Garveyism, with a membership in the United Negro Improvement Association organization numbering in the thousands; Black women played pivotal roles in building this transnational and pan-African movement in the city.[24] The South Side had been home to a number of famous Black women writers, artists, and activists, such as Ida B. Wells Barnett, Margaret Burroughs, the founder of the DuSable Museum, Lorraine Hansberry, Mahalia Jackson, and Gwendolyn Brooks, to name but a few.[25] Yet, by the mid-1970s, given antidiscrimination legislation and the emergence of a new Black middle class, many African American women had been able to move to Chicago's suburbs, where about one-third of the women on the NABF's long mailing list lived, and to many other neighborhoods, including on the North Side.[26]

Eichelberger recalls:

> We didn't have a lot of resources, so we wanted to have it as centralized as possible. Chicago is basically divided into three sides, West Side, North Side, South Side. We had it where it was centrally located so it didn't matter what side of Chicago you lived in, it was easy to get to the central part, that would be downtown Chicago, what they would call the Loop, and State Street was a major street in downtown Chicago. So my point is, people were coming in all the time. People were coming off the street, they didn't have an appointment, they would just come in. There were so many women that came and went all the time.[27]

The building at 202 South State Street also housed other cultural institutions, such as the main office of the Chicago Council on Fine Arts, as C. A. Lofton, who was a fellow of the Council at that time, recalls. The location was in fact prestigious, as it allowed the NABF to claim equality with other white activist organizations: "The people who were coming in, the people from NOW and the state representatives, when [they] heard about our office downtown, they thought it was grand. Oh wow! You got an office downtown, you must be big stuff! They had no idea."[28] By renting an office in a building in a gentrifying area, the NABF staked its claim to equality with other organizations in the movement. However, the rent represented a financial burden for the organization, which shaped NABF's activism in decisive ways.

It is worth inquiring whether locating the Center in a gentrified office building prevented poor Black women from accessing it. However, all interviewees recall that the Center was easy to locate, especially given Brenda Eichelberger's presence on the radio and in newspapers, especially in the Black media, where she gave out the Center's address, and the long mailing list that sent hundreds of brochures around the city. Elnora Washington, retired teacher and former NABF member, remembers: "It was called the Women's Center, but everybody found their way in there! Some were coming to get information, some were just passing by and wanted to know what is this about, and then they became interested!"[29] Another former NABF member, Beryl Fitzpatrick, recalls: "I just went, their office was at 202 South State Street, which is a couple of blocks from the university. After I finished my class or my studies one day, I remember during the summer, I went over and it just resonated with me." Having an easily accessible downtown space made Black feminism welcoming, in a grounded, spatial way to any Black woman, while its proximity to several universities added even more visibility. Many years after the organization ended, all former members remember the Center's address, which testifies to its prominence in their memories of the NABF.

More importantly, the Women's Center anchored and gave a physical address to the safe spaces of Black female friendship. In fact, NABF organizers encouraged potential members who attended consciousness-raising sessions to "bring at least one female friend to each session,"[30] which many members did. Washington recalls,

> I had a friend by the name of Donna Stutts, who's dead now, and she was the first one to become acquainted with the group, and she met up with them because of some theater work she was doing. I think she met

FIGURE 1. Brenda Eichelberger at the National Alliance of Black Feminists office, Chicago, Illinois, 1976. Chicago History Museum STC-000000007, Pete Peters/*Chicago Sun-Times*.

FIGURE 2. The high-rise office building at 202 South State Street, Chicago, Illinois, 1975. The Black Women's Center occupied room 1024. HB-39113, Chicago History Museum, Hedrich-Blessing Collection.

FIGURE 3. Front page of article "Black Feminists and the Equal Rights Amendment," *Sepia*, October 1979. From left to right: Sharon Wells, Theresa Abdullah, Brenda Eichelberger, Beti Ellerson, Regina Hyatt, Janie Nelson, Rebecca Fisher, Halcyon Chambers. Courtesy of the African American Museum, Dallas, Texas.

BLACK FEMINISM:
DOES IT DIVIDE

THE BLACK STRUGGLE?

Do Black women need women's liberation?

Are Black feminists merely mimicking white women?

Is the Black feminist movement dividing the Black struggle?

Should Black women abort the babies who will be our revolutionary leaders?

Are the only free people in this country white men and Black women?

SPEAKERS:

RALPH METCALFE, JR., Associate Professor
Kennedy-King College
DR. BOBBY WRIGHT, Clinical Psychologist
Administrative Director, Garfield Park
Comprehensive Community Health Center
LESLIE MAHASIN, Assistant Minister
World Community of Islam
MONICA STEWART, United Black Voters

CHICAGO STATE UNIVERSITY
95th and King Drive
Chicago, Illinois

WEDNESDAY, NOVEMBER 17, 1976
6:00 P.M. to 9:00 P.M.
Emily Douglas Library Building
Room E103

Admission $2.00

For further information contact the sponsoring organization,
the NATIONAL ALLIANCE OF BLACK FEMINISTS at 939-0107 ...where feminism is a dimension of humanism

FIGURE 4. Promotional flyer for the community forum "Black Feminism: Does it Divide the Black Struggle?," sponsored by the National Alliance of Black Feminists on November 17, 1976. Chicago History Museum, ICHi-183259.

IS THERE A CONFLICT?

YOU are cordially invited
to attend the forum,

BLACK FEMINISM, WHITE FEMINISM--IS THERE A CONFLICT?

SPEAKERS

CAROL ADAMS HENRY, Director
Women's Educational Resource Center
Northeastern Illinois University

OUIDA LINDSEY
Chicago Sun-Times Columnist

PHYLLIS NELSON
South Suburban Women's Liberation

JULIE SASS, President
Chicago Coalition on Women's Employment

CHICAGO STATE UNIVERSITY
95th and St. Lawrence
Chicago, Illinois

WEDNESDAY, DECEMBER 8, 1976
6:00 p.m. to 9:00 p.m.
Division of Cultural Studies
University Center
Building K, Room 200

Admission: $2.00

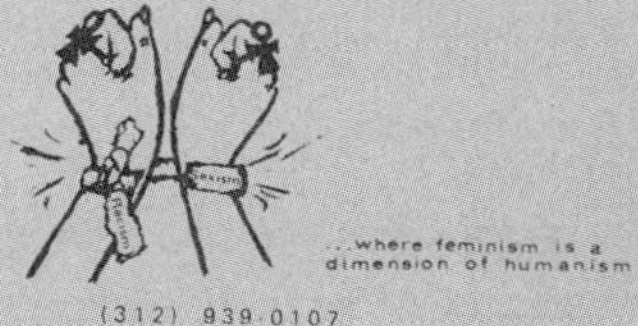

For further information contact the sponsoring organization,
the NATIONAL ALLIANCE OF BLACK FEMINISTS at 939-0107

Figure 5. Printed flyer on pink paper for a community forum titled "Black Feminism, White Feminism: Is There a Conflict?," organized by the NABF at Chicago State University. Chicago History Museum, ICHi-183516. Flyer made by National Alliance of Black Feminists.

> Brenda, or she met some people who then introduced her to Brenda, and that's how she joined and that's how I joined too.[31]

Often, meeting Eichelberger in person inspired women to join the organization. A former member, Laverne Bennett, who was active in the organization from 1976 to 1978, recalls that "Brenda Eichelberger was one of the most earnest and focused and passionate people I've ever met."[32] Eichelberger's leadership and dedication were widely viewed as crucial for the NABF's efforts, and the community she and other Black feminists created at the Center nurtured both supportive friendships and an intellectual counter-public sphere.

The Center, nevertheless, operated at a time when vicious homophobic attacks were leveled against feminist organizations of any race. The well-known tactic of "lesbian baiting" invoked the fearful specter of the man-hating lesbian and was used by conservative forces to disqualify feminists' critiques of patriarchy. Simply by identifying as feminist, NABF members could become targets of such allegations, and anyone associated with the Center could be "accused" of lesbianism. Some Black women professionals, fearful for their reputations, simply avoided joining, although their politics aligned with the NABF's. A former member recalls:

> They didn't want that lesbian identity. That's right and I can say it now . . . because I had a huge crush on [name redacted], I had a political crush on her . . . and then I tried to get her to come to the meetings, and anyway, she didn't come. She just didn't want that identity. And years later it came out that she had a [woman] lover.
>
> Interviewer: *She didn't want to be associated with being a feminist?*
>
> She was very much a feminist. She just didn't want to be associated with any women's groups. Because she was afraid that people would say that she was a lesbian. She wasn't out or anything like that. And she had a lot of power. It's just like . . . they don't give Bayard Rustin any recognition. And he organized the March on Washington. But number one, he was not considered Christian because he was a Quaker, and he was openly gay.[33]

The former member references the secondary marginalization[34] operating within African American communities, which prevented a Black feminist from attending meetings and joining the organization. The NABF itself avoided stating its public support for lesbians, although it accepted lesbian members and organized consciousness-raising groups for them.

Yet Black lesbian organizers were denied visibility and leadership, which shows the complex spatial and racial dynamic of the Black women's center.

> The complexities of black space not only highlight the role racism/white supremacy has played in the production of black space but also provide a useful means of theorizing how forms of spatial marginalization occur within black communities. Although black bodies are always read as outside the framework of whiteness . . . black gender and sexual minorities are rendered as outside the spatial formation of black communities.[35]

Black women could find a welcoming space at the Center, while Black lesbians could find a home there only if they maintained a certain secrecy about their sexuality and did not attempt to gain too much visibility. The Black Women's Center offered lesbians private support, yet the NABF refrained from formulating a critique of heteronormativity, in spite of its avowed feminist identity.

Yet, while lesbians could find some sort of a community or home at the NABF, other exclusions operated in that Black feminist space, manifested when a Black trans woman started attending meetings. C. A. Lofton recalls:

> I know she was a dark-skinned woman, she was about my complexion, probably a little lighter, and she was thick! I didn't pay any attention to it, but then someone said, "That ain't no woman." I said, "How do you know?" You know, I was just like, well, anybody said whoever they said they were, but I wasn't in no questioning mode around that time. And I certainly wasn't trying to stop anybody of color from being in the movement . . . I can't remember her name! But she did come to two or three of the meetings. At first she was well received, because she was so knowledgeable about a lot of stuff. And then the rumor started that she was not really a female. Then it became, "you tried to deceive us and might be a spy." That was the first thing. And then after it was, "Why are you here?" And then they didn't come up with a logical answer to satisfy other members of the board. Then I don't remember what happened, or how. She got away. She left on her own. Because we didn't have a precedent for putting people out.

Lofton's gendering the trans woman correctly shows that at least some NABF members felt that the trans woman belonged in a Black feminist organization. Lofton sees the movement as welcoming to all people of color, and, in contrast to some of the members of the NABF's board who questioned the trans woman's motives for joining a Black feminist organization, she valued the trans woman's being "knowledgeable" about a wide range of topics. Yet it is worth mentioning that the trans Black woman decided to leave the NABF on her own. This incident was not isolated in the movement, where feminist transphobia caused the exclusion of trans women activists, regardless of their contributions to the movement. Musician

Beth Elliott, who had started the San Francisco chapter of Daughters of Billitis, and Sandy Stone, who, given her experience as a sound engineer, was instrumental in establishing the women-only recording company Olivia Records, left the movement after transphobic attacks.[36] Both Elliott and Stone left the movement on their own; they were not simply excluded, Finn Enke argues.[37]

The Center fostered the creation of a political community while perpetuating its own exclusions. For cis-heterosexual African American women, the Center provided a space for discussions, meetings, consciousness-raising sessions, and study sessions—a community where a multiplicity of Black women's voices could emerge. The most enduring quality of these narratives is their dialogic nature. Rather than promoting a totalizing narrative of Black feminism, the NABF fostered a conversation and created an environment where this dialogue could unfold.

"Through the Power of their Pens . . . ": Creating the Black Feminist Hidden Transcript

Many potential members were attracted to the NABF, given the spirit of dialogue and collaboration that marked women's work for the organization. Beryl Fitzpatrick recalls: "I went to the building, I went to the training, and I got hooked and I wanted to be very involved. I saw these Black women working together, I saw these Black women having differences of opinion and dialogue."[38] These differences of opinion and dialogue are markers of what Nancy Fraser calls an alternative public sphere. The Black Women's Center offered the material basis for a Black feminist counterpublic, thus allowing NABF activists to weave their stories into what Catherine Squires has called the hidden transcript, a collective narrative that members of oppressed communities share with one another, but not with dominant groups. The NABF created this hidden transcript via its writing and study group, community and cultural events, then used collaborations with other entities and its own Speaker's Bureau, as well as media appearances, to disseminate its members' viewpoints to the general public.

Fraser famously defines alternative public spheres, or subaltern counter-publics, as "parallel discursive arenas where members of subordinated social groups invent and circulate counterdiscourses, which in turn permit them to formulate oppositional interpretations of their identities, interests, and needs."[39] The women's movement created an efflorescence of such spaces, such as journals, publishing companies, academic programs, conferences, conventions, and festivals, as well as bookstores, coffeehouses, and local meeting places.

While Fraser's idea of subaltern counter-publics is racially blind, in contrast, historian Michael Dawson theorizes a Black public sphere, anchored in the physical space by a multiplicity of Black institutions ranging from Black churches to secular organizations.[40] Catherine Squires develops Dawson's argument, analyzing the specific obstacles and power relations that subaltern groups, more specifically Black people, encounter when they try to disseminate their discourses among wider publics. She distinguishes between three types of counter-public spheres, all rooted in African American history. The enclave, the counter-public created by slaves in the antebellum South, had to hide its existence and discourses from the dominant public or the state. "[A]n enclave public sphere," writes Squires, "requires the maintenance of safe spaces, hidden communication networks, and group memory to safeguard against unwanted publicity of the group's true opinions, ideas, and tactics for survival."[41] When enclaved counter-publics interact with the dominant public sphere—although, usually, they are barred from accessing it as equal contributors—members of marginal groups usually conform to a "public transcript," a highly scripted way of interaction with their oppressors that avoids challenging unequal power-relations but maintains the safety of the oppressed.

The second type of marginal publics, counter-publicity, occurs at historical junctions when there is a decrease in oppression, or an increase in access to resources, and when communication between the marginal and the dominant public sphere, both mediated and face-to-face, intensifies. Squires identifies the Civil Rights and Black Power movements of the 1950s and 1960s as instances of counter-publicity, when instead of performing the "public transcript," counter-publics project the "hidden transcript," previously accessible only in enclaved spaces, into the dominant public sphere. Counter-publicity, however, presents certain risks, as members of dominant publics can have adverse reactions to marginal groups' discourses, and may attempt to silence or undermine them. Finally, the last type of marginal publics, the satellite, exemplified by the Nation of Islam, is marked by deliberate separatism from the wider publics. Desiring separateness in order to maintain its purity, this public sphere interacts with the wider public usually in moments of crisis.

The NABF's efforts to change the discourse on Black women fits the concept of counter-publicity as defined by Squires, as Black women joining the NABF created a hidden transcript of their experiences that they sometimes tried to disseminate among larger publics. Anybody joining the NABF entered a conversation about Black women's histories, experiences, and dreams of liberation, beginning with the orientation session that every potential member had to attend: "At orientation sessions, the

Black feminist movement and the women's movement are chronicled from their inception to the present," states the NABF December 1977 *Newsletter*. These conversations continued during community events and even weekend-long retreats held at resorts around Chicago,[42] which helped members from around the country to build a national network. For example, the March 1979 retreat was attended by Black feminists from Chicago, Saint Louis, Milwaukee, and Schenectady, New York.[43] Other events, such as picnics,[44] women's parties,[45] and outings with families, were also a part of the NABF's everyday life.[46]

In these counter-public spaces, NABF members produced their own accounts of their experiences, "through the power of their pens," as the NABF brochure stated, working "to eradicate the myths and distortions that surround Black women." The NABF offered both a writer's workshop and a study group, facilitated by the archive held at the Women's Center, an assorted collection of publications on topics such as employment, education, government, labor, law, manpower, civil rights, working mothers, local feminist and civil rights organizations, and others.

The study group met monthly at the Women's Center and at members' homes, debated literary and academic texts about Black women, especially new publications, and sometimes organized public forums. In the study group, NABF members discussed a wide range of texts, including founding documents such as the NABF's own Black Woman's Bill of Rights, germinal collections such as *The Black Woman* by Toni Cade,[47] and publications such as the July 1979 issue of *Off Our Backs*[48] and the February 1978 issue of *Ms. Magazine*, both dedicated to African American women. Yet these conversations focused on the experiences of heterosexual and cisgender Black women, as trans women were excluded from participating in the NABF, while queer women who joined the NABF could participate in lesbian consciousness-raising groups, but these conversations were kept private throughout the NABF's history, with one important exception that will be discussed in chapter 4.

Eichelberger encouraged members to write about their experiences, as she hoped to publish a collection of Black feminist writings.[49] Although the collection never materialized, many individual NABF members published their works in a variety of genres, both during the NABF's existence and after the organization ended. One of the most prolific writers was Eichelberger herself, whose essays were based on discussions and consciousness-raising sessions held at the NABF. When one of her articles, titled "Myths about Feminism," appeared in *Essence* magazine in November 1978, the study group met to discuss it.[50] The group also gathered to discuss excerpts from Michele Wallace's book *Black Macho and the Myth of the Superwoman*, which were printed in advance of publication,[51] and when Michele Wallace's book became available, the NABF members met again to discuss it.[52] Eichelberger reviewed the *The Black Macho . . .* in the pages of *Moving On: Monthly Magazine of the New American Movement*, thus continuing the tradition of collaborating with the leftist magazine.[53] In her review, although Eichelberger agrees with Wallace's account of the historical roots of the Black Macho (emerging from the Black movement) and the myth of the Superwoman (a stereotype of Black women originating in slavery), she nevertheless finds Wallace's generalizations about Black women and feminism worthy of critique. Eichelberger points out Wallace's analysis of the Superwoman myth is not new, but repeats similar arguments made in Toni Cade's collection *The Black Woman*.[54] Given Wallace's overall dismissal of Black feminists—stereotyped as unhappy wives, lesbians looking for a public forum, or careerists angling for a better position—Eichelberger concludes that her book is "a polemic, not a historical document or feminist treatise."[55]

The NABF often organized poetry readings and participated as a group in cultural events. They organized a book reception when poet and NABF member Carolyn Rodgers, whose distinctions included a nomination for the National Book Award and a grant from the National Endowments for the Arts (for her 1976 collection of poetry *how i got ovah*), published a new book of poetry, *The Heart as Evergreen*, in 1979.[56] When Ntozake Shange's famous choreopoem *For Colored Girls Who Have Considered Suicide When the Rainbow Is Enuf* was staged in Chicago in October 1978, NABF members attended the play as a group and moderated the discussion with the public that occurred afterwards.[57] Poet C. A. Lofton recalls that the discussion prompted defensive responses from African American men:

> I remember when *For Colored Girls . . .* first came out. There was a huge showing, we went to see the play as a Black feminist group and I remember that there were Black men who just were angered. First of all, they were angered that the play was out, and I remember that they were angered [about] "You black feminists organizing!" Because there was dialogue after the play and we were facilitating the dialogue between the Black men and the Black women. [They were saying,] "Oh, you're just denigrating Black men.[58]

The *Chicago Defender*, reporting on the event, notes that over four hundred people attended the workshop to discuss Shange's play. The newspaper portrays Black men's reaction to the debate in similar terms, although they do mention one African American male participant who declared toward the end of the debate that, while initially disliking the play, he had changed his mind after the debate and that he supported it.[59]

Ntozake Shange's choreopoem prompted intense debates in African American communities about sexism and the denial of the abuse experienced by Black women. Throughout the country, as Kimberly Springer shows in an article detailing Black women's response to Black Power, Shange's work was often met with resistance and Black feminists were accused of being "man haters."[60] This exemplifies one of the difficulties Black feminists encountered when they tried to disseminate their hidden transcript within the African American community, although the NABF tried to reach multiple audiences, ranging from university publics to mass media. The NABF's message was particularly successful in that it tailored its message for different audiences, while maintaining the complexity and dialogic nature of their own ongoing conversation about Black women.

Disseminating the Hidden Transcript

In 1973, less than three years before the opening of the Black Women's Center, the formation of the NBFO had triggered a wave of enthusiasm for Black feminism around the country, both among Black women and in the white-dominated women's liberation movement. Energized by that insight, the NABF worked to develop and disseminate a multiplicity of narratives rooted in Black women's experiences. The NABF created a Speaker's Bureau specifically to deal with that need. In addition to educating their audiences about Black feminism, the women's movement more generally, and the NABF's organizing work, the speakers volunteered both their personal experience and their professional expertise. In doing so, they examined critically how gender and race influenced their experiences in their chosen professional fields. An undated Speaker's Bureau document lists honorary members such as Reverend Willie Barrow as available to speak on topics related to women in the ministry. A. LaVerne Bennett, who was working as a school counselor at the time, was available to address rape, woman-man relationships, aloneness, and personal growth issues for young adults. Eichelberger herself, who was the most active and in-demand public speaker, gave talks about feminism, Black feminisms, Black women and the feminist movement, female sexuality, Black female sexuality, assertiveness training, and consciousness-raising for women and men. Poet C. A. Lofton discussed women and literature and offered poetry readings, while Gayle Porter, who later would pursue a career in public health, talked about counseling single female parents, friendships between men and women, and friendship between women. Monica Stewart, who was preparing for a political career, offered her expertise on the Equal Rights Amendment and women in politics, while Sharon Wells, who was working as a librarian but would soon pursue a law degree and become a judge, could educate the public about the "Feminization of the American Library Profession, The Female Law Student, and Black Woman and Sexism and Racism on the Job." In addition to reflecting, from their own personal experience, on gender and relationships, race and community, and Black women's role in the feminist movement, NABF speakers offered intersectional perspectives as professionals who were charting groundbreaking careers in fields from which they had recently been excluded.[61]

The wide variety of topics and the interest generated by Black feminism guaranteed that NABF members were constantly moving from one speaking engagement to the next. Within less than a month after the official announcement of the NABF, the Speaker's Bureau schedule included the following: a presentation on "The Relationship of the Black Feminist Movement to the Civil Rights Movement and the Women's Movement" at Northwestern University on Friday May 14, 1976; then, on May 20, Eichelberger's speaking engagement on "The Philosophy and Programs of the National Alliance of Black Feminists" at the University of Illinois at Chicago Circle;[62] on June 2, on the local station WCIU-TV, Channel 26, the NABF spoke live on a television phone-in talk show, then discussed Black feminism on June 8 on the radio station WCGS. Given that the *Chicago Defender* planned to publish a feature story on the NABF, the women were invited to the Black Women's Center to be interviewed by a journalist on June 10; finally, on June 20, the NABF participated in the Sixth International Black Writers' Conference.[63]

In most cases, the NABF's audiences were receptive and warm. A letter from the Cultural Affairs Committee at the University of Wisconsin at Madison thanked Eichelberger for a keynote lecture that had attracted an audience of five hundred attendees: "The reaction to your program was outstanding."[64] After listening to Eichelberger speak, some considered starting new local chapters. After her talk on "Sexuality . . . Or Who Says Black Women Are Liberated?" at the event "Hurray for Black Women," which took place in Detroit, in September 1977, one of the attendees, Nancy Lewers, wrote to the NABF offering to start a local chapter.[65]

In general, NABF members gladly accepted invitations to local and regional radio and television stations; however, the speakers sometimes learned that their hosts weren't always genuinely interested in learning about Black feminism. Sometimes NABF members felt they were being manipulated by their hosts. Poet C. A. Lofton remembers: "We used to call it covering two stones. In other words, 'We didn't have to talk about women's issues because they were talking about women's issues, and we wouldn't have to talk about black issues, because they were talking about black issues.' You'd get two for one." Lofton felt that instead of offering more programs that discussed gender and race, television stations used the NABF's intellectual activism to optimize their coverage. Even more, as Lofton recalls, the intentions of the radio stations, owned by white media conglomerates, could be at times manipulative, attempting to coax Black feminists into taking public positions against Black men.

C. A. LOFTON: Radio stations would call you and ask if you would come down and bring a few of your members. Then they'd grill you. What do you think about Elijah Mohammed? They'd ask us about all of these Black organizations . . . and they would make it their business to try to pit us against Black males.

INTERVIEWER: So it wasn't a friendly, supportive exchange.

C. A. LOFTON: Oh, sure they wanted us to think it was friendly. They were going to feed us, and we'd get to talk on television and give them our view. Of course, it wasn't the view they wanted to hear, because we just took a stance not to say anything negative about [Black men]. We're not one group, so there's room enough for what the Muslims are saying. We're not going to be divided like that. . . . Anyhow, I don't remember we ever took a stand against another Black person. We weren't here to fight Black people. We were here to fight racism and sexism.[66]

While consciousness-raising, during the women's liberation movement, mainly took place in small groups, a very similar process, in which audiences were invited to reflect on gender roles, occurred at public events and on the radio. For example, in 1970, WBAI-FM, a local radio station in New York City, broadcast a weekly feminist show that included a consciousness-raising session consisting of a taped session followed by call-ins from the audience.

In the NABF's case, their astute use of mass media and especially their radio programs created fleeting counter-publics and aural communities uniting Black women and general audiences throughout the Chicago area. During their shows, Black women living in the city, on the South Side, or in other urban spaces, as well as in the Chicago suburbs, could feel connected as a part of the same community. But the NABF intervened even more directly in African American spaces, by organizing community forums in Black neighborhoods.

"Is the Relationship between Black Women and Men Getting Better or Worse?"

The community forums organized by the NABF in the fall of 1976 were inspired by similar events they had created the previous year, during the short-lived Chicago NBFO chapter. The forums fulfilled multiple functions: consciousness-raising, gaining visibility, building connections, and fundraising. Addressing the difference between community fundraising and traditional fundraising, Guilloud and Cordery claim that, in contrast to fundraising with foundations, which requires competition between groups for scarce resources, community fundraising allows collaboration between organizations serving the same population. Often, these collaborations take the form of co-organized community events, where participating organizations can expand their base while charging a small amount. Unlike traditional fundraising parties, which are designed for wealthier donors, community fundraising events facilitate public discussion of new ideas within the community that the organizations serve: "The folks attending, performing, and soaking up the politics are the same folks (youth, low-income organizers, community members) who participate in the organizing projects."[67] The NABF forums embodied this type of community fundraising. They were coterminous with larger debates unfolding in the Black freedom struggle, especially within Black Power spaces, about gender roles—debates that grounded a liberatory vision that started with personal transformation. The forums also provided the space where attendees could discuss their personal experiences and reflect on the historic changes occurring in the African American community.

The first forum, in September 1976, focused on the topic of Black Woman / Man Relationship, aiming to explore heterosexual relationships in the Black community and the impact of Black feminism on the Black freedom struggle. These topics were very likely to attract a wide audience, in a context where one of the core features of Black Power's liberatory vision was reimagining gender roles.[68] According to Ashley Farmer, "Black Power organizers participated in extensive and contested conversations over the definitions and contours of Black womanhood *precisely* because they believed these new gendered ideals to be legitimate forms of political opposition and a vital component of personal and collective self-liberation."[69] The NABF brought a feminist point of view to these debates, and its audiences were excited to engage with this new perspective, although they did not always embrace it.

The forum poster, most likely created by the organizers, like many other NABF advertising materials, demonstrates in a visual way both the message they were trying to convey and their audience as they imagined it. The poster features the image of an attractive Black man and woman, smiling, looking straight at the camera, in a friendly, relaxed way. The man is wearing a dark-colored turtleneck, the woman is wearing hoop earrings; they are both sporting short Afros, showing their political credentials in a fashionable way. The man's arm appears to be draped around the woman's shoulders, in a protective way, suggesting they might be a couple. This photograph, however, is diagonally cut into two pieces, with a wide white space separating the two images, while two vertical zigzag lines crossing the white space in the middle reinforce the jagged contours of this split. A question mark at the center of the white space separating the two fragments of the photograph invites the audience to ask themselves what might have been the cause of the couple's separation.

The forum title, in all caps above and below the photo, is: "Black Feminism: Does It Divide the Black Struggle?" with the text split after the verb. The white space in the middle and the question mark at its center separate not only Black women from Black men, but also Black feminism from the Black struggle. The questions, displayed under the image, interrogate common nationalist tropes rejecting Black feminism: "Do Black women need women's liberation?" and so on. Yet the question mark in the middle of the poster reinforces the message that the forum would ask questions rather than provide answers, thereby creating the expectation of a consciousness-raising session. Although, in the poster, the Black man is separated from his partner, he is still present, demonstrating Black humanist feminism's commitment to raising Black men's consciousness and organizing together with them for the betterment of the community. The poster also depicts the event's audience as the organizers imagined it: young, fashionable, political, attractive, comfortable in their skin, and heterosexual.

An astute user of mass media, the NABF circulated press releases for each of its public events. Held at the Malcolm X College, the forums started with registration and refreshments (made possible by the participation fee of $2, the equivalent of a movie ticket at the time), followed by about one hour dedicated to presentations made by the speakers. After a short break, the floor opened to audience participation for another hour or so, after which the organizers gave out information about the NABF to interested parties.[70] The flyer for the first forum advertised "dynamic speakers" such as Don Adderton, Managing Editor for *Jet* magazine; Dr. Earle Chisolm, Lecturer at Kennedy King College; Rev. Willie Barrow, National

Vice President of PUSH; and Excell Jones, Public Affairs Director for the radio station WFYR, entities that were serving the Black community in Chicago. By collaborating with them, the NABF hoped to build lasting relationships and increase their standing among local organizations.

The event was so successful that the NABF decided to organize another forum on the same theme a month later. "Back by popular demand!" read the press release[71] announcing the event, titled "Black Woman / Man Relationships," on October 27, 1976. The forum flyer suggests a series of provocative questions:

> Is the relationship between Black women and men getting better or worse? Are Black men *really* good lovers? [emphasis in original] Are they good providers? Are Black women sexually promiscuous or sexually inhibited? Are Black women castrating Sapphires? Should women be kept barefoot and pregnant? Should men be househusbands? Is Women's Lib giving women too much independence?[72]

The questions, formulated to have maximum impact, interrogate raced and gendered stereotypes as well as clichés about the Women's Liberation Movement (presented ironically, with its derogatory name as "Women's Lib"). The specter of the imminent upending of gender relations (women becoming too independent, men as househusbands) contrasts with patriarchal stereotypes (women being kept "barefoot and pregnant"), thus inviting the audience to craft their own discourse between these extreme positions.

An undated tape preserved in the NABF archives at the Chicago History Museum, which bears the inscription Black Woman / Man Relationship Forum, allows contemporary listeners to map out the speakers' various positions relative to feminism.[73] Most of the panelists were prominent African American women of various careers, ages, and beliefs; there was one male participant. Brenda Eichelberger opened the discussion by defending the existence of Black feminism as not dividing, but strengthening the race, and restating the statistically proven fact that Black women found themselves "on the bottom of every ladder of opportunity, whether were talking about economical, educational, social, or any other kind." She then reaffirmed her definition of feminism as the social, political, and economic equality of the sexes, and of Black feminists as autonomous, assertive, self-initiating, freethinking, and, most importantly, humanists, who could not be against men because they were fighting for the liberation of all human beings.

The first speaker, Naurice Roberts, Director of News and Public Affairs for WFLV-TV Channel 32 and contributing editor to the magazine *Ebony*

Junior, spoke of her experiences as a single, professional Black woman. Roberts shared that whenever she tried to date a man, she discovered that "a lot of the brothers who find out immediately what I do, they begin to feel very, very nervous, and they feel very insecure." She also criticized the double standard of respectability: "Brothers will not allow sisters to go to the bar kind of thing by themselves." She advised African American women to seek independence and each other for support.

Representatives of the Nation of Islam were usually among the guests invited to most forums, such Sister Mary . . . [last name is unclear in the recording], who was working with the Nation of Islam's Ministers Counseling Department. A graduate of the Rutgers School of Social Work, she had joined the Peace Corps, working in Niger as a public health volunteer. In her address, she quoted the honorable Elijah Muhammad's statement that "Satan has tricked the world for centuries by naming women as materialist creatures that cannot become divine," and that these "false teachings" have shaped women's perceptions of themselves. She states that patriarchal thinking assigning women a lower place in society is both wrong and outdated: "In this year, 1976," she continued, "we can finally say that the role of the woman is only defined by the limit of a woman's own imagination." Yet, perhaps, in order to temper this potentially radical statement that envisions for women the complete freedom to define their own lives, she adds that "the creation itself is obligated to work in harmony with itself, and maybe, as women, this is what we should be working on." While celebrating the new roles for women brought about by a modern society (the year 1976), the speaker is supportive of feminism as part of the larger search for harmony within the divine creation.

The next speaker, Connie Seals, Executive Director of the Illinois Commission on Human Relations, a veteran of the Civil Rights movement, often attended NABF events and was listed in the Speaker's Bureau. Her analysis of gender and race is deeply shaped by class:

> In the 1970s, Black women, some of us, found ourselves facing two deadly monsters: racism and sexism. And we found ourselves needing allies. Our natural allies are Black men. They can no more escape racism than we can escape racism and sexism. And so, we must develop Black women and Black men who have their heads together, because there's another -ism fast on all our heels, and that is classism. Soon, it'll be Black and white against the poor.

Seals's analysis shows her awareness of the new impetus toward privatization and neoliberalism occurring in the mid-to-late 1970s. Black men's alliance with Black women is made even more urgent due to the economic transformations that would limit the prospects of vast numbers of poor people, regardless of race. Seals's narrative of Black women's experiences works as a starting point for building allyship and support across gender and race.

Furthermore, addressing the Moynihan Report's infamous contention that African American families led by single women were sources of poverty and delinquency, Seals insists that given current statistics, "there are going to be more female heads of households, not less." Thus, she concludes,

> When we talk about our relationships, they go deeper than whether or not we're going to get a good lover or whether or not we're going to get satisfied emotionally. They go a little further than that. They go down to whether or not Black women who must work and support their families are going to be able to join the workforce with dignity, make a decent salary, and move their children, boys and girls, into the mainstream.

Pointing out the increase in teenage motherhood, Seals claims that the answer, especially in Black communities, should be to "support [teenage mothers], rather than disdain them . . . why not deal with them now, humanely, rather than saying they're the curse of the race?" Seals advocates for support for teenage mothers and their families, thus challenging respectability politics.

While Seals's intersectional analysis focuses on contemporary socioeconomic trends, Thomas N. Todd,[74] civil rights attorney and the first Black professor at Northwestern Law School, invokes the memories of his own childhood spent in Alabama: "The first relationship in Alabama that I was aware of was the relationship between Black people and white people . . . more than the relationship between Black men and Black women." He underlines Black men and women's need for unity throughout history; however, in the contemporary world, "we've got so sophisticated and urbane, we've become competitors," alluding to the Great Migration, whose consequences he sees as fragmenting relationships that had guaranteed survival for Black Americans. While Todd does not have a specific answer to the question of gender equality, he cautiously expresses hope in racial unity.

The recordings preserved in the NABF archives show different analyses that participants in the forums crafted in order to discuss relationships between Black women and men. Most speakers focus on the Black family, imagined as a heterosexual unit able to provide shelter in a racist world. Other speakers point out the progress made by institutions and legal antidiscrimination provisions, or simply the fact that their lives in a large city,

Chicago, in a decade that had witnessed multiple opportunities for social change, were radically different from the experiences of their parents, who in some cases had only recently moved to the North as a result of the Great Migration. Nevertheless, one aspect of American society, according to speakers who backed their arguments with statistics, had not changed: Black women's position at the bottom of the racial, gendered, and class hierarchy.

The forums successfully created counter-public arenas in Black neighborhoods in Chicago. Brenda Eichelberger recalls that every time there was a forum, the NABF "had a packed house."[75] For the price of a movie ticket, the forums educated and entertained the audience, who were encouraged to interrogate received ideas about important aspects of their lives. Unlike the membership letters and cultural activities promoted by the NABF that often ended up mobilizing an upwardly mobile or educated audience, the forums, organized at a local institution in a neighborhood inhabited by working-class African Americans, created community-based counter-public arenas infused with Black feminist politics.

Organizers for the NABF sometimes encountered resistance in their efforts to disseminate Black feminist analyses. "Some black feminists are reluctant to spread the feminist philosophy in the black community because of the negative reaction feminism evokes," writes Eichelberger, referring to an event where she had been invited to speak, not knowing that she was only one of several panelists. She was scheduled to speak first; after listening to her, the other panelists rushed to attack her: "The black feminist finds all manner of charges being hurled at her. . . . Some appellations are: 'white feminist mimicker,' 'castrator,' petty bourgeois irrelevant,' 'black race divider,' 'pro-black genocidist,' and on and on ad nauseam." As a result, Eichelberger continues, faced with this aggressive and patronizing attitude, many potential Black feminists in the community avoid identifying publicly as feminists: "The black feminist sympathizers who were entertaining the idea of joining the movement begin to have second thoughts about their participation when they see a black woman treated in this manner."[76] While NABF organizers were always ready to disseminate their ideas, educate the Black community, and raise the feminist consciousness of their public, they often experienced the stubborn and aggressive resistance of their audience.

The NABF similarly attempted to reach a feminist movement audience, which they understood as being predominantly white. Eichelberger, who authored many essays and articles based on the collective experiences of NABF members, was able to publish her writings in prominent feminist and progressive publications, but her work was anthologized only once, and was excluded from the canon of 1970s feminist theory.

The Black Feminist Transcript and the Counter-Publics of Women's Liberation

Like many women's groups who turned the insights gained during consciousness-raising sessions into feminist writing, thus generating early feminist theory, the Black feminists who gathered in the mid-seventies in Chicago published several articles based on their experiences. In most cases, Brenda Eichelberger served as the writer and editor of these pieces; however, these texts were, in the end, collectively produced, emerging from a vivid, multidimensional dialogue. Although signed by Eichelberger, "Voices on Black Feminism," published in the journal *Quest: A Feminist Quarterly* in April 1977, is based on interviews with Bonita Kelly, Marion Fisher, Monica Stewart, Marta White, Michele Gautreaux, Rose Diggs, Cozetta Milton, and Donna Stutts. Although in latter works, Eichelberger would simply integrate other women's perspectives into her own writing, for this essay she transcribed the eight interviews she recorded, synthesized each speaker's point of view, and used direct quotations to summarize their arguments, thus presenting Black feminism not as a unitary ideology, but as a multiplicity of perspectives. *Quest* was an early and much-respected publication of the predominantly white women's movement. However, despite being one of only a handful of articles by women of color published in *Quest*, and although it included a multiplicity of perspectives, "Voices on Black Feminism" was not anthologized when *Quest* published a selection of essays from the magazine as an edited collection. Feminist publications of that time usually included a very small number of essays by women of color, sometimes only one, but these essays were rarely anthologized in books and they ended up not reaching a readership that would ensure their survival in the feminist canon. "Voices . . . " is completely forgotten today, although it provides an original account of Black women's attempts to build a Black feminist movement in the mid-1970s.

Quest: A Feminist Quarterly had been founded in 1974 by a group of movement women, including Charlotte Bunch, who had previously published *The Furies*, a lesbian feminist newsletter that circulated in 1972 and 1973. *Quest*'s intended audience was women's movement organizers, a general readership interested in feminism, and social justice activists working in adjacent fields. "Voices on Black Feminism" tries to answer a question that author Cellestine Ware had asked in her book *Woman*

Power, in 1970: why were there so few African American women in the women's liberation movement? Documenting the extent to which things had changed since the publication of *Woman Power* in 1970, the essay offers "an interpretation and analysis of the viability of a Black feminist movement." Seven years after *Woman Power*, eight African American self-identified feminists, members of a national organization, discuss their ideas and experiences, showing the continuity and evolution of the Black feminist movement.[77]

"Voices on Black Feminism" is another contribution to Black women's intellectual history in which NABF organizers develop their analysis of economic class as one of the main reasons for African American women's low participation in the movement. The interviewees perceive the feminist movement as focused on the needs of middle-class white women (searching for fulfillment in their careers) and marginalizing the concerns of women of color (economic survival). In fact, Black women's struggle for survival leaves them little free time and energy to participate in protests, marches, and consciousness-raising sessions. Fisher also points out that, as more Black women than ever are enrolled in college, this further reduces the amount of free time available for organizing.[78]

Another factor limiting Black women's participation in the predominantly white women's movement is its negative depiction in the media—the infamous stereotype of the bra-burning, manhating feminist and, perhaps the most deterring of all, the fear that "if it is known that they are associated with it they will have the stigma of being gay."[79] The article, while acknowledging that lesbian baiting was emblematic of attacks leveled against the women's liberation movement, completely avoids discussing nonheteronormative sexuality. Given the mainstream media's negative portrayal of feminism, the article similarly suggests that Black women also fear that they might "alienate black men, weaken the black family, dissipate the energies of the black struggle, and thereby fragment the black community."[80] This fear was often stated by Black women writers. As Erica Townsend-Bell has argued, many similar writings of the mid-1970s focused on defending the mere existence of women of color feminisms and rejecting arguments that the participation of women of color in the movement might result in diverting precious energies from the anti-racist struggle.[81] In addition, Black feminists quoted in "Voices . . . " argue that Black women fear that affirmative action might result in white women taking jobs away from Black men, a belief that further undermines Black women's participation in mainstream feminism.

In spite of their limited access to economic resources, Black women were still involved in various kinds of activism, in addition to their church and community work, which was often political. Yet, according to the essay's authors, they tend to avoid the predominantly white women's movement as an arena for political action because of white bias and racism. The movement has failed to challenge white institutionalized beauty standards, which contribute to Black women's devalued position not only in society at large, but even within their own communities, states Michele Gautreaux.[82] Although Black women agree with many feminist issues (equal pay for equal work, rights for single mothers and displaced homemakers, protection from sexual abuse), pervasive white racist attitudes that view Black women as a necessary constituency for the movement, but not as equal comrades, friends, or leaders, make them distrust the movement. Even more, the movement's appropriation of the symbols and tactics of the civil rights movement feels like another reminder of white privilege.

The article does not attempt to build a consensus on the issues discussed, but instead showcases a diversity of opinions. Monica Stewart, for example, privileges race in her analysis of Black women's position: "When we are viewed by the larger culture, we are not looked on in terms of our class or sex first, but in terms of our black skin." Eichelberger, on the other hand, firmly situates the politics of the NABF at the intersection of gender and race: "The eradication of racist and sexist oppression are interdependent," and the Black woman "has a personal stake in both struggles."[83]

The second half of the article strongly affirms the existence of Black feminism as a movement controlled by Black women. NABF activists debate various strategies, such as being a part of the feminist movement, focusing more on working within the Black community, or crafting a separatist position based on their specific experiences and needs. While some interviewees insist on keeping their feminist struggle within the confines of Black liberation, others acknowledge "the importance of joining forces with white feminists." Cozetta Milton, on the other hand, states that Black feminists "are not appendages of the white feminist movement but . . . we are very separate and different."[84] Yet the organizers are adamant that they are building a Black feminist movement, and that this movement has a revolutionary potential that exceeds white feminism.

All NABF activists are adamant that their movement should be initiated and controlled by Black women. This movement can help Black women actualize their potential, educate the public about their own lives, and create social change that in the end would benefit all. The essay advances a multidimensional concept of self-actualization that includes economic advancement, social relations, cultural activities, and mentoring younger women. The interviewees see educational advancement as a valid answer to economic woes, demanding training programs for unemployed Black women, on-the-job training for underemployed women, and encouraging women to explore various career opportunities.[85]

Building a feminist community, the writers note, would mean reaching out to and welcoming teenage mothers within their ranks. Marta White states, "We need to form a sisterhood with our younger black sisters offering school counseling, job counseling, and other types of services that deal with reality."[86] In addition to reaching out to high school women, the organizers recommend the formation of Black feminist organizations on university campuses. Eichelberger ends the article by wistfully noting the enormous impact that a mass movement of Black women could potentially have: "If the energy with which the Black woman has so intensely worked in the church is harnessed and channeled along Black feminist lines, there is *no* [emphasis in original] force that can block the dynamo."

Just like other writings by NABF members, "Voices on Black Feminism," despite its origin in consciousness-raising and interviews with eight Black feminist activists, has yet to be added to the canon of early feminist theory. The article was not included in the collection *Building Feminist Theory: Essays from Quest*[87], although the editors decided to reprint two essays by Charlotte Bunch. In her review of the volume for the academic feminist journal *Signs*, then in its early years, Barrie Thorne notes that although the collection presents different ideological strands of feminism, it includes only one piece by a woman of color, an essay by Michelle Russell.[88]

Including a small or very small number of essays by women of color, most often just one, was a rather common, tokenist practice for 1970s feminist collections. A similar text by a group of Black feminists, the now-famous "Black Feminist Statement" written by the Combahee River Collective, was included in the collection *Capitalist Patriarchy and the Case for Socialist Feminism*, edited by Zillah Eisenstein, and thus circulated to a larger audience. It too was the only article penned by women of color included in that particular collection of feminist theory.[89]

Yet "Voices . . . " did find its way into a collection of feminist essays. It was republished in a women's studies textbook titled *The Women Say, the Men Say: Women's Liberation and Men's Consciousness*.[90] In addition to including several men's perspectives on women's liberation, an unusual gesture for that time, the collection included several writings by women of color such as Angela Davis, Frances Beal, Martha Cotera, in addition to Eichelberger. Although the book, intended as a textbook for women's studies courses, which were beginning to be offered at American and British universities, was richly illustrated and well organized, the reviewer for the *Women's Studies International Forum* found the text "not well suited to a course whose focus is women."[91]

It is possible that the marginalization of the NABF's intellectual work contributes to its relatively unknown status today, despite the organization's regional visibility, national ambitions, and large number of publications. Inclusion in the edited collections that formed the canon of early feminist theory offered a guarantee that some writers would not be forgotten. Yet, during the second half of the 1970s, the women's movement's mainstream publications and the writings that formed the incipient discipline of women's studies were, with very few exceptions, authored by white women, who would only occasionally include women of color, as Barbara Smith recalls: "The late seventies and early eighties were the era of the 'special issue,' the response of some white feminist journals and periodicals to increasing numbers of women of color raising the issue of racism in the women's movement."[92] Eichelberger herself, when invited to join the editorial board of the journal *Quest*, offered to edit an issue by women of color; her offer was never accepted. While Eichelberger was able to find other outlets for her writings, based on the collective insights of NABF members, her work remains scattered through periodicals and has been anthologized only once, in a now-forgotten collection.

While it could easily be argued that many early feminist articles from that time are forgotten today, and perhaps rightfully so, the erasure of the NABF's intellectual labor is of a different order altogether. It signifies the *Quest* collection's failure to center intersectional feminism and it marginalizes the perspectives of a group of activists trying to build a national Black feminist movement. Yet the NABF came one step closer to achieving that goal in the fall of 1976, when Eichelberger was invited to speak on national television as part of a daytime talk show. In the aftermath of the show, the NABF received a large number of letters from around the country from Black women who were excited about Black feminism and either hoped to learn more or offered to start local chapters.

"Seeing That There Are Black Sisters Involved, Feminism Must Have an Objective Side"

Within only a few months after the NABF's founding, the organization reached national fame. On November 8, 1976, Brenda Eichelberger was invited as a guest on *The Phil Donahue Show*. She was in illustrious company: other show guests included Ntozake Shange and Martha Gillespie, and all three guests debated the status of African American women. On television screens around the country, Brenda Eichelberger appeared, standing behind a lectern bearing the name and address of the National Alliance of Black Feminists.

In the aftermath of the show, the NABF was inundated with letters from viewers. Many were impressed with Eichelberger's intellectual prowess and political astuteness. "On this program," wrote a teacher from Omaha, Nebraska, "three Black women expressed their feelings in a way that white Americans usually do not see."[93] Others were willing to translate their enthusiasm for Eichelberger into joining the NABF or starting a local chapter: "I saw your president on the Donahue show and was most impressed," wrote a woman from San Diego, California. She requested information about the San Diego chapter of the NABF and volunteered to start a chapter.[94] Many women asked for information about local chapters or, like one of the writers, a student enrolled in the Teacher Education Program at San Diego State University, about a Black women's conference.[95] From Buffalo, New York, a viewer asked about Black feminist organizations in the area, and for information on how she could begin to organize.[96] From Houston, Texas, another writer wanted to know how she could join a local chapter.[97] One correspondent from Philadelphia expressed her surprise at the existence of a Black feminist organization, and mentioned that, prior to the show, she had associated feminism with "white middle class women, who hated men . . . [but] seeing that there are Black sisters involved, feminism must have an objective side. I hope you will be able to explain it to me." The writer also requested literature about the organization, while enclosing a copy of the pamphlet *The Dialectics of Rape*, by "sister Angela,"[98] which shows that the writer was familiar with the work of Black women radicals. The NABF openly identifying as feminist gave legitimacy to the women's movement for this Black woman viewer.

Beyond merely requesting information, some writers penned their analyses of the situation of Black women in their communities. A 22-year-old Black woman from Omaha, Nebraska, stated that "The Black women in our city are in need of additional help in regards to themselves and their families."[99] Many letter writers hoped that Black feminism would empower them or help them deal with adversity in their own lives. From Phoenix, Arizona, a housewife confessed that she had used her home as a sanctuary to protect herself from the "ignorance and prejudice" she encountered; after watching the television show, she wanted to improve herself "not just as a woman, but as a Black woman who loves her people very much."[100] Another writer, from Rockford, Illinois, who identified as a "Black woman in trouble" without giving specific details, expressed her wish to study engineering and asked about resources that would allow her to start college while also caring for her three-year-old son.[101] A student at Columbia College wrote that by joining the organization she was hoping to "sort some of these things out, learn some new things, and continue to believe in myself."[102] These writers identified Black feminism as a potential source of empowerment and as an answer to many of their real-life problems.

Conclusion

One of the most unique features of the NABF's contributions to the Black feminist movement lies in its creation of an alternative public space at its Black Women's Center. A meeting space, library, archive, announcement board, service provider, and classroom, the room at 202 South State Street offered a material grounding to the NABF's counter-publicity, the process whereby its Black feminist community created its transcript and attempted to disseminate it to larger counter-publics.

The NABF worked hard to publicize the hidden transcript of Black women's lives and experiences in the predominantly white women's movement, in Black communities in Chicago, and via mass media to the general public. Their experiences were decidedly mixed. Sometimes they encountered support, other times vocal rejection and critique, or even, in the women's movement, tokenization and marginalization.

Nevertheless, one group had the strongest positive reaction to the NABF's message: Black women themselves. In their letters to the organization, they talked about their lives and confessed their personal ways of dealing with sexism and racism. They shared their critiques of their own families, communities, the Black freedom struggle, and the women's movement. Most importantly, they gave voice to their desire for community and liberation.

As Deborah Gray White states in her groundbreaking study, the emergence of Black feminism broke the silence about African American women's experiences.[103] Wishing to build the Black feminist counter-public at the local, regional, and national levels, the NABF enthusiastically answered every letter, sending its materials around the country and encouraging women who expressed their interest to submit an application for membership and start a local chapter. An undated membership letter mentions the voluminous correspondence handled by the organization (a mailing list of about one thousand at the time of the letter and growing by about two hundred every month).[104] The wave of letters received in the fall of 1976 strengthened NABF activists' conviction that they could build a national Black feminist movement. To take advantage of that momentum, they decided to organize a national conference. Titled "A Meeting of the Minds," the conference, which took place over three days in October 1977, showcased both the NABF's ability to reach large numbers of Black women around the country and the obstacles it encountered in its efforts to build a mass following.

CHAPTER 4

Mapping the Black Feminist Movement

> If the energy with which the Black woman has so intensely worked in the church is harnessed and channeled along Black feminist lines, there is no force that can block the dynamo.[1]
>
> —Brenda Eichelberger

Introduction

By the beginning of 1977, NABF activists felt confident that they could build a national following, and were ready to organize an event that would bring together Black women from around the country: a national conference. The wave of letters received by the NABF at the end of 1976 had demonstrated again that interest in Black feminism came from all regions of the United States. National Black women's conferences such as the ones organized by the NBFO in New York in 1973 and in Detroit two years later had been well attended, including by some NABF members, who had joined audiences numbering in the hundreds.[2] By organizing a national conference, the NABF intended to position itself as the leader of the Black women's liberation movement and craft a comprehensive agenda for action.

"A Meeting of the Minds: A Conference for, by, and about Black Women" was a three-day consciousness-raising session with more than two hundred attendees. The conference both celebrated the achievements of professional Black women, who were charting new career paths in fields that had until recently excluded them, and collectively designed a wide-ranging list of resolutions addressing the needs of Black women from all walks of life. The long list of resolutions, based on consciousness-raising principles during the conference, makes "A Meeting of the Minds" a unique event in the history of 1970s Black feminism. In addition, Eichelberger documented the event by recording the conference proceedings, thus giving contemporary researchers an unparalleled view into debates that unfolded almost five decades ago.

In spite of their efforts, a concerted national Black feminist movement led by the NABF did not materialize in the aftermath of the conference. However, the criteria of success versus failure does not capture the transformative effects of the conference for the participants. Nor does such an evaluation indicate, in the end, the amplitude of the Black feminist movement that was unfolding throughout the country during the 1970s. The NABF gave rise to several local chapters and affiliates throughout the West and the Midwest. Mapping their geographical distribution, and adding them to Black women's groups and organizations that are already documented, helps demonstrate the existence of a national Black women's liberation movement simultaneous with, yet independent from, the predominantly white women's liberation movement.

In addition, the NABF briefly connected to a transnational Black women's movement when they received the visit of a delegation from the Organization of Women of African and Asian Descent, a British umbrella group, which encouraged American activists to identify as women of color, in solidarity with their sisters across the ocean. During that meeting, which left lasting memories for the participants, NABF organizers saw themselves not only as Black American women within a specific national history, but as part of a global network of sisters, located in the West, yet hailing from all parts of the African diaspora.

A Meeting of the Minds

The NABF's preparations for the "Meeting of the Minds" conference started in January 1977, with a two-day retreat used to plan the major activities for that year,[3] and continued unabated until the fall. In the spring, the NABF started reaching out to nationally known African American women, such as Democratic Congresswoman Cardiss Collins,[4] Illinois native and the first Black woman to be elected to the House of Representatives, as well as Angela Davis,[5] Ntozake Shange,[6] and Toni Morrison,[7] who were invited to deliver keynote talks. Although these women were unable to attend, the NABF assembled a long list of prominent African American women activists, intellectuals, professionals, and entrepreneurs as plenary speakers and workshop leaders, including the NABF's own honorary members, such as Rev. Willie Barrow, National President of PUSH; Aileen Hernandez, former president of NOW; Connie Seals, Executive Director of the Illinois Commission on Human Relations; and Addie Wyatt, National Vice-President of the Coalition of Labor Union Women and International

Women's Year Commissioner. Writers such as Verta Mae Grosvenor and Sonia Sanchez participated in the conference, leading workshops and reading from their works.[8] In addition, the conference boasted the participation of local media professionals, such as Lillian Bell, Professor of Journalism at Northern Illinois University, and Naurice Roberts, Public Affairs Manager for WFLD-TV, who ensured that the conference would be extensively covered in the regional media.

The conference offered NABF activists an opportunity to reconnect with similar organizations. In her invitation to Aileen Hernandez, former president of NOW, then working with the San Francisco–based Black Women Organized for Action (BWOA), Eichelberger notes that the Black Women's Center had been collecting BWOA's newsletter *What It Is* and that BWOA editors had published a profile of the NABF in May 1976.[9] At the conference, Hernandez spoke about Women in Management and Women Entrepreneurs.[10] Similarly, Eichelberger invited M. A. Terry, who was active in the New York–based Black Women United for Political Action, to join the panel working on the International Women's Year / Black Women's Caucus.[11]

The conference took place at the elegant Midland Hotel, a venue built in 1928 as a private club for wealthy business owners.[12] The choice of the venue was a spatial articulation of the celebratory mood of the event. "A Meeting of the Minds" intended to both acclaim high-achieving Black women and to build a national agenda based on shared experiences: "There are certain issues that are related to us all," states the conference flyer. However, the way these commonalities were articulated tended to privilege the experiences of middle-class, educated, or professional Black women, while pointing out the discriminations they still endured, despite their advancements: "On the average, Black women earn less money than other wage earners," states the program. Other shared experiences, as seen by the organizers, referenced lack of day care facilities, negative media representation, and the increasing number of female-headed households. The conference flyer, while claiming that the conference aimed to identify the "needs and concerns of Black women" in general, unwittingly assumed a subject that was gainfully employed instead of unemployed or on welfare.[13] The conference debates, as reported in the media, evaluation forms, and conference resolutions, tended to privilege racism and sexism, the issues that united Black women, to the detriment of class and sexuality, identity axes that divided them, although the latter were debated in several panels and included in their resolutions.

The conference started on Friday, October 21, with a workshop on consciousness-raising and assertiveness training led by Brenda Eichelberger and Sharon Scoby (who, together with Marta White, co-chaired the conference). The first day of the conference was dedicated to celebrating African American women's success in career fields where, during the mid-1970s, they were making inroads in unprecedented ways: management, the arts, government, media, health care, and business. Given that participating in the conference required travel and lodging expenses, and because the organizers had to charge a conference fee to cover the costs related to renting the venue, most attendees tended to be middle-class and professional women. The conference provided multiple opportunities for socializing and networking (a reception, a banquet, and a cocktail hour), and ended with a plenary session that passed a series of resolutions based on discussions held during the workshops.[14] Only registered Black women received voting privileges. Other registered attendees, regardless of race or gender, were allowed "voice privileges" only during the workshop question-and-answer time, and at the discretion of the workshop chair.[15]

On the second day of the conference, which started with Eichelberger delivering the keynote address on the history and current state of Black feminism, fourteen workshops explored Black women's lives, discussing topics such as education, civil and criminal justice, women's health care, economics, lifestyles, female adolescents, women relating to women, accurate media portrayal, and women relating to men. Each workshop lasted two hours, and at the end, workshop participants adopted resolutions based on their discussions. On Sunday, the final day of the conference, during the closing plenary session, participants voted to adopt all the workshop resolutions. The resulting list was sent to all registered delegates after the conference. The organizers intended to present it at the International Women's Year Conference in Houston, Texas, the following month.[16]

Local media and progressive regional publications covered the event extensively. News outlets such as the *Defender*, *Chicago Sun-Times*, *Chicago Metro News*, and *Chicago Tribune* featured articles and interviewed the more notable participants. *Chicago Metro News* quoted conference co-chairperson Sharon Scoby as saying that "Black women from all walks of life will come together around the commonness of our mutually shared experiences as women and Blacks."[17] Barbara Merrill, regional representative for the Amalgamated Clothing and Textile Workers' Union, focused on class issues in her address, by stating that she "felt the need for the concerns of the working woman to be addressed. Women, especially Black women, don't work because they do not have anything else to do. Black women work because they have to work!"[18] In addition to economic issues, participants were concerned with cultural stereotypes. In her interview with the press, poet Sonia Sanchez expressed her concern with Black women's portrayal in the media: "Every Black woman you see on TV is always super-sexy, or super-crazy, or a big, fat mammy again." Verta Mae Grosvenor, culinary anthropologist, was quoted as stating that "we hope, as writers, we can change this image. It is starting to change, but only because people make it change."[19] The event's extensive coverage in the local and regional media documented the diversity of participants' interests and helped burnish the NABF's image and reputation as the leader of a Black feminist movement.

The participants adopted a list of twenty-eight resolutions, and, in most cases, tasked the NABF with creating mechanisms to implement them. The NABF committed to develop resources for Black female inmates and ex-offenders and, in the area of education, to work to create sex education workshops that "promote an awareness of a freedom to choose alternative lifestyle[s]." The NABF vowed to fight, both independently and together with other organizations, "for abortion rights for all women, against sterilization abuse, and for the right[s] of gays." The health care workshop resolution expressed participants' concerns with women's alcoholism and their support for national education campaigns on its effects on women. The workshop on political awareness passed a resolution endorsing the creation of a Black Women's Political Caucus that would sponsor political education forums and assist Black women running for political office. The participants demanded accurate representation of Black women in the media, as well as support for Black women working in the arts, issues that the NABF was already working to address. In addition, the NABF vowed to continue the forums on Black women and men's relationships and to develop resources for Black women in management positions and Black women exposed to sexual harassment.

Occasionally, the resolutions encouraged participants to organize on their own or in their own local communities. During the workshop on education, conference participants decided to work together with community organizations in order to protect African American children who often suffered threats and bullying in newly integrated schools. At the "Women Relating to Women" workshop, participants pledged to acknowledge and support other Black women and to boycott companies advertising in racist and sexist publications, thus engaging in consumer activism. The NABF assumed the responsibility to implement most of the resolutions in its activism, a tall order, given the wide range of issues discussed at the conference and the NABF's limited resources.

The resolutions, while centered on specific topics that explore Black women's experiences in a variety of contexts, nevertheless articulated an intersectional analysis that included sexuality and class in addition to gender and race. Although the word "lesbian" does not appear in any of the workshop titles, the resolutions expressed support for Black lesbians in multiple ways, and the correspondence preserved in the archive, as well as the articles published in the media, show that discussions on sexuality took place in several panels. The workshop on lifestyles, for example, discussed what the organizers deemed "nontraditional lifestyles," in terms of age, marital status, and sexuality. The first panelist discussed her experiences as an elderly African American woman, and the second shared her insights about her life after divorce. The last speaker, Madonna Perkins, talks at length about her life as a Black lesbian. She begins by sharing the feelings of shame she experienced while growing up: "When I first felt that I was attracted to women, it was very upsetting, I started thinking about all the things that I was told that were wrong about me . . . A myth is that the way [lesbians] make love is unnatural, and my answer to that is, by whose standards is it unnatural?" Perkins shares with the audience her long and painful path toward self-acceptance in a society that saw lesbianism as an illness and placed Black women on the lowest social level. She discusses in detail the homophobic treatment she experienced from family members and her family's path toward acceptance:

> I was paranoid all the time, and then I finally got to the point where I did tell my mother, and she took it like most mothers would take it, "where did I go wrong?" And we lost communication for a while. And I understood that there was a problem there, so I tried to help her along, I would talk to her, I would try to explain to her, I'm the same person, I just happen to be different from what society says I should be, and it's nothing wrong with the way you brought me up, in fact you brought me up very well! We finally came to a point, just very recently, and I've been a lesbian for about six years, and my mother started asking questions like "Why is it that you feel this way?" She wants to know things, and I can talk to her at another level now, and we discovered that we love each other very much, and that I am her daughter and that she is my mother, and now we're at the point in time to get my sisters and brothers to understand, which will take time.[20]

Perkins delivers the heart-wrenching truths of her experience in a quiet, measured voice. Attempting to educate her audience, Perkins shows empathy toward her mother and explains the long path toward reciprocal understanding between a mother and daughter whose bond is stronger than social prejudice.

While acceptance by her own family seemed possible, being an out lesbian at work carried specific dangers at the time of the Briggs Initiative, or the infamous California Proposition 8, which intended to ban gays and lesbians from working in California's public schools. As many African American women who acquired college degrees worked as teachers or school counselors, Perkins warned her audience that coming out at work could lead to loss of employment.

> At work, it was the same way . . . and I decided it was not important, and unless you have an intimate job relationship where it might be necessary to tell people that you're a lesbian, I don't think it's necessary to tell, because you're there to do a job first. And the job comes first. Especially with the movements in California about teachers and I suppose not only related to teachers but every woman or in a job situation and you're found out to be a lesbian, you just may be fired. The work situation I think is still very controversial.[21]

If coming out at work proved risky, in her social life, Perkins often experienced rejection, even from close friends:

> The peer pressure of other women, as Sharon was talking about women not being able to deal with other women because they feel threatened, because they feel that, that if they deal with a lesbian woman, by mere association they might be looked upon as lesbians, and they will feel pressure from their peers and their families. And at this point I believe that we're growing and we need to get together and relate to each other regardless of whether we are lesbian or not, straight women or lesbians.[22]

Perkins maintains an empathetic tone toward other women, and, like many other speakers at NABF events, reiterates her awareness that Black women's worlds were changing. Yet, she recalls that some her female friends choose to avoid being seen with her in public. Invited to attend Perkins's talk, one of her close friends stated her fear that male colleagues might see her there. This homophobic fear contrasts with Perkins's own courage to come out and discuss her experience at a public conference. The public's reaction was warm and sympathetic, as they applauded the speaker and showed their support through their questions and comments. The adopted resolution recommended developing sex education programs and supporting the right of any woman "to exercise her sexuality in a manner which is fulfilling to her."[23] Other panels identified sexuality as an axis of oppression affecting Black women's lives. According to an article in *The Militant*, a left-leaning publication, the debate around the health care resolution referred to "the discrimination experienced by lesbians in the healthcare system"[24] and pledged to fight against all forms of inequality affecting Black women.

In addition to sexuality, the participants engaged with the topics of economic class, poverty, and welfare in several different workshops. The conference flyer announced a workshop on public assistance and one on economics, and the conference program detailed the first as "an examination and explanation of various welfare programs," their criteria for eligibility, and recipients' rights. One of the announced panelists was Ruby Mabry, a long-term activist for welfare rights, president of the Illinois Welfare Rights Organization. Participants discussed poverty and welfare on other occasions during the conference. The workshop on political awareness, for example, recognized that the Hyde Amendment, which prohibited the use of Medicaid and public funds for abortion, would predominantly affect African American and poor women.[25] At the "Women's Health Care" workshop, in addition to demanding reproductive rights and an end to sterilization abuse, participants decided that the NABF would examine the use of funds by the Department of Health, Education, and Welfare and the "plight of Black and working class women in federally funded programs."[26]

Members agreed about the historical significance of the event, although their evaluation of conference participation differed. Monica Faith Stewart, an NABF member who would later be elected Illinois State Representative, wrote in the Chicago-based feminist publication *Women's News . . . For a Change* that the conference had been a "historic first," given the large number of participants from San Francisco, Detroit, Denver, Cleveland, Washington, Kansas City, Saint Louis, Milwaukee, and "cities in between," and the platform built on their insights.[27] However, others contended that the conference fee prevented more Black women from attending the conference. Willie Mae Reid, member of both the NABF and the Socialist Workers Party, in her article published in *The Militant*, estimates the number of attendants at two hundred women. In her view, the conference fee ($12.50 for preregistration and $15.00 on the day of the conference for adult women, $7.00 and $9.50, respectively, for "female youth"[28]) had the unfortunate effect of limiting the number of poor women and students who could participate in the conference.

From the organizers' perspective, the number of two hundred attendees appears to have fallen short of their expectations. Interviewed a few days before the conference by the *Chicago Daily News*, Eichelberger expressed her belief that "more than 1,000 black women" were going to participate.[29] If that was indeed the number the organizers had in mind, then the actual attendance figure, at around two hundred, must have felt disappointing. In addition, rather than mobilizing Black women from around the country, conference participants came mostly from the Midwest, which meant that the NABF consolidated its regional, rather than national, reputation. In her article in the *Militant*, Reid also claimed that most of the attendees were professional women, underlining the limits of the NABF's appeal.

In the aftermath of the conference, some NABF members attended the "International Women's Year" conference in Houston, Texas.[30] The NABF had planned to use the document adopted at the "Meeting of the Minds" conference as an inspiration for similar resolutions adopted by the Minority Women's Plank. It seems that NABF delegates were either not included or their perspectives were marginalized in the group of African American women leaders who authored a position paper titled "Black Women's Action Plan," which served as the basis for a "Black women's agenda" drafted by a group of Black women led by Dorothy Height, president of the National Council of Negro Women. The group did not include Brenda Eichelberger, nor any other delegates from the NABF.

The Black women's agenda served as basis for discussion and creation of language to be included in the Minority Women's Plank, adopted by the full assembly of the Houston conference. The Minority Women's Plank included issues specific to Native American, Asian American, Hispanic, and African American women.[31] The issues listed by African American women referred to quality education, housing, and employment for low-income women.[32] They overlap partially with the much more comprehensive resolutions passed at the "Meeting of the Minds" conference.

While in many respects the NABF's conference was a success, in other ways its impact on the organization was not entirely positive. The amount of effort needed to organize the conference meant that the NABF had very little time and energy left for other projects that year. Activists mailed hundreds of letters, invitations, and flyers to prospective speakers and attendees, organized press conferences, reserved the space, selected caterers, and answered questions from participants. Although the NABF worked hard to raise funds for conference expenses through participation fees and by selling exhibit space to local businesses,[33] the organization incurred a rather significant debt to the Midland Hotel, which the NABF was still struggling to pay almost a year later.[34]

These negative aspects seem small compared to what the conference managed to accomplish. Former members recall the "Meeting of the Minds" conference with affection and pride, as a transformative moment similar to their experience of intersectional consciousness-raising. Decades later, former member Helen Whigham recalls the conference as a highlight of her work for the NABF:

> I think for me, when we had the "Meeting of the Minds"—as a matter of fact, there's an organization here now. It's called Today's Black Woman—it was a concept of what we did when we had our women's conference. It's the same identical concept of what we did.
>
> We were way ahead of our time. We had this "Meeting of the Mind[s]," we had fantastic speakers to come in, we had workshops, and the women were really engaged. Women were really excited about it. In some of the workshops, you could actually feel some of the pain that some of the women were experiencing. It was a great organization and I truly, truly believe that it should still be around today, and it should be in every state.[35]

This vivid recollection is similar to many other accounts of former members, who recall the thrill of seeing so many Black women talking about their experiences in a collective setting, and of enjoying the sense of solidarity and community at the conference. In the memory of former activists, the national conference appears as one of the defining moments of their political engagement with Black feminism.

A National Organization

The national conference "A Meeting of the Minds" was the culmination of a long-term effort by the NABF to build a Black feminist movement that extended beyond the region. The NABF had members, affiliates, and chapters around the country, and this network, when added to Black feminist groups and organizations that historians have already studied (groups that may or may not have adopted the label "feminist"), helps document the geographic spread of a national movement.

In an interview from 1977, Eichelberger estimates the NABF's membership at two hundred and fifty nationwide, while noting that many came from the Chicago area.[36] The NABF maintained a long mailing list that included correspondents from places as far as California, New Jersey, and Alaska, who received the NABF's newsletter and invitations to events happening in Chicago. Whenever Eichelberger traveled for speaking engagements, she helped local groups organize. In Wilmington, Ohio, during Eichelberger's visit in May 1975, a group of students decided to start a consciousness-raising group.[37] After Eichelberger's visit to Philadelphia in June 1976, a local newspaper reported that the attendees were planning to start a local chapter.[38]

Black feminist groups inspired by the NABF met independently, maintained their connection with the Chicago-based headquarters, and sent members to the national conference or annual NABF retreats. Myrtlene

Clark, one of the first NABF members, led a group in Denver, Colorado, after Eichelberger taught a workshop on the Black woman, followed by brunch and a rap session, over one weekend in June 1976.[39] By January 1977, the members from Denver acquired an office and a phone number.[40] A few months later, Eichelberger met for a rap session with women interested in creating a local chapter in Washington, DC.[41] In Cleveland, Ohio, NABF member LaVerna Caldwell started a consciousness-raising group in 1976, which continued until 1979. Based on her experience leading small groups, Caldwell collaborated with other Chicago-based members in creating guidelines for intersectional consciousness-raising.[42]

In some cities, Black women formed local organizations that joined the NABF as affiliate members, preserving their independence, but receiving guidance from the NABF. A group from East Saint Louis, Illinois, and Saint Louis, Missouri, two suburbs located across the river from each other, started a Women's Self-Help Center in 1978 and received an NABF delegate who spoke on the topic "Black and White Women Working Together for Change."[43] The goals of the Saint Louis group were consciousness-raising, building community, and cultivating political awareness among Black women. Similar to the NABF, the Saint Louis group decided to accept only African American women as members, although they planned future events open to white women and the public at large.[44]

Other groups were located in upstate New York, such as Introspect Counseling Services, from Rochester, New York, which became an institutional affiliate in June 1979. That summer, Brenda Eichelberger delivered a speech titled "Black Feminism and Today's Black Woman" at a seminar sponsored by Introspect, followed by a discussion about Black woman / Black man relationships led by Introspect members Susan Goodwin Humphrey, Gaya Shakes, and Furelise Smith.[45] Another affiliate group formed not far from Rochester, in the New York tri-city area of Albany, Schenectady, and Troy. The women listed as the purpose of their meeting "to study literature by and about Black women and give each other support." In July 1979, the New York TriCity Area Black Feminists was meeting every other week at the home of Elizabeth Campbell, an NABF member who was involved in developing consciousness-raising guidelines for Black women.[46]

Inspired by the NABF, Black women gathered in small groups in different parts of the country and were concerned with similar questions. Elizabeth Campbell, who lived in upstate New York, and LaVerna Caldwell, from Cleveland, Ohio joined Chicago-based NABF activists who were working to develop consciousness-raising guidelines for Black women. Intersectional consciousness-raising emerged as a pivotal topic, as organizers were convinced that they could build a national movement by fostering a feminist consciousness. Although some of the groups were isolated or short-lived, it is possible that many more groups might have formed who did not necessarily affiliate with a larger organization, make headlines in newspapers, or leave much more than faint archival traces. These local groups of Black feminist activists, sprinkled throughout middle America, in addition to the groups continuing their work on the East Coast and the West Coast (the Third World Women's Alliance, Combahee River Collective, and Black Women Organized for Action), show the national reach of the Black women's liberation movement. Organizers for the NABF soon learned that their movement had transnational dimensions, as Black women's groups across the Atlantic used similar organizing strategies and confronted similar issues.

Expanding the Bonds of Sisterhood

When Stella Dadzie and Gerlin Bean, activists for the London-based Organization of Women of African and Asian Descent (OWAAD), visited the Black Women's Center in Chicago, they discovered many similarities, in their personal experiences as well as in their organizing work, between them and their American counterparts. Formed in 1978 at the University of Warwick by students active in the African Student Organization,[47] OWAAD emerged as an umbrella organization uniting minority women's groups from around the country, and faced similar challenges to the NABF. In England as much as in the United States, Black feminists were accused of dividing the larger Black freedom struggle. From the outside, critics insisted that Black British feminism was an elite movement, irrelevant for poor and working-class women, while internally, tensions about class and sexuality surfaced multiple times. These divisions, coupled with the general lack of resources and an unwelcoming environment in both the predominantly white women's movement and in the Black community, limited both groups' ability to enact the wider social changes that they envisioned.

The OWAAD emerged out of the similarity of the experiences of Black and Asian women living in England. After the end of World War II, citizens from the former British colonies in Africa and the Caribbean were invited to contribute to the rebuilding of war-torn England. African and Afro-Caribbean women arrived both as wives of male workers and as workers ready to participate in the national reconstruction effort. However, once in the metropolis, they encountered discrimination in the job market and a generally unwelcoming atmosphere that at times erupted in racist riots.[48] Based on these experiences, Black women immigrants such as Stella Thomas and Claudia Jones, political organizers and writers, brought a gendered view to debates occurring in the anticolonial and leftist movements. In the 1970s, Black nationalist, gendered expectations marginalized the work of Black women, who in turn formed women's caucuses and independent groups, such as the Brixton Black Women's Group, formed in 1973. The group acquired a space in 1980, and, much like the Chicago-based Black Women's Center operated by the NABF, provided a resource center, a meeting space, study groups, and a library.[49]

The OWAAD emerged out of the efforts of the Brixton Black Women's Group, AWAZ (an Asian women's organization), the East London Black Women's Organization, and others to unite in their efforts and build a coalition based on similar experiences.[50] The OWAAD was built as an umbrella organization, uniting existing groups, although after their first conference, attended by two hundred and fifty women, new groups started forming in London and around the country.[51] The OWAAD's politics derived from its members' experiences and was rooted in their identity, just like the NABF's. However, unlike the NABF, the OWAAD saw the shared history of colonialism as a basis for organizing together with women of Asian descent, recent immigrants from postcolonial African nations, and Afro-Caribbean women: "An organization of African and Afro-Caribbean sisters could not take up the issue of racism without responding to the questions raised by our Asian sisters."[52] Their political ideology of gendered political Blackness,[53] as interpreted by Nydia A. Swaby, shaped their activism against unfair immigration laws that granted secondary status to immigrants of color, against police harassing Black youth, and for education reform.[54]

Recorded tapes of the consciousness-raising session held by the American and British feminists of color show the organizers' shared concerns on both sides of the Atlantic, and intersectional analyses that revealed the participants' similar experiences. In their presentation, British feminists stated that the OWAAD's intersectional analysis included class in addition to gender and race: "We define ourselves within our organization as being triply oppressed, I've seen here that you have sexism and racism, we add another dimension to that, we see ourselves as triply oppressed, as economically oppressed, as racially oppressed, and sexually oppressed. As Black women, we come to the bottom of the ladder because of that." Asked by one of the American feminists about their own class backgrounds, Gerlin Bean explained:

> I came from Jamaica at the age of 18, and I come from a working-class background. As you get more educated, the system puts you into a class. Now I don't accept that, but they will say middle class or something like that, because I work in an educational institution and I get a certain amount of salary. In our groups, we have got students, people who work in factories, who work in offices, who work in schools, we've got married women, we've got divorced women, single women with children, all that.

Eichelberger then marveled at the extent to which British Black feminist concerns echoed those of their American counterparts, who in many cases came from working class backgrounds and, although upwardly mobile through their ability to acquire an education, still understood poverty in ways that women from majority ethnic groups could not. For the NABF, economic class, although not explicitly stated, was nonetheless included in their race and gender analysis, as one American organizer put it: "We don't have classism up there, but one of the things that we know is that as Black women is that we are at the very bottom of the ladder and it doesn't matter how upwardly mobile other groups become, we either stand still or tend to go backwards."[55] Black women organizers, unlike white feminists, could have "a total appreciation of what it's like to be seriously poor, not just talking about being poor, but to have poverty as a way of life set out for you. That can be very difficult for other people to understand," stated another NABF member.[56]

Both NABF and OWAAD organizers compared their experiences trying to mobilize working-class Black women. On both sides of the Atlantic, married women who might have been interested in joining a feminist organization often refrained from doing so because of their husbands' resistance. More generally, working-class women who were busy raising a family rarely found the time and energy to join activist groups. Other similar concerns were related to media representation and violence against Black women.

One major obstacle encountered by Black women organizing for themselves on both sides of the Atlantic was the accusation of splitting the Black movement. In addition, they felt that so-called "lesbian baiting," the fearful specter the manhating lesbian, prevented women from joining feminist groups. Within the predominantly white movement, British Black women felt marginalized because the campaign for "wages for housework" promoted by white feminists did not address the discrimination Black women experienced in the workforce, and the emphasis on abortion did not address forced sterilization and the racism of the medical establishment.[57] Initially, Black women working within the Brixton group had felt that feminism represented a white ideology,[58] although by the early 1980s,

Black women organizers started embracing the label, as the fourth and final OWAAD conference was titled "Black Feminism."[59]

Both groups felt that their transnational connection had to continue, and the OWAAD became an international affiliate of the NABF. This affiliation, as the membership letter stated, "officially connects us with hundreds of our sisters abroad . . . As our bonds of sisterhood expand throughout other parts of the world, they herald the decade for women of color."[60] It is worth noting that, although the NABF was firmly rooted in the experiences of African American women, on this occasion, they saw themselves as part of a transnational coalition of women of color, thus expanding their political identity.

The NABF and the OWAAD occupied similar positions as multiple-issue organizations of women of color, although the NABF tried to create a national movement, while the OWAAD emerged to coordinate at the national level the activist projects created by local groups. Their history unfolded in similar ways. Both the OWAAD and the NABF ended around 1983, due to conflicts over issues of sexuality and leadership, compounded by lack of resources, long before they managed to create the far-reaching social changes they had envisioned.

Toward a History of the Black Women's Liberation Movement

Former NABF activists often decry the limitations of 1970s Black feminism. In an interview, Janie Nelson recalls, "The women who were . . . educated, they were already inspired. They were already closet feminists . . . I'm used to going out and stirring the people up . . . Going to the church, stirring them up, like Martin Luther King did. We weren't doing it. We were strictly intellectuals."[61]

Nelson's statement sets up several binary oppositions: between intellect and emotion; education and authenticity; individuals and collective social movement. Nelson claims that the NABF failed to reach masses of African American women throughout the country and instead mobilized only a small constituency of educated women. In the 1970s, Eichelberger had wistfully imagined what might happen if Black women invested in feminism the seemingly endless energy they usually dedicated to their churches. Many years later, Nelson points out the impossibility of such a dream.

However, there were many Black women who did, in fact, dedicate their energies to building Black feminism. If we try to map the locations of the national organizations, local chapters, and informal groups documented in the archives, we learn that self-identified Black feminists were active in all regions of the United States throughout the 1970s. The NBFO had started eight local chapters, in Atlanta; Buffalo, New York; Kansas City; Los Angeles; Philadelphia; Raleigh, North Carolina; Washington, DC; and Westchester, New York. According to the proceedings, their Detroit conference, held in 1975, was attended by representatives from other places such as Oakland, Cleveland, Lansing, and Richmond, Virginia, thus showing that Black feminist groups either were active or in the process of being formed in these locations at that time. In New York, a collective of Black lesbian writers named Jemima, who was organizing public readings and published a collection of their poems, was meeting in the mid-1970s.[62] In the Bay Area, Black Women Organized for Action started in 1973 and lasted until 1980, while in the Boston area, the widely known Combahee River Collective was active throughout the decade.

The Combahee River Collective, the most famous 1970s Black feminist group, dedicated its efforts to activism and consciousness-raising, but never intended to create a national following.[63] In 1974, Barbara Smith, her sister Beverly Smith, and Demita Frazier planned to form a Boston-based chapter of the NBFO. They soon realized that they were looking for a more radical anti-capitalist and anti-imperialist philosophy than the NBFO's arguably reformist stance. Joined by Margo Okazawa Rey and Mercedes Tompkins, they adopted a decentered structure, held retreats, organized in support of Black women's health and reproductive rights, and protested the murders of Black women in Boston.[64] Their Black Feminist Statement outlined a political vision rooted in Black women's experiences: identity politics, and a radical vision of socialist and anti-imperialist Black feminism, which Robin D. G. Kelley, in his history, titled *Freedom Dreams: The Black Radical Imagination*, has described as "a vision of liberation expansive enough for all," or as radical humanism.[65]

The Third World Women's Alliance, an organization with roots going back to the Student Non-Violent Coordinating Committee, engaged in a similar combination of social and intellectual activism, although their writings, published in their periodical *Triple Jeopardy*, never reached the popularity of the "Black Feminist Statement." The Third World Women's Alliance started as the Black Women's Liberation Caucus within the Student Non-Violent Coordinating Committee (SNCC), with Frances Beal, Mae Patton, and Mae Jackson as founding members, in 1968. A year later, they renamed themselves the Black Women's Alliance, then later on opened the organization, which was growing, to women of color more generally, as the Third World Women's Alliance, and started publishing its newspaper, *Triple Jeopardy*, which ran for the next five years. Alliance members who moved to the West Coast started a chapter in the Bay Area, which the New York chapter recognized in 1972. Like its East Coast counterpart, the West Coast TWWA published position papers in *Triple Jeopardy*, and were active on a wide range of issues, such as organizing against the Vietnam War, for affirmative action, against sterilization abuse, and building alliances with other radical organizations for the next nine years, until 1980.[66] There were many other groups, as Linda Burnham recalls in an interview with Christina Greene, that did not leave any records behind: "You know, there were probably hundreds of groups . . . across the country. That's the kind of history that really does get lost."[67]

If we add these organizations, their chapters, and other local groups mentioned in the archives to the map of the Chicago-based NABF and its affiliates in Wilmington, Philadelphia, Denver, Cleveland, Saint Louis, Rochester, and Albany, New York, we learn that there were rather few urban places with significant African American populations in the 1970s where some sort of interest in feminism did *not* develop. There were local consciousness-raising groups that left few records of their existence, activists that organized a handful of events in their communities, groups that published several issues of a newsletter, or full-fledged organizations with stable headquarters. Both the geographic spread and the diversity in size, longevity, politics, and focus of Black feminist organizations and groups show that, throughout the 1970s, Black feminism was a national movement.

These multiple groups and organizations preferred to stay independent of white women's liberation, at least at the organizational level. Some included other women of color, while others, like the NABF, focused their organizing efforts on Black American women. Yet the Black feminist groups and organizations very often pursued a politics of coalition-building with both other feminists of color and with predominantly white women's organizations. These coalitions with white feminists were often fragile and short-lived, as white women liberationists were rather reluctant to accept Black women's leadership in the movement, interrogate white privilege, or decenter colorblind feminism.

CHAPTER 5

The NABF, Coalition Politics, and Colorblind Feminism in the Late 1970s

> You don't go into coalition because you just like it. The only reason you would want to team up with someone who could possibly kill you is because that's the only way you can figure you can stay alive.
>
> —Bernice Johnson Reagon, "Coalition Politics: Turning the Century"

Faithful to the principles of Black humanist feminism, the NABF continuously attempted to build coalitions and work together with individuals and groups from all backgrounds, regardless of race, gender, or ethnicity. In their feminist coalitions, when successful, NABF activists were able to create truly multicultural activist events that responded to the needs of diverse populations. In many such cases, given the NABF's expertise, visibility, and access to resources such as the Black Women's Center, NABF activists, and Eichelberger especially, rose to positions of leadership. The NABF collaborated seamlessly with other women of color groups, such as the Mujeres Latinas en Acción, and local institutions. However, in their interactions with white feminists, the NABF learned the limits of coalition politics. The NABF's intersectional analysis defied a feminist worldview centered on gender equality and thus made white privilege visible. Challenged in their conviction that they were victims rather than oppressors, white feminists either marginalized the NABF, or, when confronted with an unflattering image of their actions, censored their writings.

In her analysis of coalition theorizing in the work of 1970s feminists of color, Liza Taylor defines coalition as "the intentional coming together of diverse or heterogeneous parts for the purpose of struggling toward a shared political commitment." Taylor's account of coalition is based on a close reading, from the point of view of political theory, of texts by feminists of color such as Bernice Johnson Reagon, Audre Lorde, the Combahee River Collective, Barbara Smith, Gloria Anzaldúa, Chela Sandoval, and Minnie Bruce Pratt. These writers see coalition as a transformative process. In Taylor's reading, the "crucial components of this process include the notions of *struggle, shared self-reflexive political commitment,* and the fact of profound *existential transformation* through such a process [emphasis in original]."[1] The concept of struggle, in Taylor's view, accounts for the power differentials among unequally situated feminists. A shared and self-reflective political commitment signifies that a political goal is paramount to coalition formation, although participants in that coalition might hold different perceptions of that goal dependent on their situation in the matrix of gender, race, and class. Finally, the profound existential transformation underscores the discomfort, pain, and profound realignment of values required by coalition work.

Taylor's reading of Bernice Johnson Reagon's germinal text informs her emphasis on the profound discomfort and occasionally painful reconstruction of the self required by coalition work. In her famous speech, Reagon differentiates between home and coalition. Home, in her view, is "little barred rooms" where people with similar identities can congregate, be themselves, and find nurturance and understanding among people with similar experiences. Coalition, on the other hand, is dangerous: "you shouldn't look for comfort" or even a "refuge place" in a coalition.[2] In Taylor's interpretation, only commitment to political struggle can compel us to enter these encounters filled with all sorts of existential perils, including that "one might lose a sense of oneself through coalitional work. The most successful activists, [Bernice Johnson Reagon] tells us, were those who were open to self-transformation through the process of coalescing."[3]

In this chapter, I explore the evolution of coalition theory and practice in the works of NABF activists, with a special emphasis on Brenda Eichelberger. The NABF moved between "home" and "coalition" throughout the organization's life. Their "home," the Black Women's Center, was a space where they could be vulnerable, articulate a collective perspective out of disparate experiences, and maintain the focus on the interlocking oppressions that shaped their daily lives. Coalition work, on the other hand, could have different dimensions. It could mean organizing events or projects across racial and ethnic lines, or participating in academic conferences together with women from other ethnic groups. Coalition work for the NABF could also mean that sometimes Eichelberger facilitated consciousness-raising sessions or assertiveness-training sessions for groups of Black and white women. She often learned that white women rejected the discomfort and the profound self-transformation that cross-racial coalition required.

Publishing was, of course, a form of women's liberation activism, as feminists published multi-genre collections, periodicals, and women's novels—including texts that earned the label of the consciousness-raising novel—as activist endeavors.[4] The NABF had its own plans to edit a collection of Black feminist writings, which never materialized. The limits of coalition politics became painfully obvious when in 1978, a Chicago-based, lesbian-owned periodical contracted a series of articles by Brenda Eichelberger. Titled Anglogynophobia!, the series, based on insights generated during consciousness-raising and rap sessions held at the Women's Center, explored the feelings that Black women had toward white women based on the myriad ways in which the racism manifest in their lives extended into the women's movement. Eichelberger saw the series as a step toward personal transformation for both Black and white feminists, a precondition for coalition work. However, the periodical cut the series short, after three installments, without much of an explanation, an instance of censorship of Black women's voices and of refusal of coalition work.

Cross-Racial Coalitions and Feminist Activism in 1970s Chicago

The NABF worked hard to build coalitions with a host of local entities in Chicago and often assumed leadership on issues ranging from antirape and reproductive rights to solidarity campaigns with incarcerated Black women. In November 1978, the NABF joined the Chicago Council on Crimes Against Women (CCCAW), a citywide interagency collaboration that intended to study and address rape and violence against women[5] and sexual harassment in schools, and planned to compile a list of legislative suggestions to address these forms of abuse.[6] Eichelberger was one of the three codirectors of the new umbrella organization, which included representatives of the Chicago NOW, the North Side Rape Crisis Line, Mujeres Latinas en Acción, Women for Racial and Economic Equality, the Chicago Abused Women Coalition, and many other entities.[7]

While the women's movement had been to a certain extent successful at changing the discourse about rape and providing victims with various forms of assistance, NABF activists felt that Black women's experiences and needs had been marginalized in such efforts. For example, Rape Victim Advocacy (RVA) programs were established throughout Chicago, especially on the North Side, in predominantly white neighborhoods. Volunteers for RVA met women in the emergency rooms and worked on their behalf by explaining hospital and legal procedures and by following up with the victims. Yet the RVA program at Billings Hospital, on the South Side of Chicago, was staffed by students of local area divinity schools, mostly young white men. The NABF insisted that local Black women would make more appropriate advocates, and started training volunteers in the fall of 1979.[8]

The NABF was recognized as a leader in the local movement against violence against women. The organization co-sponsored Take Back the Night marches and rallies,[9] which in Chicago were truly coalitional, multicultural events. Written in both English and Spanish, the NABF's flyers announced the march as fighting back against abuse and rape, and unifying "our struggle as women of different colors, classes, ages, and political philosophies."[10] In 1980, as one of the key organizers, Eichelberger invited Carol Moseley Braun, Illinois State Representative, to speak about the victimization of women, violent crimes, and the threat to physical safety experienced by African American women.[11]

In addition to antiviolence activism, the NABF consistently tried to build coalitions in their reproductive rights organizing. In their attempt to identify and respond to Black women's reproductive needs, they created the Reproductive Health Task Force, led by Madonna Perkins and Regina Hyatt. They attended meetings of pro-choice groups in New York City and Washington, DC, while Eichelberger and Gayle Porter received training in self-help techniques at the Abortion Rights Movement Self Help clinic in Washington, DC. Other members received self-help training at various feminist centers in Chicago, as the NABF was hoping to open a self-help clinic in the fall of 1979. However, there are no records in the archives that document the existence of the clinic, which means that the NABF might have either abandoned the project or perhaps provided these services in an intermittent fashion.

The NABF's approach to reproductive rights, grounded in the experiences of Black women, clashed with the politics of the predominantly white groups active in the reproductive rights movement. Historians have documented the tensions between white feminists, who demanded unrestricted access to abortion and sterilization, and women of color, whose more comprehensive agenda included, in addition to abortion, an end to forced sterilization, affordable prenatal care, childcare, and health care for both women and children.[12] These tensions surfaced during the planning period for the Abortion Rights Week in Chicago in October 1979, a series of educational events followed by a rally. The NABF invited several white feminist groups to a planning meeting at the Black Women's Center, but the white groups ignored the invitation and met in a different place,

FRIDAY, SEPTEMBER 26
RALLY AND MARCH * ASSEMBLE 7 PM, DALEY PLAZA, CHICAGO
(RANDOLPH AND CLARK)
*REUNION Y MARCHA * A LAS 7 EN LA NOCHE*

WOMEN UNITE!
take back the night

¡MUJERES UNIDOS!
en reclamo por la noche

Are you afraid to go out at night?
To stay home alone?

Are you tired of sexual harrassment on the job?
Catcalls on the street?

Have you been abused or beaten by a husband, father, friend, brother, boyfriend?

This march is organized for and by women to demonstrate our independence; to fight back against rape and abuse of women; to unify our struggle as women of different colors, classes, ages, and political philosophies. This night we will assert our right to walk the streets unafraid. By marching together we multiply our individual power and in solidarity determine our lives.

Did you know?

• The advice most commonly given to women on avoiding rape limits our lives and activities.

• A study has shown that 3 out of 4 women sucessfull resist being raped.

• Women are most successful in avoiding rape by screaming and physically struggling.

Join with us to demand an end to all violence against women!

The rally and march will be held rain or shine. Escorts will see women safely to transportation after the march, and we will provide childcare.

For more information, call Southwest Women Working Together - 436-0550.

¿Tiene miedo salir en la noche?
O quedarse en casa sola?

¿Esta ud. cansada de ser sexualmente acosada en el trabajo?
Chiflidos en la calle?

¿Ha sido ud. abusada o golpeada por su marido, padre, amigo, hermano o novio?

Esta marcha fue organizada por mujeres para demostrar nuestra independencia; para luchar contra la violacion y abuso de las mujeres; para unificar nuestra lucha como mujeres de diferente colores, clases, edades y filosofias politicas. Esta noche afirmaremos nuestro derecho a caminar por las calles sin temor. Marchando juntas multiplicaremos nuestro poder individual y en solidaridad determinaremos nuestras vidas.

¿Sabe Usted?

• *El consejo que comunmente se les da a la mujer para evitar ser violadas limita nuestras vidas y actividades.*

• *Un estudio ha mostrado que tres de cada quatro mujeres han resistido con exito la violacion.*

• *Las mujeres han tenido mucho mas exito en evitar la violacion gritando y defendiendose fisicamente.*

¡Juntense con Nostras para reclamar un fin toda violencia contra mujeres!

La marcha se hara sin importarnos el tiempo—Despues de la marcha, seran acompanadas sin peligro a los sitios de transportacion. Tenemos facilidad para el cuidado de sus ninos.

Para mas information, llame Southwest Women Working Together - 436-0550.

Endorsers:

Catalyst
Center for Lesbian Affairs—Northwestern University
Chicago Abused Women's Coalition
Chicago Circle Women's Studies
Chicago Gray Panthers
Chicago Women Against Rape
Chicago Women in Research
Chimera, Inc., Self Defense for Women
Ecumenical Women's Center
Great American Lesbian Art Show
HERS—Health Evaluation Referral Service
Hull House
Jane Addams Book Store
Lesbian and Gay Socialists of Chicago
Lesbian Community Center
Loop Center YWCA
Midwest Women's Center
Mujeres Latinas en Accion
National Alliance of Black Feminists
Southwest Women Working Together
Women and Children First Book Store
WICCA—Women in Crisis Can Act
Women in Music
Women's Graphics
Women's Rape Services Network
Women's Studies Program—Northeastern Illinois University

FIGURE 7. The Alternative School course titled Feminism, taught by NABF instructors at the Black Women's Center, in 1979. The course image depicts a movement led by Black women, in coalition with white and Latina women. "National Alliance of Black Feminists Alternative School Program, page Feminism," National Alliance of Black Feminists collection, Box 1, Folder 1, Special Collections and University Archives, University of Illinois at Chicago.

FIGURE 6. (Opposite page) Flyer for Women Unite! Take Back the Night rally and march in Chicago, Illinois, on September 26, 1980, in English and Spanish. The National Alliance of Black Feminists is among the event's sponsors. Chicago History Museum, ICHi-183518, Chicago. Designed by Women's Graphics Collective.

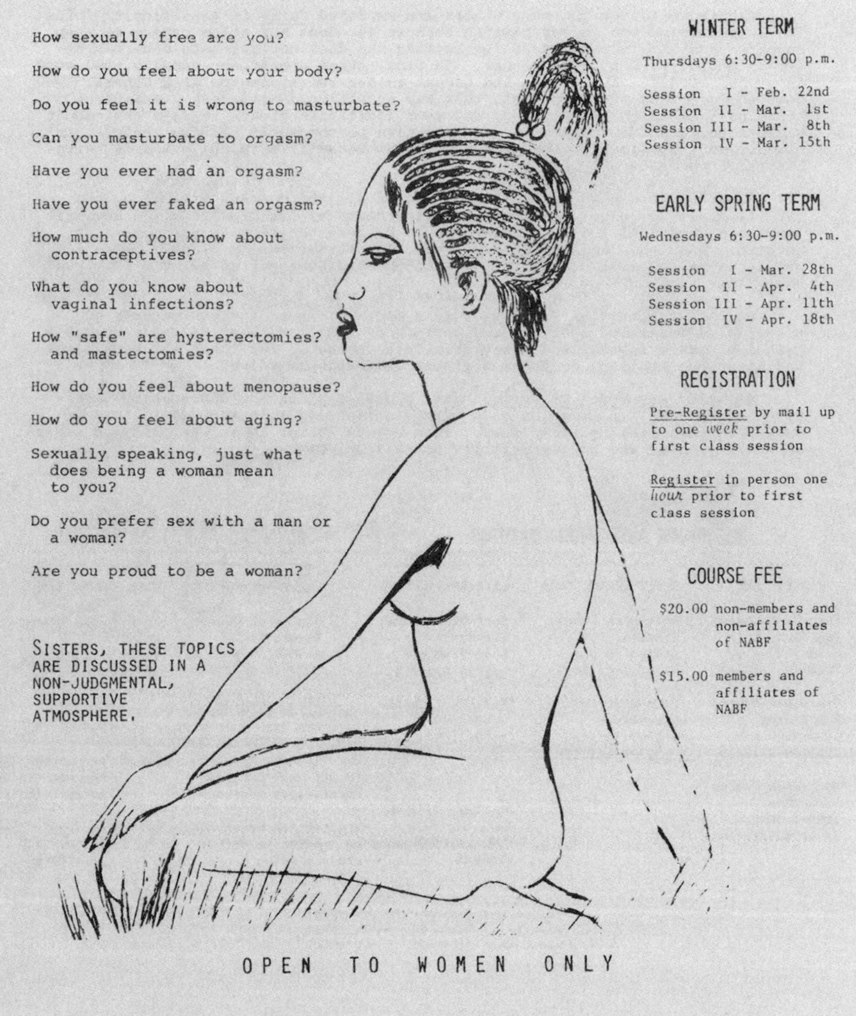

FIGURE 8. The Alternative School course titled Female Sexuality, taught by NABF instructors at the Black Women's Center, in 1979. The course centers the experiences of Black women and offers medical information often unavailable to women of color. "National Alliance of Black Feminists Alternative School Program, page Female Sexuality," National Alliance of Black Feminists collection, Box 1, Folder 1, Special Collections and University Archives, University of Illinois at Chicago.

without notifying the NABF. Black feminists, although disappointed with this act of exclusion, were absolutely convinced that the public needed to hear their perspective on reproductive issues. They organized a separate forum on October 26, the day before the rally,[13] titled "Health Care Issues in the Black Community—Abortion and Reproductive Rights." The speakers were Elyzabeth Dungey, a health educator from PUSH; Gayle Porter, NABF chairperson,[14] who would later pursue a career in public health fueled by her insights into the experiences of Black women during her work for NABF; and a representative for the Chicago Welfare Rights Organization. Their choice of speakers shows the NABF's understanding of reproductive rights in the wider context of class, in addition to race and gender.

The NABF was tireless in building coalitions with various institutions and groups across lines of race and ethnicity, in order to bring a Black feminist perspective to issues that otherwise would have reflected only the experiences of white and predominantly middle-class women. Yet when they challenged white feminist narratives, critiquing their narrow focus rooted in white women's experiences, Black activists were simply excluded. The NABF documented in their membership letter white feminists' attempt to marginalize them and organized their own, independent event, one that widened the frame of reproductive activism.

The Alternative School

The NABF's intellectual activism was another arena for coalition work, as Black feminists sought always to stay abreast of new feminist discourses generated in the women's movement and bring their own perspectives to feminist educational initiatives, whether inside or outside formal educational establishments. In the summer of 1979, Eichelberger learned about an upcoming women's history institute from Barbara Omolade, who was involved with Women's Action Alliance.[15] The Institute on Women's History, held at Sarah Lawrence College and directed by Gerda Lerner,[16] granted Brenda Eichelberger and Gayle Porter scholarships to participate in the two-week program. In the report written after their return to Chicago, Eichelberger and Porter noted the relatively diverse backgrounds of the attendees: out of forty-five women, seven were African American, three were Chicana, and one was Native American, while the remaining thirty-four were white. However, the faculty consisted entirely of white women. Even more, when the program occasionally addressed the experiences of women of color, these histories were not integrated into the program's structure. "If Black and other women of color had been involved in the planning and implementing of the Institute, we are certain that the material presented would have been more reflective of the role all women have played in American history," concluded the writers.[17] In fact, Barbara Omolade, active in the Women's Action Alliance, was the coordinator of the Institute; however, the faculty teaching the courses, Alice Kessler-Harris, Gerda Lerner, and Amy Swerdlow, were all white.

The Institute for Women's History was a landmark event in the process of building the canon of a new field of inquiry: women's history. However, given the structure of the seminar and the race of the instructors, the Institute de facto defined women's history as white history. It is particularly telling that activists from women of color organizations, who had vocally criticized racism in the women's movement, were invited to participate in an institute that taught them mostly white women's history, where the teaching body was white, and where the occasional mention of race was relegated to decontextualized examples. Eichelberger and Porter's experience at the Women's History Institute was in fact part of a larger pattern in the women's liberation movement, where women of color were welcome as students but not teachers, consumers but not producers of feminist knowledge, and followers but not leaders.

The 1970s witnessed the arrival of feminist courses on university campuses, where consciousness-raising groups initiated by students and professors institutionalized as Women's Studies programs. Inheriting the knowledge production of the women's liberation movement, these disciplinary formations often centered the idea of sisterhood and similarity of women's experiences, while neglecting race. Barbara Winkler claims that women's studies programs shared "white bias both with the universities and colleges and the feminist movement of which they [were] a part."[18] The University of Illinois at Chicago, for example, offered women's and gender studies courses, yet few if any of these courses focused on the experiences of Black women.[19] At the University at Buffalo, a Women's Studies College was founded in 1971.[20] Only women could enroll, and its leadership was predominantly white.[21] Throughout the seventies, its curriculum "both underrepresented and misrepresented the history and culture of racially oppressed groups."[22] In Kum Kum Bhavnani's words, the discipline of women's studies as it emerged on college campuses was overall "racially unselfconscious," as women of color were excluded from leadership positions and marginalized in academic feminism.[23]

The whiteness of this emergent field of study did not consolidate because of Black women's lack of interest in academic feminism; on the contrary, throughout the 1970s Black feminist intellectuals were present on college campuses. They presented at feminist conferences, lectured on a part-time basis, and were enthusiastically received as guest speakers. Yet they did not find a permanent home in academe. Eichelberger received multiple invitations to speak at conferences and events. She supported the academic labor of the few African American women who were teaching courses on Black women, and herself taught a course on Black women at Governors State University. She used the advanced technology of that time to include a multitude of activist voices in her course, as guest lecturers (experienced Black women activists) could call in and lecture to students from remote locations. Yet, in all these circumstances, academic feminists welcomed Black women's intellectual labor only in a temporary fashion (one could argue, in today's parlance, that they were adjunct instructors). Black feminism consolidated its position in the university in the 1980s, when it started enjoying access to unprecedented resources.

The social movements of the 1960s and 1970s worked to disseminate their insights beyond college campuses. A larger movement for community-based education was unfolding around the country. In Southern California, feminist education camps for adult women were organized from 1975 until 1987.[24] The Black Panther Party's Oakland Community School, active until 1982, was widely viewed as a model of progressive education for poor and minority children.[25] In the early 1970s, alternative schools for African American children founded in upstate New York were based on Afrocentric consciousness-raising as a model for education.[26] They were a part of a larger network of alternative schools for Black children organized by Black Power organizations.[27] The NABF started its own Alternative School, which offered courses rooted in a Black feminist perspective, available for a small fee to anybody interested. Yet like most of the public-facing NABF events, the Alternative School offerings, while politically progressive on issues of gender and race, remained grounded in a heteronormative perspective and within a year from the School's opening, its initial slate of courses was drastically reduced.

The Alternative School, announced on February 13, 1979, with a press release and an open house, offered courses such as Beginning and Advanced Assertion Training (one of the most popular offerings), Female Sexuality, Human Sexuality, Woman/Man Relationships, Feminism, The Black Woman, and Black Feminism. The school had six short semesters of four weeks each, two in the spring and fall, one in winter and one in the summer, and the classes, scheduled in the afternoons and on weekends, were open to the public—with the exception of the Female Sexuality class, which was open only to women.[28] The school offered a learning environment that was open and relaxed, and a tuition so low that virtually anyone could afford it ($15 for members, $20 for nonmembers). Registration forms point out the NABF's attempt to diversify its courses by suggesting assertiveness training for parents, teachers, young adults, and even children.[29] Nevertheless, out of the wide range of courses envisioned, only two topics proved to enjoy lasting popularity: female sexuality and assertiveness training.[30] In 1980, about a year after the opening of the Alternative School, the NABF offered only assertiveness training classes.[31]

The Alternative School courses relied on consciousness-raising techniques, similar to the earlier community forums. The course titled The Black Woman critically interrogated stereotypes ("Are Black women 'matriarchs' and 'castrating Sapphires'?"), invited the audience to find out more about Black women's history, and discussed issues such as teenage pregnancy and Black women's economic status. Any reference to Black women's love relationships, however, assumed a heterosexual framework ("Should Black women take lessons from white women on how to treat a man?").[32] The seminar on Black feminism defended the existence of the Black women's movement ("Is there a need for Black feminism? Is the Black woman already liberated?"); refuted the accusation that Black feminism could divide the Black community ("Are Black women taking jobs away from Black men? Is the Black woman's place 'behind' her man?"); and placed Black feminism within the larger context of women's liberation ("Are Black feminists mere mimickers of white feminists? Which is the Black feminist first, *Black* or *woman*?" [emphasis in original]). These community-based courses provided a cultural, historical, and political analysis of Black women's position in society, offering important information at a time when university-level courses in Black women's studies were very rare or simply did not exist, to an audience that might not have had access to college-level courses.

The courses took as a starting point the Black experience. The advertising page for the course on Woman/Man Relationships includes two drawings of a Black couple, a man and a woman with their backs to each other on the left-hand side of the page, and facing each other, communicating, on the right-hand side. The course centers Black heterosexual relationships, while the topics announced seem applicable to a general audience ("Can you be honest and open with your mate?" "Are you uptight about interracial dating?"). The flyer for the Female Sexuality course, one of the most popular offerings, presents a drawing of a Black woman at the center on the page, thus recentering womanhood as Black. The questions listed on both sides of the image, in consciousness-raising style, reference sexual freedom and pleasure ("How sexually free are you?" "Have you ever had an orgasm?" "Do you prefer sex with a man or a woman?") alongside contraceptive and medical information ("What do you know about vaginal infections?" "How do you feel about menopause?"),[33] thus continuing the referral work done at the Center.

However, just like most of the NABF's public-facing events, the Alternative School courses generally stayed within a heteronormative framework. In the seminar on "Human Sexuality," the questions guiding the discussion seem to challenge heteronormative assumptions ("Why are so many 'straight' men threatened by gay men?," "Why are so many men threatened by lesbians?"), yet the visual economy of the program reinforces heteronormativity by presenting two human nudes, one of an African American man, one of an African American woman, facing each other.[34] The flyer for the course on assertiveness training centers an image of a Black woman kneeling in front a Black man sitting in an armchair, with a crown on his head and a scepter in his right hand, with a cigarette dangling from his mouth and a beer can propped on his round belly. The image suggests that assertiveness might rearrange gender roles that subordinated Black women to their less-than-seductive partners.

The NABF's most popular course offering, the assertiveness training classes, were indeed popular not only among the organization's constituents but also with the general public. Given her status as a trained psychologist and her expertise in the movement, Eichelberger was invited to teach AT seminars, as they were called at the time, at a variety of institutions around Chicago. In these settings, consisting of multiracial audiences, Eichelberger learned that Black and white women's understandings of feminist assertiveness training, like many other issues, diverged rather sharply. While Black women learned from assertiveness training to be assertive in terms of gender and race, white feminists resisted any discussion of their racial privilege and embraced colorblindness instead.

"Can You Say No without Feeling Guilty?"

In their search for a new organizing practice that could consolidate the wins of consciousness-raising, women's movement activists embraced assertiveness training, a behavioral modification technique popular in the 1970s. Feminist psychologists were enthusiastic about its potential to foster women's "growth," as Patricia Jacubowski-Spector put it in a much-quoted article and film.[35] Major women's organizations published and circulated manuals such as Elan Cummings's *Woman, Assert Yourself: An Instructive Handbook about Assertiveness Training for Women*, printed in 1974 with the support of the Seattle King County chapter of NOW; *Assertive Training for Women* and *The Assertive Woman*, reprinted three times within less than a year of its publication (1975); and *The New Assertive Woman* (published that same year). In the terms of a manual widely circulating in the movement, assertiveness training was built on reinforcing the "tactful skills" women already had and aiming to provide them with the "problem-solving skills" men had been trained to use, in order to "enable women, finally, to be equal partners with men."[36] Of course, the implied subject of feminist assertiveness training was white.

Assertiveness training had become popular by the mid-1970s due to a series of bestsellers with titles such as *Your Perfect Self*; *When I Say No, I Feel Guilty*; and *Don't Say Yes When You Want to Say No* published in quick succession.[37] Even *Time* magazine featured an article on AT, as it was abbreviated at the time, thus popularizing the practice.[38] In small groups led by one or two facilitators, participants usually determined a set of individual rights,[39] and then role-played various situations in which they upheld these rights. The practice drew criticism as well, as psychologists cautioned that a narrow focus on individual rights could promote asocial behavior, and that newly acquired assertive behaviors might disrupt participants' lives.[40]

Similar to their engagement with consciousness-raising, the NABF theorized intersectional assertiveness training by analyzing assertiveness in terms of race and gender and evaluating the contexts in which assertive acts were supposed to occur from an intersectional perspective. The NABF saw assertiveness training for Black women as part of a larger project of collective struggle for social change. NABF member Janie Nelson wrote a dissertation in which she examines the transformative effects of assertiveness training and consciousness-raising on Black women, while Eichelberger taught assertiveness seminars at a host of institutions around Chicago. When teaching interracial groups, she learned that while assertiveness could be a vehicle for liberation for Black women, white women interpreted assertiveness as a way to demand gender equality while asserting white privilege.[41]

Yet there were significant differences between consciousness-raising and assertiveness training, although both used psychological expertise in the service of social change. Assertiveness training was structured where consciousness-raising had been fluid; led by an expert, while consciousness-raising was emphatically nonhierarchical; and it had a well-defined, even measurable goal, while feminist CR could end in activist projects, writing, publishing, personal empowerment, and everything in between. Most importantly, assertiveness training assumed that reaching equality depended on changing women's behavior, rather than society.

The NABF offered its first assertiveness training to its members in June 1976, with Marge Witty from the Chicago Counseling and Psychotherapy Center (an offshoot of the Counseling and Psychotherapy Research Center founded by Carl Rogers in 1945 at the University of Chicago). These seminars became a source of much needed revenue for the NABF, who delivered them not only through the Alternative School, but also onsite at various Chicago institutions,[42] such as Credit Women International[43] and the Argonne National Laboratories in Argonne, Illinois, through the Federal Women's Program of the U. S. Department of Energy.[44]

As part of the Alternative School offering, the assertiveness training seminars promoted the overall humanist philosophy that the NABF embraced. "We seek to unshackle ourselves from our 'place' as Black women to become individuals free to live to the fullest of our potential," states the Philosophy of the NABF section of the Alternative School Program. Yet rather than limiting the effects of liberation to changes in one's life and the pursuits of elusive equality with men, Black feminists saw personal freedom as a first step toward collective change: "These programs are designed to help foster our personal growth and development, thereby encouraging us to take individual action, and to help foster societal growth and development by encouraging us to take collective action."[45] For the NABF, assertiveness training promoted a new, liberated Black woman, empowered to create social change not only in her personal life, but in society as well.[46]

Trainers for the NABF popularized the knowledge dispensed in the self-help assertiveness training manuals designed for white women. Black female students might or might not have recognized themselves in, for example, the Characterological Lifechart of People We All Know. This handout describes Doris Doormat, a paragon of passive behavior, who allows others to make decisions for her and is highly critical of herself; Agatha Aggressive, who often overreacts and acts aggressively toward others; Iris Indirect, who wins by manipulating the people in her life; and, finally, the much more likeable April Assertive, whose attitude is "I'm OK and you're OK," who makes decisions for herself, is respected by others, "acts directly," and "wins honestly."[47] Of course, Doris, Agatha, Iris, and April are presumably white, although their behaviors, didactically portrayed, could be recognized as general patterns.

But did the skills taught in assertiveness training, in fact, help Black women improve their lives? "Can you . . . say no without feeling guilty?" asks the NABF Alternative School Program on the page advertising assertiveness training courses.[48] Practitioners claimed that the ability to deny a request represented an assertive skill: "The assertive woman can say no to requests when she is already busy, and she can give herself time to decide when she will do."[49] As Kimberly Springer argues, assertiveness could in fact address Black women's needs, given their long history of unsung labor for their communities and society at large.[50]

Furthermore, a closer look at the materials used in the NABF's assertiveness classes shows that they might have allowed students to engage in an intersectional analysis of their experiences, in a context not entirely different from a consciousness-raising group. The seminars started with a discussion of assertiveness and women's particular assertiveness problems, followed by "role playing alternative responses to difficult situations in small groups."[51] The assertiveness inventory, completed at the beginning of each class, asked participants to analyze interactions in a variety of contexts, as consumers, patients, students, family members, and members of the community, and develop an assertive (as opposed to passive or aggressive) response. A professional (unraced) woman responding to a male collaborator's comments on her looks; a customer standing her ground in front of a rude salesperson; a returning female student demanding feedback from a professor ready to ignore her work—these situations, for which assertiveness training attempted to develop polite yet firm responses could be recognized as instances of microaggressions by participants. After all, Black women had the historical experience of being viewed as sexually available, discriminated against as customers because of their race (not just their gender), and considered less intellectually gifted than their peers.

The NABF supplemented their feminist textbooks with exercises such as the Survival Ladder, borrowed from *Assertive Black . . . Puzzled White: A Black Perspective on Assertive Behavior* (1976), a manual that analyzed assertiveness from the perspective of race.[52] The author, an African American psychologist, warned that in their interactions with white people, African Americans were in danger of being perceived as too assertive, rather than not assertive enough. The Survival Ladder handout used by the NABF listed various situations in terms of power relations between African Americans and whites and correlated it with the level of assertiveness that they could safely express[53] in a society where white supremacy was maintained through violence both direct and mediated.

Although the NABF's seminars attracted many Black women, thereby helping the organization generate much needed revenue, it is nevertheless easy to imagine the limitations of this method. The NABF followed Jacubowski-Spector's[54] definition of assertiveness as a way of defending one's rights:

> Assertion is the kind of behavior in which a person stands up for her legitimate rights in such a way that the rights of others are not violated. Assertive behavior is an honest, direct, and appropriate expression of one's beliefs and needs, in a way that communicates respect—though not deference or submission—toward the other person.[55]

This type of interaction presupposes a certain level of shared concern for each other's rights and, up to a point, a relationship among equals. It is not necessarily true that African American women's superiors, coworkers, or even community and family members were eager to uphold Black women's rights. Even worse, in interactions with white people, as Donald Cheek states, African Americans' assertiveness is perceived differently: "There are readymade words for assertive blacks—impudent, impolite, arrogant, hostile, aggressive, and abrasive."[56] Even if fluent in the communicative codes of dominant society, African Americans could still be perceived as aggressive when trying to stand for their legitimate rights. The NABF claimed that assertiveness training could teach Black women to respond to microaggressions ("Can you respond with humor to someone's putdown of you?"), yet the onus of developing these humorous responses that could hopefully deflect unequal power relations falls on Black women after all.

The most comprehensive assessment of assertiveness training's potential for personal change was written at the very time the NABF was offering these courses, by NABF Board of Directors member Janie Nelson. After joining the organization as a graduate student doing fieldwork for her doctoral dissertation, she articulated a different critique of assertiveness training. In her thesis, she compared the attitudes and behaviors of Black women who identified as feminists and of "traditional women"—the members of the Ladies' Group of the Sacrament Society of the Holy Angels, a Catholic African American church.[57] Did women who attended consciousness-raising groups, participated in assertiveness training seminars, and read women's liberation literature have different attitudes and behaviors[58] compared with women from more "traditional" backgrounds?

Nelson distributed one hundred questionnaires to each group and received fifty-four completed forms from the NABF and an unspecified number from the Ladies' Group of the Sacrament Society. Nelson's research allows the contemporary historian a peek into the demographic data of the feminists who had joined NABF. From the questionnaires, we learn that most Black feminists were married, between twenty-one and thirty-four years old (there were similar percentages of women older than thirty-four), college educated, and employed, and had participated in both consciousness-raising and assertiveness training seminars. In the church group, most women were married (although in a smaller percentage than the feminists—53% versus 79%), high school educated, employed, over the age of forty, and had not participated in either consciousness-raising or assertiveness training.

Unsurprisingly, perhaps, Nelson discovered that NABF members' experience in consciousness-raising and assertiveness training correlated with more liberal attitudes toward gender and with their self-perception as assertive, which Nelson confirmed based on her observations that NABF activists were indeed more likely to act assertively in various situations than the church group. Nevertheless, as Nelson points out, her findings had certain limitations. In the absence of an assessment conducted before Black feminists' participation in the NABF, it was not entirely clear that more liberal attitudes toward women followed women's participation in political activism. A favorable attitude toward feminism also correlated with a higher educational level,[59] which allows for the alternative explanation that Black feminists were more likely to act assertively due to their level of educational attainment rather than their movement experience. The church group is simply labeled as "traditional women" and the research does not explore the possibility that a different denomination could have had different behavioral expectations or gender roles.[60] Finally, in the discussion of her results, Nelson differentiates between assertiveness training and real-life situations: "the average testing situation is probably very different from the normal situation of coercive social forces in which attitudes are expressed,"[61] thus echoing warnings formulated by practitioners about possible unwanted consequences of assertion.

While assertiveness training might have been useful, in a limited way, for African American women, could it perhaps help Black and white women build coalitions? Eichelberger was adept at using consciousness-raising in order to discuss both gender and race, in mixed groups of men and women. For example, her proposal for the 1976 American Personnel and Guidance Association Conference includes a workshop where participants could choose to be in one of four groups: Black women, Black men, women only, and African Americans only, allowing individuals with multiple identities to decide what issues they preferred to discuss in that context. The participants were asked to break out and talk and then report to the larger group. Eichelberger used a similar strategy in her assertiveness-training seminars, which she sometimes taught to both Black and white women. What kind of conversations about race occurred between Black and white women in the 1970s in the workplaces where Eichelberger taught assertiveness training? Twenty-four completed assertiveness-training handouts (seven by white women, seventeen by African Americans women) are stored in the archives, and they offer a glimpse into how women of different races understood assertiveness.[62]

The undated, untitled handout asks participants to define assertiveness in general, from a gender perspective, and from a racial perspective. Given the general level of information and the similarity of some responses, it appears as if the forms were completed after the participants had acquired at least a basic understanding of assertiveness and had spent some time imagining its uses in their lives. Each participant self-identified by writing B or W in the upper right corner. Most writers understand assertiveness, defined generally, in similar ways: expressing one's views, standing up to a group of people, not feeling guilty, saying no, or, more specifically, asking people not to smoke in one's car. From a gendered perspective, some respondents, both Black and white, define assertiveness as asking their husbands to take on more housework or participate in childcare. Others mention initiating sex, buying a drink for a male colleague, and refusing to make coffee or assume traditional female roles at work. Some feel that being assertive in gender terms would mean being able to act "feminine" and not being judged for it. A Black woman sees being assertive from a gender perspective as being compensated for caring for her children.

From a racial perspective, Black and white women's understandings of assertiveness diverge sharply. African American women define it in a variety of ways. Some explain it as expressing individual tastes and not being judged for them ("being able to have so called white lifestyles, not being put down by Black peers"), while others liken it with the ability to avoid stereotypes ("responding as oneself and not playing the racial role of compliance or noncompliance because of race but rather as an individual. Ex. Being able to say, 'I'm not a fan of Jesse Jackson'"). Several responders see assertiveness as the ability to stand for one's rights in a racist society ("insisting on my right to be waited on next in line when overlooked by clerk who asks the person behind you what you want"; "responding to a white woman I don't know addressing me by my first name"). Others define assertiveness as being competitive in a white world ("choosing a white sorority while being in residence in an all-white dorm," "showing whites I am as competent and knowledgeable as they are"), or as being comfortable with their white friends ("inviting your white friends to your black neighborhood"). One respondent saw assertiveness as rethinking old assumptions about race and class ("Not assuming the white person is the doctor and the black person is the janitor when I don't know which is which"). Others had a hopeful definition of assertiveness as "making a difference in the world we live [in] so that race relations are improved" or as "being able to express my love for all people, be they purple . . . starving in India or living next door to me and making people feel comfortable with this expression." These women imagine an alternative world without racial injustice.

The responses submitted by white women show that white women did not consider racism as something that affected them personally. One white woman defines assertiveness from a racial point of view as not engaging in tokenism, while another one defines it as establishing "bonds of communication" and a good, easy rapport with African Americans. Another white woman understands assertiveness from a racial point of view as "having black friends and being able to view the race condition in a humorous / loving way. Learning from them how they feel about their condition." This responder expects to learn from African Americans how they feel about "their condition" instead of trying to educate herself. Finally, some white women understood assertiveness from the point of view of race as upholding white privilege by being able to tell Black women "I believe you are not open or frank" or, even worse, as "offering a watermelon to a black." While white women who attended the assertiveness training session were fewer than the Black women, their responses show that some define assertiveness as willingness to learn from a different perspective—albeit expecting people of color to teach them. For other white women, assertiveness means claiming equality with men while upholding white privilege, thereby indicating white women's lack of desire to learn the uncomfortable truths that would lead to the self-transformation required by coalition work. This attitude was rather widespread among feminists as well, a lesson NABF activists learned when they tried to publish a series of articles dealing specifically with racism in the movement.

Theorizing Anglogynophobia and Dispelling the Myths of Cross-Race Sisterhood

Black feminists attempting to contribute to the knowledge production of the women's liberation movement often experienced the hard limits of coalition work. White women controlled most movement publications, while lack of resources limited Black feminists' access to publishing, although many desired to edit independent collections.[63] When Eichelberger was offered the opportunity to a write series of essays by the Chicago-based feminist periodical *Women's News . . . for a Change*, she gladly suggested a series of articles theorizing coalition work by analyzing both Black women's response to white women's racism in the movement and suggesting changes for both Black and white women in order to work together. The series was titled Anglogynophobia!, a neologism that captured the fear and resentment of Black women toward their white counterparts—feelings that had surfaced repeatedly in the rap sessions held by the NABF. Although, generally, lesbian spaces often were more open to criticisms of racism in the movement formulated by Black women, in this instance, the publication fell short of this ideal. The series provides a chilling account of white privilege, how it is exercised and defended by white women in their daily interactions with Black women and men, and of white feminists' inability to engage with the discomfort inherent to coalition work.[64]

The first article in the series frames the project as an attempt to share sharp emotional truths engendered by centuries of racism—truths that had not yet been engaged by the white women's movement. The neologism Anglo+gyno+phobia translates as "hatred of or aversion to white women" and describes a "visceral reaction" some Black women have toward white women based on historical and sociological conditions that the series planned to explore. While the series title is written in bold letters, followed by an exclamation mark that implies it is a widespread, alarming phenomenon, Eichelberger's minute analysis of its causes points toward the profoundly uncomfortable personal transformation that women, white as well as Black, needed to undergo in order to do feminist coalition work.

The first essay lists white women representing institutionalized beauty standards as one of the reasons for Black women's feelings of resentment. Eichelberger analyzes this as an entry point to explore gendered and racialized biases that devalue Black women, placing them at the bottom of racial and gender hierarchies in American society. Beauty standards, as Eichelberger insists, are institutionalized through advertising, media, and culture. At the time of the essay, the Miss America contest had never been won by a Black woman: "Physically speaking, the black woman can never be the 'All American girl,' for subliminally, the implication is that she is *foreign* [emphasis in original]."[65] Exclusion from traditional beauty standards renders Black women valueless in a sexist and racist society, which expects white men to excel intellectually, Black men to exercise "brute strength," and white women to share in white men's privilege on the basis of their beauty. Placed at the bottom of this hierarchy, Black women are completely devalued. Despite claims that Black women benefit from their double minority status on the job market, Eichelberger points out that white women benefit far more from affirmative action programs, providing another reason for Anglogynophobia.

In the second article in this series, Eichelberger examines how sexism and racism generate difficulties for Black women who desire long-term (heterosexual) relationships: "In a patriarchal society where many women are male defined, it is quite common for competition to be higher among women than it is among men." By foregrounding competition among women, Eichelberger challenges the premise of sisterhood, then celebrated within the white women's movement. She also extends the parameters of competition beyond educational and employment opportunity to focus on intimate relationships. Indeed, she points out that finding a romantic partner is difficult for heterosexual Black women, not only because of statistical imbalance (47% of Black people are male), but also due to high rates of incarceration and addiction. The increased (although by no means complete) acceptance of interracial relationships has exacerbated gender imbalances within the Black community as Black men, usually middle class, marry white women, thus reducing the number of possible partners for Black women: "Like a hunter, the white woman snares her prey with her hair of silk, eyes of blue, and skin of milk, the entrapments of which no black woman can ever match."[66] Beauty standards grounded in whiteness appear to completely erase Black women's attractiveness.

Eichelberger further emphasizes that norms of hypergamy (that is, "marrying up" or seeking a marital partner of a higher socioeconomic class) have left few options for Black women looking for a life partner. Given the place of Black women at the bottom of the socioeconomic hierarchy, dating white men was not a valid option as very few white men were willing to treat Black women as equal partners. Moreover, same-sex relationships would subject Black women "to censure from society in general and black society in particular," thus openly acknowledging the additional marginalization experienced by Black lesbians.[67]

Eichelberger's argument was based on conversations and consciousness-raising sessions held at the Black Women's Center. These debates were rooted in analyses that combined gender, race, and class. Gayle Porter remembers the complexity of these debates:

> One of the strangest experiences was [that] one of the women came in and she said how she had seen this interracial couple coming out of the Roosevelt, and she had slapped the woman, because when she looked at the woman, the woman was Caucasian. She thought about all of the years of white women misusing Black women and taking our men, and I was waiting, and hoping that the group would react. And they did! And they said, "Wait a minute, tell us again. You saw her and you saw him. Did she have a gun on him?" She said, "No." "And you hit her? You hit this strange woman who might have had a gun and shot you back?"
>
> It was wonderful to hear them help her to look at how crazy her behavior was, how dangerous it was, but to look at where it came from. This

> woman wasn't making him do anything, but I think that is an area that we still don't do enough exploring of. What is the impact on the psyche of Black women who see a pattern of Black men, often Black men who are affluent for one reason or another choosing to become involved with and/or marry women who are outside of the race? What is the message that is given? I shared then that my belief was only that if two people are really in love with one another, that is what everybody is hoping for, and if they are not, Black women have enough to struggle with without getting a man who really doesn't think that they are good enough.[68]

Black feminists, while critical of upwardly mobile Black men who chose their partners based on internalized racism and sexism, were, however, convinced that Black women needed partners who would appreciate them.

These discussions mirror similar ones unfolding in the Black freedom struggle. In her contribution to the *Black Scholar* forum on Black male/female relationships, poet and theorist Audre Lorde noted that "Black men with middle-class aspirations frequently turn to white women" for their alleged ability to fit the model of "femininity"; however, she insisted that "freedom and future for Blacks does not mean absorbing the dominant white male disease" of sexism and male domination.[69] Like Lorde, Eichelberger linked her critique of interracial dating to oppressive notions of white beauty and femininity, as well as norms of womanhood tied to docility and submissiveness, attributes that Black feminists could not and would not seek for themselves.

As explored in another installment in the series, white women's "superiority complex" is another reason for Anglogynophobia. Despite their insistence that they are not racist, white women enact white supremacy and defend white privilege. To support this view, Eichelberger provides several kinds of evidence. In the workplace, white women have a condescending attitude toward Black women who hold subordinate positions. When white women serve as their counselors or advisors, Black women feel white women's lack of empathy. If Black and white women inhabit similar positions in the workforce, white women act surprised when Black women manifest their access to the trappings of middle-class life. Even worse, when Black women are in a supervisory position, white women rarely perform at their highest capacity. Examples of the persistence and pervasiveness of these inequities surfaced regularly during NABF consciousness-raising sessions, encompassing multiple aspects of white women's racial privilege—cultural, economic, and interpersonal. Yet, when Black women tried to raise these power dynamics with white feminists, they encountered a stone wall. Thus, Eichelberger pointed out, not only do white women never admit to or voice criticism of white privilege, but they are deeply invested in protecting it. The NABF's insights, then, linked Black women's anger not only to centuries of racial oppression that have gone unacknowledged in white American history and society, but also to white feminists' refusal to address how white privilege continues to play out in the women's movement.[70]

Eichelberger's articulation of Black women's feelings expressed during NABF rap sessions likely angered the editors of *Women's News*, who decided to cut the series short after the third installment. Eichelberger was allowed to publish a fourth article, subtitled "Conclusion," which defended her choice of subject matter, insisting that a feminist periodical was the best venue for such difficult conversations to occur, so that Black and white women could start doing the arduous work of coalition building: "If the bonds of sisterhood are to be strengthened, women of the same color need to explore their antipathetic feelings, but women of different colors need to explore theirs as well!"[71] She then listed six causes of Anglogynophobia, noting that she had been given the opportunity to explore only the first four, and that "space limitations" prevented her from developing the last two on the list: "a) representing institutionalized beauty, b) receiving preferential treatment, c) mating Black men, d) appearing to possess a superiority complex, e) seeming to exploit black women, and f) acting overtly racist." The feminist canon is depleted because censorship prevented publication of the last article, exploring dimensions of racism and white privilege as perceived by NABF activists.

Fortunately, the National Alliance of Black Feminists archives hold a copy of the last one of Eichelberger's essays, which, according to marginal notes by the author, was never submitted to *Women's News*.[72] Based on recorded conversations between Black women, the essay states that another cause of Anglogynophobia is "the perception many Black women [have] that white women exploit them. This exploitation is viewed as existing on both a mass scale and in individual relationships between Black and white women." The examples supporting this statement range from economic appropriation (white women discovering a cosmetic product used in the Black community, marketing it, and capitalizing on it) to intellectual appropriation of Black women's contributions to the feminist movement, which happens while Black women are still tokenized and advised to relinquish their concerns with race and instead focus on sexism. The double standard that views only white women as vulnerable prompted public support for "displaced homemakers." In response, Eichelberger quotes from an interviewee who states that Black women "have been displaced homemakers all [their] lives" but had never received any kind of empathy or support.

The unpublished essay includes more direct quotations from Eichelberger's interviews, which speak directly about how overt racism by white women is likely to fuel Anglogynophobia: "Remember in Chicago when they were busing kids early in the school year, the majority of those people yelling, 'Kill those n . . . !' and things like that were white women. They weren't big gruffy white men, they were white women, and that got televised!" While the interviewee does not recommend working together with white women based on gender solidarity, Eichelberger still concludes that although Anglogynophobia has deep roots, there are ways to reduce it, a topic she promises to discuss in a future essay.

It is worth noting that Eichelberger herself also attempted to tone down the feelings of Anglogynophobia expressed by her interlocutors. In an early draft, she quotes in full a Black woman who discussed white women segregationists: "I don't think it's necessarily unhealthy for Black women to have a phobia about dealing with white women. White women have, with few exceptions, on the bottom line they have sided with their men, just as the white working class or the lower white working class sides with the male power structure. I don't suggest trying to make friends based on the woman's struggle." Aware of the deep mistrust engendered by centuries of racial exploitation and years in a movement where white women refused to engage with their racism, Eichelberger still believed in the importance and necessity of coalition work. For that purpose, Eichelberger redacted this more radical statement, although to no avail. Her series was cut short anyway.

This instance of censorship of the NABF is surprising because Eichelberger was neither the first nor the only Black woman to state that Black women held feelings of mistrust and fear toward white women. "What do Black women feel about Women's Lib? Distrust. It is white, therefore suspect," states Toni Morrison in an essay published in the *New York Times Magazine* in 1971.[73] In her analysis, the women's liberation movement appears as little more than a family quarrel between white women and men. Black women already enjoyed most of the freedoms that white women were searching for in their liberation (jobs, independence, sexual freedom, power within their own families)—yet not as freedoms but as unrewarded responsibilities. Toward white women, Black women felt animosity; they "look at white women and see the enemy, for they know that racism is not confined to white men and that there are more white women than men in this country."[74] Yet, Morrison sees hope in a women's movement that can claim political power. Black women organizers such as Shirley Chisholm, Fannie Lou Hamer, and Beulah Sanders, working in the National Women's Political Caucus, could turn the movement toward "human rights rather than sexual rights—something other than a family quarrel, and the air is shivery with possibilities."[75]

Just like Morrison, Eichelberger planned to conclude an argument that started with seemingly harsh criticism of white women in the movement by outlining ways of overcoming Anglogynophobia in order to build cross-racial coalitions. The editorial board's decision to censor this series is even more surprising, considering the NABF and *Women's News* had developed a working relationship. NABF members had contributed articles to the magazine, which in turn had published announcements about NABF events. In another article, written less than a year later, Margaret Simmons noted that this incident represented another failed attempt at interracial dialogue in the women's liberation movement, in which the editors of *Women's News* censored the series of articles instead of welcoming it as an opportunity for meaningful exchange.[76]

Decades later, Eichelberger still believed that Black women's critiques of racism within the women's movement had to be voiced and explored in order for the movement to thrive:

> I was pointing out how a lot of Black women felt about white women, because I would talk to them and, being Black, they felt comfortable telling me how they felt. And it certainly wasn't isolated, not just one Black woman here and a Black woman there, there was a strong enmity by many Black women against white women. . . . I wanted to end [the series] on how we need to get together to work together, but maybe [the editors] felt that I was too slow in making that point. But I felt that I needed to get out all the negative feelings, to get them all out in the publication, and that's why I did the series, and they stopped me before I was able to do that.[77]

Given Eichelberger's years of experience in the movement, she was familiar with the difficulty of overcoming profound feelings of anger at white women's racism. The statement that Black and white women need "to get together to work together" points toward the self-reflective political commitment to gender justice, one where Black and white women have to meet one another by first acknowledging their feelings engendered by centuries of racial exploitation. This is a dangerous encounter. While Eichelberger acknowledges the white editors' inability to experience their discomfort for too long, she still believes in the importance of coalition work.

Believing in the value of the ideas expressed in "Anglogynophobia!" Eichelberger offered to revise the series for *Ms. Magazine*, who never published it. She also proposed a book on the topic to Follett Publishing Company, who at the time were looking for manuscripts about the women's movement. In her cover letter, Eichelberger states that her book exploring relationships between Black and white women "is quite comprehensive, I feel, because it covers every area imaginable regarding the way black and white women relate to each other. In addition to its informative aspect, it carries with it the aspect of self-help, as solutions are offered in which women, individually as well as collectively, can improve their relationships with other women both intra-ethnically and inter-ethnically."[78] Follett rejected the proposal for reasons worth examining. In the rejection letter, the acquisitions editor states that "Although the topic has considerable merit, it was thought that the audience was too limited.... I think you are an excellent writer and would be happy to consider any other idea with you that you might have, but I believe we will have to keep the material in the feminist realm without going into other areas."[79] The rejection reasons had nothing to do with the quality of writing or the author's ability to write a thought-provoking book. It was the book's topic, relationships between Black and white women in the feminist movement, that the editor felt would not attract enough of an audience interested in women's liberation. According to Follett, the "feminist realm" did not include an analysis of racism or power relations between white and Black women. Thus, Anglogynophobia was censored again.

Conclusion

As Christina Greene argues, during the 1970s, Black feminists were both *apart from and a part of* the women's movement.[80] They preferred to have their own independent organizations, but engaged deeply in coalition politics. Antiviolence activist events such as Take Back the Night, co-chaired by Eichelberger, were truly multicultural due to collaborations with other women of color groups, white feminist groups, and local institutions. Yet in their attempts to work together with white feminists, the NABF sometimes encountered rejection and censorship.

Eichelberger attempted to go beyond publishing the occasional essay by writing article series and a book proposal as a way to solidify the NABF's intellectual legacy. Yet with few notable exceptions such as the novelist, essayist, and Random House editor Toni Morrison, the feminists making strides in the mainstream publishing establishment were white and their vision of feminism grounded in colorblind gender equality. As feminism became institutionalized on college campuses via women's studies programs and academic feminism in the 1970s, the white women who were at the forefront of this expansion into academe erased, marginalized, or misrepresented women of color and their critiques of racism in the movement.

The whitewashing of women's liberation did not originate in the historical work published in the 1980s about the movement. It manifested during the movement years, via a myriad of small and not-so-small decisions made by white feminists. Whether in social activism or in feminist publishing, white feminists often suppressed Black women's voices. These processes took multiple shapes: editorial decisions not to anthologize more than one essay by women of color; organizing that prioritized white women's needs; a stubborn refusal to engage with white privilege; direct censorship; and an insistence on centering colorblind feminism, with race considered at best a marginal particularity and at worst something outside of its realm.

Many Black feminists—although not all—believed in coalition work, despite disappointing responses from white women. Eichelberger's response to the censorship she experienced was, as we will see in chapter 7, to double down on the need for coalition work, and to continue to advocate for cross-racial coalitions led by African Americans as a strategy for passing the Equal Rights Amendment in the aftermath of Reagan's election in 1980.

By the end of the decade, a series of crises made the NABF's work increasingly difficult. The organization had to contend with outside factors, such as rising rents in the downtown area where the Black Women's Center was located, as well as a shortage of dues-paying members. Internal tensions within the organization, between lesbian and heterosexual members, were amplified by respectability politics and the more general lesbian baiting of feminist organizations. Although the NABF offered lesbians private support while maintaining public silence, a lesbian-straight split reduced the organization's membership at a time when it needed the most support.

CHAPTER 6

Between Public Silence and Private Support

Black Lesbians and the NABF's Politics of Sexuality

> Heterosexual privilege is usually the only privilege that Black women have . . . Being out, particularly out in print, is the final renunciation of any claim to the crumbs of tolerance that nonthreatening "ladylike" Black women are sometimes fed . . .
>
> —Barbara Smith, "Building Black Women's Studies"

Soon after announcing their presence in 1974, the NABF's predecessor, the Chicago chapter of the NBFO, received multiple letters from African American women who identified as lesbians and were excited to learn about a new Black women's organization. Writers came out in their letters ("since accepting my homosexuality I am a much happier person") and expressed their intention to be active in the Black women's liberation movement.[1] One woman, who identified as "Black, twenty-six years old female, strictly gay,"[2] was willing to relocate to Illinois from Florida. These writers felt that a Black feminist organization could offer support and community and looked forward to finding a place where they could belong and a movement that spoke to their needs and aspirations.

Yet the NABF rarely stated its support for Black lesbians openly,[3] failed to challenge heteronormativity in its theoretical analysis, and seldom debated same-sex desire at public-facing NABF events. The NABF's community forums, their most successful public events for Black audiences, reinforced heteronormative discourse through their focus on relationships between Black women and men. When addressing predominantly white and feminist audiences, especially in academic settings, the NABF's leadership tended to depict Black female sexuality as heterosexual and oriented toward forming long-term relationships.

The NABF's public silence about same-sex desire hid a much more complex internal reality. Black lesbians were a vibrant part of the organization, formed friendships and relationships with other members, and participated in their own small group discussions. Behind closed doors, in consciousness-raising sessions that specifically explored their experiences, lesbian activists talked about their relationships, their lives, building community, the threat of stigmatization, and dealing with rejection and violence. This is another example of counter-publicity as defined by Catherine Squires, where subaltern groups, in this case Black lesbian members of the NABF, created a "hidden transcript," as she outlined. Based on historical analysis, Squires proposes three types of subaltern spheres, based on the relationships between the marginal group and larger, more public groups. Counter-publicity describes a relationship where marginalized groups, such as Black lesbians in this situation, create a "hidden transcript" by discussing experiences that would challenge public narratives about race, gender, and sexuality. In some cases of counter-publicity, marginalized groups can disseminate their hidden transcripts to larger publics, in this case the Black freedom struggle, the women's movement, and the American public at large.[4] Yet the collective narratives created by Black lesbians in the NABF never reached larger publics.

The NABF's history shows a profound contrast between its vibrant lesbian community and the intense internal debates that occurred on the topic of sexuality, on the one hand, and the image of a professional organization that obeyed the dictates of heteronormativity and respectability politics, on the other. The contradictions inherent in the NABF's stance of private support and public silence, in the context of increased lesbian visibility in the organization, created tensions that negatively affected the organization.

The history of lesbian NABF members helps us better understand the differences between the Black feminist movement and the predominantly white women's liberation movement. Black and white women of similar ages who were a part of the same movement experienced the same circumstances: lesbian baiting used to discredit the movement, the intense affective energy that lesbians brought to the movement, and the possibility of sexual liberation. Yet the widely diverging experiences of white and Black women, especially respectability politics, prompted different responses and led to very different lesbian herstories.

Respectability Politics and Public Silence

Respectability politics was a strategy devised by Black Baptist women at the beginning of the twentieth century in order to refute the racist stereotypes that influenced their lives: "Respectability demanded that every individual in the black community assume responsibility for behavioral self-regulation and self-improvement along moral, educational, and economic lines."[5] A big part of this moral self-regulation was connected with performing (hetero)sexuality the right way, as reproductive and within the bounds of marriage. The NABF constantly challenged respectability politics, by leading public conversations about issues such as reproductive rights, rape, single motherhood, or incarcerated women. Yet the NABF avoided challenging heteronormativity.

"I don't say gay women don't belong in the movement, but the discussion of gay rights belongs in the homosexual movement,"[6] states NABF founder Brenda Eichelberger, in an interview taken during a visit to Philadelphia in 1976. While the Black feminist movement would accept lesbians among their ranks (the double negative "don't say . . . don't belong" indicates wariness and ambivalence toward the question as well as a cautious welcome), the question of same-sex desire was displaced onto the gay liberation movement. This position might seem odd for a self-designated feminist organization, especially given that the predominantly white women's liberation movement had given visibility to lesbians, promoted a wide range of discourses surrounding women's sexuality, and launched a frontal critique of heteronormativity. However, African Americans experienced the postwar history of American sexuality differently.

According to sociologist Patricia Hill Collins, while Black communities in the 1950s tacitly accepted gay and lesbian individuals, they disapproved of homosexuality itself.[7] According to Alexis DeVeaux, Queer African Americans were seen as "sexual outsiders" in Black communities.[8] Even when Black periodicals such as *Ebony* and *Jet* published celebratory coverage of drag balls, thus presenting the experiences of queers of color in a more positive light than the mainstream media, "coverage notably soured," as E. James-West put it, once these depictions of a glamorous "gay fantastic" overstepped the limits of ballroom space and threatened everyday respectability.[9] Especially toward the end of the decade, as the Civil Rights movement, in its search for integration, adopted and disseminated its "norms of heterosexual citizenship," the Black press mostly stopped publishing positive accounts of homosexuality. Gay activists such as Bayard Rustin, the architect of the March on Washington, were not excluded from the movement, but their leadership was circumscribed and their influence limited by respectability politics.[10] Although Black Panther Party leader Huey Newton expressed support for gays and saw them as potential allies in the Black freedom struggle, heteronormative ideas dominated the Black Power movement.[11] Some Black nationalists notably agreed with the infamous Moynihan Report that saw African American women as sources of pathology in their families and communities. While the report itself did not mention homosexuality, it defined masculinity as the ability to support a woman.[12]

During the 1970s, Black consumer magazines both amplified respectability politics and created a space where it could occasionally be challenged. *Ebony*, specifically designed for a middle-class audience, published multiple articles by experts such as Alvin Poussaint and Winston Moore, who pathologized homosexuality and saw it predominantly as a male issue. While these articles decried male homosexuality's pernicious effects on the Black family, the African American reproductive rate, and overall racial uplift, *Ebony* nevertheless published a number of letters to the editor that presented a different narrative. The writers of these letters proudly identified as gay or criticized homophobic discourses, including those published in the magazine. In contrast to *Ebony*, the magazine *Jet*, which was also designed for African American readers, occasionally featured Black lesbian couples in a normalizing context.[13]

Black consumer periodicals also discussed, in detail, contemporary evolving mores, such as the so-called sexual revolution. "Has the Sexual Revolution Bypassed Blacks?" asked sociologist Robert Staples, provocatively, in the pages of *Ebony* in April 1974.[14] His essay was one of a range of articles in the Black press discussing the complex relationship of African Americans to the wide-ranging changes in sexual morality unfolding in 1960s and 1970s America. As literary critic Trimiko Melancon argues, "the black sexual revolution embodied a complexity that spans a continuum, not only in terms of the varied sexual expressions, loving, or sex purely for sex's sake; but also in its multifaceted effort to narrate and iterate the varieties of black sexual expressions and experiences."[15]

Despite these instances of sexual liberation expressing an expansive view of sexuality, Black feminists were exposed to relentless media attacks that portrayed feminists as "manhating lesbians." This was particularly barbed for Black women, as it signified not only the pathologization of lesbian desire, but also the very serious accusation of race betrayal. When asked about sexual minorities and their role in the NABF, the first thing all interviewees recall is the unrelenting homophobia they experienced.

Elnora Washington recalls: "The only negative thing . . . was not within the group, but with the onlookers. I think it was a deliberate ploy, trying to end the feminist movement by associating it with the lesbian aspect, because that did stop a lot of people from participating."[16] The politics of respectability prevented the NABF from reaching a larger audience among Black women, as even the suspicion that the organization might have supported lesbians was likely to trigger disapproval from community and family members. Helen Whigham recalls: "We even heard that from my father: 'You know, that's a lesbian organization. Why would you want to be a part of it?' You understand? That was their perception."[17]

These stereotypes further pressured Black women, especially educated women who had only recently made inroads into professional careers, to conform to respectability norms.[18] Gay and lesbian professionals, especially if they were working in the public school system, like many African American women did, feared persecution, legal and otherwise. In 1977, singer Anita Bryant spearheaded a backlash against the ordinances that would have protected gay rights in Miami-Dade County. The following year, spurred by Bryant's charges that gay rights activists were recruiting children to their lifestyles, a referendum was initiated in California that would have prohibited openly gay teachers from working in the public school system. Although the referendum was narrowly defeated, similar local initiatives occurred throughout the country. In Chicago, a voter-registration program for high school students denied openly gay activists the opportunity to serve as registrars.[19] NABF lesbians were aware of facing heightened dangers to their careers and livelihoods if they were to come out. Janie Nelson recalls, "But it was dangerous. It was dangerous because they—because I mean she [name redacted] had this career, she had all this. There were a lot of reasons why people wouldn't want to come out."[20]

White women's history of sexuality was rather differently shaped by the 1960s sexual revolution and the women's movement. As historian David Allyn shows, the sexual revolution, which unfolded over the twentieth century, during the 1960s and 1970s, brought about profound changes in sexual behaviors, from rejecting Victorian values and challenging heterosexual marriage as the only sanctioned locus of sexuality to contesting taboos on premarital sex, masturbation, homosexuality, polyamory, open marriages, interracial sex, and group sex. A series of legal changes enabled new attitudes toward sexuality, from the FDA approval of the birth-control pill in 1960 to a series of Supreme Court decisions that struck down laws banning contraception (1965) and interracial marriage (1967), and decriminalized abortion (1973).[21] For white women, the sexual revolution brought about a wider acceptance of women's sexual desires,[22] although the women's liberation movement rightfully saw the sexual revolution as yet another vehicle for male domination.

Women's liberationists emphasized women's sexual autonomy, centering clitoral pleasure as opposed to the myth of the vaginal orgasm.[23] A certain segment of the movement centered not only female pleasure, but lesbian relationships as well. Historian Ruth Rosen claims that the movement liberated some women to "embrace the identity of lesbian with pride" and provided others "a safe space in which to explore a different sexual preference."[24] For lesbians living in the closet, the women's movement was to a certain extent liberating, although movement women tended to frown upon butch-femme roles, practiced by predominantly working-class lesbians,[25] as reproducing heterosexual arrangements. Instead, they embraced a vision of lesbian relationships as nurturing and egalitarian, a joyful way of fighting patriarchy in the bedroom as well as in the streets. Especially in the large cities in the Northeast, in the early seventies, participants in women's liberation experienced lesbian feminism as "the political choice du jour." It was not uncommon for women to become "political lesbians," as a way to avoid sleeping with the enemy (men) and thus to continue the feminist revolution in their everyday lives.[26] After the movement ended, some women returned to heterosexual relationships; others did not.

Yet, beyond the radical circles in large urban areas, the women's movement itself was not unambiguously supportive of lesbians. In 1969, Betty Friedan, President of the National Organization for Women, had infamously denounced lesbianism as a "lavender herring" likely to deter the revolutionary potential of the movement by giving its enemies the chance to accuse feminists of being "manhating lesbians." Shortly after that, the group Radicalesbians, who initially named themselves Lavender Menace, staged a protest, forcing NOW to confront homophobia among its ranks.[27] Although this event is often presented as a watershed moment that put an end to the homophobia in the movement, such an optimistic account fails to grapple with residual tensions and lesbian-straight splits that persisted within feminism for decades, threatening and in some cases putting an end to women's organizations or groups.[28] The Memphis chapter of NOW, for example, split in 1982 over the issue of sexuality.[29] To avoid a similar outcome, the Columbus, Ohio, chapter of the same organization decided not to hold a public meeting on lesbianism until 1985.[30]

Yet, within certain neighborhoods in Chicago, sexual minorities could live openly gay lives during the 1970s. Sexual minorities were able to escape the closet in Hyde Park, an integrated neighborhood on the South Side, and near Lincoln Park on the North Side. Women's centers anchored these communities, such as the Women's Center in Lakeview and the larger Chicago Women's Liberation Union, one of the earliest women's organizations, which started in 1969. A lesbian bar subculture also thrived in Chicago,[31] and during the 1970s, the city's LGBT community gradually became a political force. A turning point was the June 1977 protest at Anita Bryant's concert, when five thousand gays and lesbians from all ethnic groups gathered outside the stadium where she was performing, a protest larger than her audience. Chicago gays and lesbians achieved increased visibility over the course of the decade by running independent campaigns for office and participating in gay pride parades. Although predominantly white, gays and lesbians on the North Side often compared their social position with that of ethnic minority groups. They gradually acquired a measure of political power. By the end of the 1970s, in certain areas on the North Side of Chicago, it had become routine to ask political candidates about their stance on gay rights.[32]

The local women's liberation movement offered a supportive space for lesbians. Women living in women-only communities attempted to create lives independent of patriarchy, embracing a grassroots ethos that emphasized do-it-yourself skills, such as auto-mechanics and self-defense, and cultural and creative pursuits.

Black lesbians sometimes embraced the ethos of sisterhood within these separatist communities, and other times insisted on maintaining their connections with their local racial communities and becoming visible in these spaces. Historian Timothy Stewart-Winter claims that the Chicago lesbian subculture was more racially mixed than the segregated neighborhoods where both Black and white women had been raised. For this reason, "the lesbian-feminist movement was at least partly open to racial dialogues that were of an intensity rarely seen in the broader society."[33] Yet interracial collaborations, alliances, and relationships also evinced racial tensions, as Black lesbians complained about the casual racism they encountered.[34] The NABF both collaborated with lesbian publications based on the North Side and experienced the racial tensions that were characteristic of such relationships, as I show in chapter 5. Yet the NABF's commitment was to organizing primarily in the Black community, although they were always open to joining efforts with other feminists, regardless of race.

At the NABF, public-facing discussions of Black female sexuality and Black sexuality often ended up reinforcing heteronormativity. Eichelberger describes a seminar that she was planning to teach at the University of Illinois as follows: "In the Black Sexuality workshop I plan to explore ways in which Black men and women can be sexually-fulfilled human beings, giving special emphasis to the paradox Black women face based on the acute shortage of Black men."[35] Although the questions guiding the seminar discussion seemingly challenged heteronormative assumptions ("Why are so many 'straight' men threatened by gay men?" "Why are so many men threatened by lesbians?"), the visual economy of the pamphlet associated with the seminar reinforces heteronormativity through a drawing of two nudes, a man and a woman, facing each other.[36] Occasionally, public events allowed for small openings where the NABF would fleetingly address Black lesbianism, before returning to heteronormative ground. For example, when the NABF opened its Alternative School in 1978, its course on female sexuality advertised topics such as "How sexually free are you?" and "Do you prefer sex with a man or a woman?," but most of the materials, nevertheless, focused on the experiences of heterosexual women.[37] The "Meeting of the Minds" Conference was one instance where the NABF adopted a resolution stating that the NABF would be "supportive of each woman's right to exercise her sexuality in a manner which is fulfilling to her."[38]

According to political scientist Cathy Cohen, respectability politics takes a particular toll on members of Black communities who are "thought to fulfill stereotypes of black sexuality as deviant or 'other.'" These people suffer a "*secondary process of marginalization* [emphasis in original], this time imposed by their own group."[39] Although Black feminists associated with the NABF challenged the norms of respectability in the African American community, Black lesbians suffered secondary marginalization within the NABF.

Unlike the NABF, the Combahee River Collective took an open stance against "heterosexual oppression" in their Black Feminist Statement (1977). It was, of course, a "courageous and revolutionary move," as Kimberly Springer argues. Yet the statement did not analyze the effects of heteronormativity on Black women's identities, nor the Black community's contribution to perpetuating it.[40] The CRC was not the only Black lesbian group. Founder Barbara Smith mentions a New York–based collective of Black lesbian writers named Jemima, who in the mid-1970s were organizing public readings and published a collection of their poems.[41] According to Donna Allegra, Black lesbian writer, dancer, radio producer, and former member of Jemima, the collective started meeting in 1974. They were "the first self-conscious Black lesbian writers' group."[42]

Lesbian politics within Black women's organizations was rather complex and even, at times, contradictory. In 1972, the New York chapter of the Third World Women's Alliance published a statement in their periodical *Triple Jeopardy*, stating that "the oppression and dehumanizing ostracism that homosexuals face must be rejected and their right to exist as dignified human beings must be defended."[43] Nevertheless, it appears that the

West Coast chapter of the TWWA experienced a lesbian-straight split, one that led to the departure of key members of the chapter.[44] The NBFO did not mention lesbians in its Statement of Purpose, but former members recall a committee titled Triple Oppression: Being Black, Female, and Lesbian, dedicated to gay issues. The San Francisco–based Black Women Organized for Action "included discussions of sexuality . . . but they did not interrogate heterosexism as an oppressive force in Black women's lives, regardless of sexual orientation."[45] As many other groups around the country left few archival traces, it is difficult to ascertain the relationship between Black heterosexual and lesbian feminists, whether the groups supported their members who were sexual minorities, and how these relationships evolved over time. However, as the NABF's history alongside the history of other women of color organizations demonstrates, lesbians were active everywhere in the Black feminist movement, with or without their organizations' open support.

Private Support

The NABF's lesbian members were actively involved in organizing on a variety of issues that were not related to their lesbian identity. While some NABF members led openly lesbian lives, others avoided coming out. Yet they formed their own community within the organization, and occasionally participated in their own consciousness-raising sessions. An audio tape titled "Black Lesbians" contains the recording of a rap session or consciousness-raising session where a group of lesbians affiliated with the NABF talk about relationships, community, violence, and stereotyping.[46] Unlike other tapes stored in the NABF archives, this one does not bear the name of the participants, which shows the organization's commitment to protect the identities of its lesbian members.

In the following, I am going to quote extensively from the "Black Lesbians" tape because of the in-depth conversations that were recorded. These conversations challenge the narrative that the women's liberation movement made it safe for all lesbians (especially lesbians of color) to come out. Instead, they document the existence and resilience of Black same-sex love and relationships alongside a longer historical continuum and the struggles that Black lesbians faced due to sexuality in addition to race (and implicitly class) and gender. Challenging a tidy narrative of Black lesbian unified identity, the tape also documents the experiences and narratives of bisexual Black women and of Black women who did not identify as lesbian (or "gay," the term that many used) and yet had primary relationships with other women. Furthermore, the recorded consciousness-raising session engages deeply with trauma and violence in same-sex relationships among women of color, a topic considered too explosive even for white gays and lesbians, who did not publicly discuss it until the late 1980s.

The lively conversation captures both the bonds between the women and the tensions brought by class politics within lesbian communities, as well as their attitude toward role-playing and identifying as gay under the pressure of respectability politics and pathologization by the medical establishment. Some of the speakers appear to be working-class, as they reference their physical prowess acquired through years of labor, while others use the language of psychotherapy easily, which might or might not indicate a college education. Some speakers refer to moving from out of state, others talk about growing up in Chicago, and many reference the local gay bar subculture. The session may have taken place at someone's house or at the Center. Participants share food and beverages and seem to be familiar with each other. The exchange is spontaneous; speakers interrupt each other, make jokes, share intimate stories that uncover their vulnerability, laugh uproariously, and occasionally ask to turn off the tape. These moments are telling as the speakers seem to either avoid recording confessions that would render them too vulnerable or find the dialogue too transgressive for respectability politics or even feminist expectations.

The participants follow the protocol of consciousness-raising. One speaker suggests a question, then participants take turns and answer it. Some discussion topics are similar to the ones usually suggested in consciousness-raising group guidelines, such as housework or violence in relationships, but other topics appear as well, such as lesbian bars. If, during consciousness-raising sessions, women learned to disentangle the operations of patriarchy in their everyday lives, in this lesbian-centered session, speakers engage with heteronormativity in their daily lives, especially when compounded by class, racism, sexism, and respectability politics.

A significant part of the conversation revolves around participants' search for a Black lesbian community both within and away from bar culture, thus outlining a Black lesbian geography of the city. While some speakers feel comfortable navigating the bar scene, with its overt sexuality and physicality, others prefer to socialize in quieter settings:

> *I do not particularly go out to gay bars. I've been out to a couple.*
>
> *Right, I hear you . . . I don't either . . .*
>
> *Sometimes the folks up in there, 'cause you see there are not too many gay bars for black women. Period. The gay bars are usually frequented by white women, and I don't particularly dig white women. But the thing about it is this: when you go to a bar, whether it's gay or straight, people*

> *have a tendency to believe that every time when you step into a bar, that you're going there to find a mate. A single woman cannot be there to socialize. Two women that are going together, the heterosexual crowd sees you as both going out to check out a scene to get a man or somebody. And I'm not into that. I'd rather have a close kinship with other women that feel the same way as I do, and I feel more comfortable with that. I don't believe in going out a lot . . . I prefer a different kind of a situation, like when you go to a play together, like when I know what's expected.* [. . .]
>
> *I never had anything started when my ladies and I went out to a gay bar . . . Ok, it was a mutual respect, I didn't touch theirs and they didn't touch mine . . .*
>
> *But you can't always get that, baby, cause some of these places are something else . . .*
>
> *I don't know which ones you're going to!*

The women are both critical and supportive of bar culture. One of the speakers sees little difference between gay and heterosexual bars, as places that objectify women, and expresses her preference for quiet dates and building relationships. One speaker criticizes gay bars as frequented by white lesbians, women toward whom she doesn't feel much of an attraction. Others defend bar culture by stating that an atmosphere of mutual respect prevented other patrons from "touching" their ladies. Below, the speaker references "role-playing," the butch-femme roles in lesbian relationships as documented by Elizabeth Kennedy in Buffalo, New York, in the 1950s and 1960s. In these lesbian bars, many catering to a working-class and interracial clientele, middle-class heteronormative ideas of respectability were transgressed ("some of these places are something else"), as patrons fought, sometimes physically, to protect their partners. Another speaker trains the lens of respectability discourse back upon the previous speaker ("I don't know which ones you're going to").

The women participating in the session debate role-playing and its effects on their relationships. Aware that women liberationists preferred an egalitarian model of same-sex love, one participant jokingly asks to stop the tape during an exchange about housework. The recording restarts in the middle of the animated discussion:

> *She was sloppy . . . I lived with her for two years! For two years I cleaned up, I did the dishes, I cleaned the kitchen, and I cooked dinner! Because I hate a sloppy house.*
>
> *You're gonna hear when it's my turn . . .*
>
> *I'm like this: My lady has to clean up . . .*
>
> *Stop the tape! Role-playing! (laughter)*
>
> *Because I was working . . .*

But why did you do it?
I did it because I had to!
But why did she have to do a thing?
I did it because I had to! I might be sloppy, but I want my house clean . . . I don't want any company to come and see my house out of order!
And what happened?
Because of her sloppiness, because of her unneatness . . .
"Unneatness"! Now that's a new word! (laughter)
. . . She was fired. (uproarious laughter)
You know, that is one of the things that get in the way with relationships . . .
So then what was your point?
Somebody's got to be neat, ok?
(tape is turned off and then back on)
That thing about the housecleaning gets into all kinds of relationships . . . the thing about the shared duties, shared responsibilities, that is an issue that comes up especially in lesbian relationships!
Because it's like two women in one kitchen!
And two women in the same kitchen spoils the broth! (laughter)

The participants question role-playing in lesbian relationships ("Why did she have to do a thing?") and share their own stories of conflict over housework. Challenging narratives of lesbian relationships as havens from patriarchy, the speakers see conflict as a foundational aspect of all human relations, including lesbian ones. The conversation moves playfully between exploring and subverting both gender roles and heteronormativity. They subvert tropes of traditional expectations that define women as competing for control over spaces of gendered labor (the kitchen), as the speakers seem to avoid rather than vie for household responsibilities, and provide a subversive reading to a traditional saying that codifies gendered expectations and heteronormative family arrangements.

The speakers are critical of the pathologization of same-sex desire, at a time when homosexuality had been removed from the Diagnostics and Statistics Manual only for several years.[47] While some of the participants readily identify as "gay," others, including one woman who had relationships with men in the past, balk at the label, although she appears ready to assume her relationship with a woman in other ways, as a sexual choice rather than an identity. Some point out psychotherapeutic knowledge that labels same-sex relationships as deviant, while others are critical of the stereotype of the manhating lesbian:

I don't believe that we are lesbians, I don't believe that we are gay, I don't believe that we are homosexuals. I believe that we are just two women.

Why do you have to be labeled?

I love men as much as I love women, but I have a sexual partner that is a WOMAN. And I don't care for this, when you say gays, I don't like this. I'm not gay.

Well, I'll be gay because my preference is.

I don't like it that now I'm supposed to be a freak, "abnormal" . . . I'm still me! Why does that have to be wrong? I have had the opportunity to experience both, male and female, and my preference is that I choose to be with a woman. Who has the right to say that you should go to a psychiatrist and get your head together?

Because the same thing that it took to build a relationship in a heterosexual relationship, the same thing it takes to build a relationship between two women!

Even more so!

Participants see sexual attraction toward a woman as a preference, rather than innate or constrained by biology. Some speakers point out their painful awareness of lost heterosexual privilege and the heightened social scrutiny they experienced once they had a woman as a partner ("I'm still me!). Some participants reject the label "gay" or "lesbian," while one participant readily identifies as such ("because my preference is").

Participants see conflict and violence stemming from past trauma as inherent to all relationships. The most emotionally wrenching exchange takes place when one of the speakers suggests the topic of violence:

How do you handle a relationship where the two women begin to fight?

The last relationship that I was in, for the first three years we were living together and everything was cool, and then . . . the last couple of years it was really . . . a violent type of a relationship, namely because . . . I couldn't understand what she was going through and vice versa. So . . . it was a thing when I took out all my frustrations on her . . . and only I could see the problem was to recognize the fact that our relationship was really over. I was trying to hold on. And I had tried all other methods, like the kindness, the understanding, the gentleness, giving . . . all of this stuff. But it was not enough. So I resorted to violence, and I discovered that I wound up more hurt, I would imagine, than she did, because I would hurt her! So what I did was . . . pack my things and left the state and came over here.

Because you can't solve that with violence.

You know, it has to do with the person and their own thing about violence.

Ok, you have your turn.

I was listening.

My view is I've never hit any of my women. Not any one. And that's because . . .

You were able to walk away?

Yeah . . .

And she would accept the fact that you were able to walk away?

What I wanted to say was that I've always respected my women.

That's got nothing to do with respect. It's about rejection, all other things.

That's right.

But wait a minute . . . I felt all of that! I just didn't think it was necessary for me to hit any woman. She and I got in a fight, ok? It was verbal at first, ok? And then she grabbed me. Rather than me hitting her, I picked her up, and put her on the pool table, and walked out the door. Because if I would have hit that woman, I would have killed her! And I knew it, because I knew what kind of work I was doing and what kind of hands I have. And the thing was, I knew that if I would have hit her, she would have been dead . . . and this is the way I am. I cannot afford to hit a woman. And if I love a woman so much, I don't care how much she hurts me . . . I put everything into it that I can . . . because to me it's important that I share a part of me and they share a part of themselves with me. And when you get in tune like that, that's love. And the thing is . . . how can you hit . . . yourself? And when you're in tune like that, that other person is a part of yourself.

And then again, if you're perfectly in tune, then you don't have that kind of friction . . .

That's true, but it can come up . . .

There's no such thing as being perfectly in tune with somebody . . .

But when you're starting to feel all of these different emotions, you're feeling rejection, you're feeling anger, you're feeling frustration, you know, it feels like everything that you're doing is in vain! For the relationship . . . love was not the issue. I did love her. But there were a lot of different emotions in play . . . And then the only thing I had left was violence. And rather than continuing to destroy what was happening inside of me, this monster inside of me that was making me react the way I was reacting . . . I could not deal with it being there with her, not even in the same state . . . so I left! And after I left, it still took me two years, I've been here three! And even two years after I left I was still going through the same thing, and it was interesting because about three weeks ago I had come to the point where I could pick up the phone and talk to her and I know that during this conversation that everything was alright and I no longer held the hostility and the bitterness that I had at the time when I took this anger out on her. And now she's a friend! And that's it! And no more hurt, no more nothing!

That's a very hard thing to do, until we learn to find a different way to handle our hurt and our frustration, the only way we have been conditioned to deal with it is through violence! And people need to understand that that is not because I don't love you, but that is not a part of love! That's a part of your anger, your frustration, your rejection . . .

Ok, your turn . . .

I don't think there's any place in a relationship where two people really appreciate each other for violence.

Have you ever been involved in a relationship that was violent? Where either you hit a woman or a woman hit you?

One that lasted for seven and a half or eight years, and we've gotten to a point where we really couldn't communicate anymore. But I think before not being able to communicate anymore, I think we reached the point where we couldn't grow up any further. And I think that once you lose that growth potential with an individual, once you lose the things, the values that you started out with, before you even get to this fog . . . that . . . you're trying to get control of a person by fighting, you can't control them like that! Either the person wants to be with you or they don't. If they don't what the hell, they don't! But . . . let it go! And maybe that's not even the issue, maybe, well that's just personal situations, I never want to be in a relationship where I have . . . physically hurt a person.

I don't think anybody goes into a relationship for that![48]

The speakers' stories document the resilience and intensity of same-sex relationships between Black women, as the speakers refer to living together for many years. They acknowledge that violence can be intergenerational and that a person's experience, "their own thing about violence," can shape a woman's unreflective use of violence against a loved one; yet the speakers struggle to break the cycle, occasionally even leaving the state to start anew somewhere else. They narrate their struggles to redefine love as empathy with another woman and as sharing something deep and personal that ideally should make it impossible to hurt someone dear. While recognizing the difficulty of dealing with rejection and anger, in addition to multiple societal oppressions, the women share their hard work to process their feelings, work toward a peaceful resolution, and move on with their lives. In contrast to a vision of lesbian relationships promoted in the movement as an egalitarian space away from violence, the women see violence as rooted in generational trauma, a learned defense mechanism that they had to work hard to overcome.

The consciousness-raising tape thus contains the blueprint of another hidden transcript, one that the NABF never disseminated. The rich narratives of personal experiences shared by the women who attended the session and the wide range of topics such as identifying as gay, butch-femme roles, and violence in relationships could have formed the basis for either activism or writings that would have discussed issues left unaddressed by the white feminist movement. For example, public discussions of violence in same-sex relationships did not occur until the late 1980s. It was another instance when the NABF was very much ahead of its time.

Yet, the mere fact that some members of the NABF met separately from the rest of the membership, in meetings where they shared important aspects of their lives that they did not feel comfortable sharing with the members outside their circle, was bound to create tensions in the organization. Increased lesbian visibility and the ongoing possibility that the NABF could move from silent support to a more public stance in support of lesbians created further tensions. These pressures further strained an organization that was already struggling with lack of financial resources and dwindling membership.

A Lesbian-Straight Split

The NABF's discussions of lesbianism were not limited to lesbian-only consciousness-raising groups. In fact, both heterosexual and lesbian Black feminists engaged in multiple discussions that addressed homophobia in the organization and communications between lesbian and heterosexual members. Beryl Fitzpatrick recalls: "I remember those very productive dialogues [in the organization] about being sensitive, about not denigrating a person because of their sexuality and their choices." These internal dialogues did not surface in public statements by the NABF, but they shaped the responses that members gave to the homophobia and lesbian-baiting that surrounded Black feminism.

In the absence of a public stance on same-sex relationships, individual NABF members devised personal responses to homophobic attacks. Some pointed out that sexuality was not the most important issue the NABF was fighting for. Helen Whigham, former NABF treasurer, recalls that when family members questioned her decision to join the NABF, she described the organization's social activism: "[I] would try to explain to them, 'That is not what this organization is about. It is not about that. We're talking about sexism. We talk about racism. We're talking about equality. This is what we're talking about.' People would get caught up because they heard the word feminist and they felt that we were against men, we hated men."[49] The misogynistic and homophobic reaction against feminism, widespread in mainstream society, echoed within the African American community. Members felt frustrated with these unrelenting attacks. Gayle Porter recalls: "Feminism was so often associated with lesbianism, and how could Black women feel comfortable talking about being a feminist and not feel that they had to defend their sexuality, that they didn't have to say, 'And I am not gay' or 'I am not a man hater.'"[50] These members felt that engaging their opponents' accusations of being "manhating lesbians" completely derailed the discussion from the feminist message they were trying to convey. Some also felt uncomfortable being reminded of lesbianism as a sexual identity.

Other activists tried to educate their audience by turning the tables on their homophobic interlocutors. Beryl Fitzpatrick, who after the NABF worked with the Black Women's Health Project, recalls:

> What I remember about that was that there was a misperception that outside people would have, that we were a bunch of lesbians. I remember formulating language to be able to say to people . . . if people would say, "Are you a lesbian?" I remember saying, "No, but I could pass." Because lesbian women were always passing for straight or non-lesbian women. When people would ask me direct questions about my sexuality, I was proud to say that I identify with Black women who were lesbians who were being discriminated against in our community. . . . You would not ask a person that you believe to be heterosexual, "Are you heterosexual?" It's not an appropriate question to ask. I remember developing this language where I would say . . . at that time, Macy's used to be Marshall Field and I would say to people, "You don't wear your pajamas and your sleeping coat to match to shop at Marshall Field."[51]

Rather than answer the question, Fitzpatrick chooses to highlight its inappropriateness. Other times, when responding directly to homophobic attacks, Fitzpatrick chooses to express solidarity with her lesbian sisters and to highlight the oppression they faced every day.

Yet there were unresolved tensions between members who were apprehensive of feminism's association with lesbianism and lesbian Black feminists who needed the solidarity of their sisters. Sometimes the tensions within the organization related to members' misinterpreting one another's behavior; other times, the debates echoed other conversations occurring within the movement about lesbianism as a choice or as a possibility opened by feminist consciousness-raising. Gayle Porter recalls:

> INTERVIEWER: Did you ever talk about sexuality and were there groups for lesbians or did you ever talk about that?
>
> GAYLE PORTER: Oh yeah, in fact I will never forget. I tend to be very physically affectionate and I am a hugger and I kiss and all of that, and I remember, because there were a number of gay women who were very active in the organization, and I will never forget I had a gay woman say to me, "Gayle, I have been watching you and at first I felt that you were just kind of flirty." She said, "I really see that that's just how you are. You hug and you are affectionate. You really need to think about that here because when you do that, for some of the women, you are getting a mixed signal and we need to talk about it," and we did. How can we be affectionate without giving a mixed message?

> There was a responsibility on both parts and we had to talk about what that means and how could we express it. . . . Another piece of it, I think, too, was also saying that because you weren't gay and you might not even be bisexual, that somehow that meant that you were simply not very open to your full range of feelings. There were a number of discussions in that way.[52]

Porter notes that the discussions on sexuality did not occur only once ("there were a number of discussions") and that tensions existed within the NABF, like in other feminist organizations, regarding the limits of liberation: were Black women who were fighting patriarchy in society at large supposed to continue that struggle, like some of their white sisters, in their personal relationships, thus becoming political lesbians? Was consciousness-raising, after all, expected to denaturalize heterosexual attraction as the default option of sexual choice and instead allow members to open themselves to a "full range of feelings"? These conversations show that, like in other feminist organizations in the 1970s, lesbians and heterosexual women in the NABF continuously debated their own boundaries and guidelines for acceptable communication.

The tensions evinced by the conversations Porter remembers echo in Janie Nelson's even sharper recollection of passionate relationships among NABF supporters that occasionally resulted in bruised feelings that were bound to affect the organization. Like the lesbians who wrote to the Chicago Black feminists early on, some women joining the organization expected it to be supportive of lesbians and bisexual women, while other women thought that a Black feminist movement should be a safe space where they could experiment with their sexuality. Nelson recalls:

> What I'm saying is that there were three types of people there. There were the straight women, there were the lesbians that were in closet, there were the lesbians that were out of the closet and then there were people that were just curious about the organization. See, there were different levels, different types of people in that organization, and you had to know how to navigate between the different ones. You see what I'm saying? You didn't want to disrespect anybody as a person. As a straight woman, I didn't want to disrespect anybody.
>
> But let me tell you, that lesbian stuff, it was something else. It was something else. And people joined the organization just to find out about lesbians and do all that kind of stuff, whatever. And some of them were married or had boyfriends but they just wanted to experiment with a different lifestyle. That's where they were coming from. You see what I'm saying? . . . And so they would come in, and people who were really, really lesbians and everything might like them or fall in love with them,

> but this person would think that they just wanted to experiment, and they had a husband or boyfriend or whatever. But it was a lot of drama going on in that organization. A lot of drama.[53]

The "drama" that Nelson mentions refers to the intense emotional ties that women formed with other women within the feminist movement. In the case of the NABF, like in other women's organizations, some of the women who joined were lesbians who had lived openly as such prior to the movement; others attempted to be open to their whole range of feelings toward another woman as part of their political awakening; some women were living in the closet, others were bisexual; and there were members who were simply experimenting with their sexuality. Members' affective ties fueled their commitment to feminism. Yet relationships could not only energize members, who would happily dedicate their free time and often material resources to the NABF, but also undermine the organization once these emotional bonds frayed.

Thus, the emotional intensities of forming and breaking relationships, coupled with the secrecy that some members felt they had to preserve in order to avoid the perception of a "lesbian organization," soon became a volatile mix. Former members recall that at a certain point in the organization's history, various disagreements on the issue of sexuality led to conflicts that resulted in some members leaving the organization. Helen Whigham remembers:

> We didn't have a problem [with] whether the person was gay, straight, or whatever, but a lot of, I'll just use the term gay women, started to join the organization. I think it made some people feel uncomfortable. At that time, if you stop and think, that was almost forty years ago. I think that bothered a lot of people, and a lot of women didn't want to be associated with it, because then they started looking like this was a gay organization.

> INTERVIEWER: You mean that a lot of lesbian women joined the organization, and then there was this sort of, perhaps, discussion or conflict about what direction the organization should take and whether it should support more openly its lesbian members?
>
> HELEN WHIGHAM: I think it was the influx of more gay women beginning to join the organization. Some people may have felt that it was beginning to go on a different direction that they felt uncomfortable with. That was not it, but I think a lot of people started to feel that way. . . . Let me tell you basically, I think that some people felt that they should not be in the organization, let me put it that way. Because they were there . . . some people had a problem with it. I think some women, not all, but some women left because of that.[54]

Respectability politics shaped some NABF members' reaction to the perceived influx of lesbians in the organization and perhaps their increased visibility, which threatened the delicate balance between public silence and private support.

In a follow-up interview, Whigham recalls:

> [Sexuality] brought a divide in the organization. A lot of women started getting out of the organization because they didn't feel comfortable around lesbian women. A lot of women were married, and my husband and a lot of other women's husbands started saying that it [the NABF] was a bunch of lesbians. And a lot of women didn't want to be associated with that, because of the stigma. That kind of killed the organization, to be honest with you, because were doing great before that. We had a lot of powerful women there and the organization should have grown, but it didn't. Now, we have the Black Women's Expo,[55] and we could have been like that.

Whigham places her recollection of the lesbian-straight split at the NABF within the context of members' differing expectations of what the organization could be. For some professional and heterosexual members, whom the NABF needed to attract given their ability to contribute financially to the organization, Black feminism was an opportunity for networking and empowerment, for solidarity and support as professionals, as the comparison with the Black Women's Expo reveals. Given the multiple layers of secrecy that surrounded the lesbian members' presence in the NABF, the presence of lesbians among the NABF ranks came as a surprise for some heterosexual women:

> INTERVIEWER: How did the shift happen?
>
> HELEN WHIGHAM: We went out of town [at the Interlaken retreat in 1979] and we started having conversations, and I was kind of surprised when some women started talking that they had slept with a woman. I wasn't offended by that, but a lot of other women were. And they didn't want to be associated with that. A lot of people were open, and I was among those who stayed, but you could feel that there was a kind of a shift.
>
> But you have to think about the times and people were not as open as now. That was kind of taboo. There were a lot of [gay] people, but they stayed in the closet. I would definitely say that that was the turning point in our organization. Brenda wasn't like that, but there were a lot of professional women, and I'm not saying all, but some of the people that I knew wouldn't want to be associated with [being lesbian].[56]

Heterosexual Black women had the privilege of leaving an organization that they feared would affect their career opportunities. Whigham's assessment of that time period as more homophobic than today is supported by legal victories such as the legalization of same-sex marriage in 2016, and contradicted by the persistence of homophobia in many spaces. Yet at the time, the veil of secrecy surrounding the mere existence of lesbians in a Black feminist organization was thick enough that many members were unaware of their presence. Fearful for the loss of their heterosexual privilege, the only privilege they had as Black women, these professional women decided to withdraw from the NABF. Coupled with chronic lack of resources and other difficulties experienced by the organization, this split contributed to its end.

Conclusion

Like many other women's liberation organizations, the NABF experienced conflicts related to sexuality and the position of lesbians within the organization. Their struggles around this topic were compounded by Black women's historical experiences of respectability politics, campaigns against LGBTQ rights, and targeting gay professionals, in addition to members' own affective ties formed within the organization. Over time, these pressures proved challenging for the policy of public silence and private support that the NABF adopted, which simply proved inadequate as the decade advanced. The lesbian-straight split that took place prompted some members to withdraw from the organization, and thus limited the NABF's capability to continue its work at a time of dwindling resources.

Of the former NABF members I interviewed, the one Black feminist who identified as a lesbian during interviews declined to be out in the book. I was not to publish the many stories, jokes, and pieces of gossip that she shared with me. They were secret, just like the identities of lesbian members had been protected in the NABF. As a historian, my duty is to respect her wish. The recorded tape is as close as I could come to a primary source that abundantly documents the passion, joy, pain, political savviness, and stories of Black lesbians associated with the NABF, without the danger of publicizing anyone's identity.

As a historian, my duty is also to work against the erasure of Black lesbian lives, activism, joy, love, brilliance, while avoiding any possible connection with the identities of former members. Black lesbians were very much present and active both in the NABF and in the Black feminist movement, despite suffering from the multiple burdens of respectability politics, racism and poverty, exploitation and erasure. The few who decided to come out, in the movement, in print, and in their personal lives, showed the courage of true revolutionaries.

The NABF's case is particular in the Black women's liberation movement due to the contrast between its vibrant lesbian community and the intense internal debates that occurred on the topic of sexuality, on the one hand, and the heteronormative-compliant facade the organization projected, on the other. The NABF's growth and increased visibility, especially in the aftermath of its national conference, attracted many professional Black women—by all means a measure of success, as the NABF could always use their membership dues and pledges, organizing work, and their expertise that widened the organization's mission and appeal. For them, the NABF represented a chance to network, support each other, and celebrate their unprecedented career success. The way they imagined their feminist liberation did not include challenging respectability politics, or going too far in their challenge. Black feminist organizations who tried to build a national movement had to shed the stigma of dividing the Black community, of imitating white women uncritically, of lacking connection with true Black womanhood, in addition to the homophobic attacks they had to continuously fend off. The different levels of secrecy within the organization allowed the NABF, who was trying to build a national movement, to continue to project an image and political philosophy that did not challenge homophobia in the Black community—their primary supporters—or in society at large.

About her own experience in the Black freedom struggle, Barbara Smith, one of the few Black feminists who came out in print in 1979, wrote that "Peaceful coexistence between Black homosexuals and heterosexuals is bought at the exorbitant price of our silence. The same sisters and brothers to whom racial passing would be anathema expect Black lesbians and gays to pass as straight and endure similar devastation of the spirit."[57] The NABF expected its members to derive their politics from their own experiences, yet these experiences could only go this far in challenging respectability politics.

Black lesbians participating in the NABF were supposed to generate political insights based on their experience, like all feminists who joined consciousness-raising groups. If they expected community and support in joining the NABF, they may have found other Black lesbians interested in feminism, yet the NABF would only give them private support. They could organize, but not about lesbian issues; even hold leadership positions in the organization, if they mostly stayed in the closet; and overall donate their time and energy and the few resources that they had to an organization that would refrain from openly recognizing their existence. They could work alongside and build community with sisters who engaged in secondary marginalization.

It is worth imagining what sort of political project the NABF could have created, based on the insights generated in lesbian consciousness-raising sessions such as those outlined above. Would they have tried to raise the Black community's consciousness about homophobia and respectability? Would they have addressed, for example, violence in same-sex relationships, a topic not discussed publicly in the LGBT movement at large until the late 1980s? The hidden transcript generated by Black lesbians through their consciousness-raising groups remained secret, and as a result, the NABF lesbians could not bring their full lives to political activism. Black lesbian feminists and professional heterosexual women who felt they needed to protect their careers by obeying the dictates of respectability politics held deeply contradictory visions of Black feminism and of the NABF. If, initially, the NABF's strength was to represent multiple things to Black women from all walks of life, attract them to a community of like-minded sisters, and convince them to work for social change together, this strength turned into a liability as soon as these differing member expectations collided, due to their contradictory nature.

These tensions, rather common in the women's movement, had a disproportionate effect on the NABF, as its cadre of organizers struggled with reduced membership and, hence, resources. Skyrocketing rents in the business district amplified these losses, as the NABF struggled to continue to rent the space of the Black Women's Center. A more general turn toward conservativism by the end of the decade further limited the NABF's appeal. Yet, even in the aftermath of Ronald Reagan's election in 1980, a core group of Black feminists were determined to continue their organizing work.

CHAPTER 7

Beyond the Equal Rights Amendments

Black Feminism in the Aftermath of Women's Liberation

> As Blacks, we are the missing link to the ERA passage chain. And as strong multiracial coalitions, we hold the key which securely locks the chain.
>
> —Brenda Eichelberger, "The Missing Link to Passage of the Equal Rights Amendment"

Introduction

The rise of the NABF in the mid-1970s occurred in the context of nationwide coalitional activism for the passage of the Equal Rights Amendment. Introduced first in 1923 by the Woman's Party, and every year after that for nearly five decades, the Equal Rights Amendment passed Congress with bipartisan support on March 22, 1972. By mid-1973, thirty states had ratified it,[1] and the amendment seemed well poised to pass before the 1979 deadline given by Congress.[2] Yet the ERA's seemingly unstoppable progress toward ratification surprisingly slowed down, then came to a halt by the end of the decade, as conservative activists mobilized by Illinois native Phyllis Schlafly mounted a national campaign to stop its ratification. Schlafly's loosely organized, single-issue network (STOP ERA) mobilized religious white women from around the country, who pressured state legislatures to defend the amendment by appealing to traditional notions of womanhood and by evoking the frightful specters of unisex bathrooms, same-sex marriage, and women enrolled in active combat. The ERA's supporters included, in addition to NOW and women's liberation groups, all sorts of progressive organizations, political personalities such as First Lady Betty Ford, Hollywood stars, and an array of wealthy donors.

Galvanizing the energies of feminist activists nationwide, the ERA was a rallying point for all feminist organizations and groups, be they small or large, local or national, predominantly white or women of color. The National Organization of Women started lobbying for the ERA in 1966, thus signaling its commitment to serve as a vanguard feminist organization.[3] Throughout its long life, stretching over almost a decade (1974–1983), the NABF itself was involved in coalitional organizing for passing the ERA. Eichelberger recalls: "We really worked hard to get the ERA passed, and we worked together with other women's organizations. The organization could have been all white women, it didn't matter. We tried, we did whatever we could, we went to a lot of rallies, especially in downtown Chicago . . . anytime there was any type of rally for the ERA, we were there."[4]

The NABF's commitment, working in coalition to attain equal rights, was grounded in their philosophy of Black humanist feminism, which demanded human rights for Black women and envisioned coalition work as being among the tools to achieve their goals. Black humanist feminism advocated for political-ethical coalitions as defined by Liza Taylor, political projects grounded in personal experience of oppressed individuals, intersectional analysis, and border thinking, and the need for a profound personal transformation for those involved in building these coalitions.[5] In November 1980, immediately after Ronald Reagan's electoral victory, the NABF self-published a position paper written by Eichelberger, arguing for the relevance of continued political work for ERA ratification within a cross-racial coalition led by Black people.

The paper demonstrates that despite many setbacks, NABF organizers were determined to continue their political work at the beginning of the 1980s. Nevertheless, the increasing rents in the Chicago loop and a decrease in membership threatened the NABF's very existence. The NABF's attempts to secure grants from the state of Illinois were only partially successful, and two large grants submitted in 1981 were rejected. Although unsuccessful, the grant applications demonstrate the breadth of the NABF's organizing vision. The loss of the Center in 1982 severely limited the NABF's ability to attract new members, and a year later it lost its nonprofit status. Many individual members continued their Black feminist work, while others used the NABF's lessons in their everyday lives.

"In the Forefront of Support for Human Rights Legislation": African Americans and the Struggle for the ERA

The ERA battle was intensifying toward the end of the 1970s, as Phyllis Schlafly's STOP ERA (Stop Taking Our Privileges) organization managed to slow down the momentum of the amendment's passing. In her 1972 manifesto "What's Wrong with 'Equal Rights' for Women?," Schlafly directly states her vision of gender, race, and nation, beginning with the opening sentence: "Of all the classes of people who ever lived, the American woman is the most privileged." The screed lays out the arguments that would guide opposition to the ERA for the next decade. In Schlafly's view, ratifying the ERA would have major negative consequences for women's lives, such as turning them into subjects of the draft, eliminating child support and alimony, and destroying the American family, while not giving women any new benefits or job opportunities that existing legislation did not already cover.[6] The feminist, pro-ERA agenda, she claimed, was "antifamily, antichildren, and proabortion."[7]

Schlafly's STOP ERA organization held its first national conference in 1972, and by the following year already had chapters in twenty-six states, with strongholds in states that were essential for ratification: Arizona, Florida, Illinois, Louisiana, Missouri, Ohio, Oklahoma, Utah, Nevada, North and South Carolina, and Virginia.[8] STOP ERA mobilized mostly white, middle-class women for whom organized religion played an important role, as 98 percent claimed church membership. Evangelical women's activism for STOP ERA was inspired by their profound belief in divinely ordained differences between women and men.[9] Although feminists erroneously believed that Schlafly and STOP ERA were associated with the John Birch Society and the KKK, the movement was remarkably diverse, mobilizing evangelicals, Baptists, Roman Catholics, Jewish Orthodox women, and even some African American ministers.[10]

Illinois, the only industrial state that did not ratify the ERA, was both a stronghold of the progressive movement and the home state of Phyllis Schlafly. It naturally emerged as a battleground in the struggle over the ERA. Marches and rallies were routinely organized in Springfield, the state capital, and the NABF, alongside other progressive organizations (such as the AAUP, the ACLU, the National Council of Negro Women, the Socialist Workers Party, local chapters of NOW, the Coalition of Labor Union Women, etc.), enthusiastically mobilized its members to attend coalition events such as the ERA National March and Rally, held on Sunday, May 16, 1976.[11] A year later, the NABF was among the more active organizers of another ERA March and Rally, scheduled for May 14, 1977, offering the Women's Center for weekly meetings and reaching out to other groups. Through their Black Women Task Force, led by Sharon Scoby, they reached out to the African American community in Chicago.[12] The event was typical of ERA coalition politics, uniting a wide range of organizations: the American Association of University Women, the American Civil Liberties Union, the Grey Panthers, and the National Organization for Women, among a long list of national organizations concerned with social justice, including the Chicago branch of the National Council of Negro Women. Eichelberger's leadership was well recognized as she was invited to serve as Master of Ceremonies at the rally.

Yet, in their ERA organizing, like in other contexts, NABF members experienced marginalization and occasionally the complete erasure of their work. Despite their visible position as organizers of the May 1977 rally, both press and television coverage failed to acknowledge the work of Black feminists, as Eichelberger recalls in an article. At the press conference, reporters asked questions mostly to white women participants, while the televised coverage erased Black women's presence. The camera footage failed to show the event's MC (Eichelberger), the NABF group sitting in the front row, two Black women speakers, and a Black woman singer, instead dwelling at length on the faces of the white women sitting in the audience.[13]

By the end of the 1970s, the ERA appeared to face insurmountable obstacles, even though, in 1978, Congress extended the deadline for the amendment's ratification to 1982. The election of Ronald Reagan further dampened feminist hopes that the amendment would pass. Reagan ran on a platform of economic conservativism and criticism of his predecessor's foreign policy failures, and benefitted from the support of the recently energized Christian Right, including religious and conservative women. The feminist movement perceived his landslide victory as a stunning loss.[14]

In addition to energetic feminist activism, the 1970s were marked by a stagnant economy, high unemployment, especially among the working class, and an international energy crisis that, coupled with inflation, eroded Americans' optimism regarding their economic future. Reagan ran on a platform that emphasized self-reliance, individualism, and patriotism in face of the diminishing fortunes of the American economy.[15] While Reagan claimed a landslide victory and the Republican Party took control of the House and Senate, only 28 percent of the potential electorate voted in the 1980 election, with the lowest turnout among blue-collar workers.[16]

Aware of these facts, the NABF refused to consider itself, the ERA struggle, or the women's movement defeated, and continued its intellectual activism. They published a position paper titled "The Missing Link to Passage of the Equal Rights Amendment," in which they argued that the ERA still could pass, with the help of a politically active coalition of African Americans and other minorities. Signed by Eichelberger, the document, like other writings, is based on collective insights, as honorary members and NABF leadership provided feedback to manuscript drafts: Rev. Willie Barrow, Dr. Arnita Young Boswell, Dr. Janie Nelson, Dr. Gayle Porter, and Illinois State Representative Monica Faith Stewart.[17] "The Missing Link" is a piece of interdisciplinary scholarship that combines history, sociology, and political science in an analysis centered on African American contributions to ERA organizing. More than previous writings by Eichelberger, the position paper uses scholarly information and employs a more academic voice, thus mirroring the transition toward academic feminism occurring within the women's movement at the time.

Published in November 1980, after Reagan's election win, the paper argues that ERA supporters should not despair in an unfavorable political climate, as Reagan's victory reflected voter concerns with the economy and unemployment. Pointing out that women and African Americans had made significant gains as elected officials in both the House and the Senate, Eichelberger predicts a new phase for the Black freedom struggle and the women's movement: an entry into the political arena. The missing link for the passage of the ERA lies in the mobilization of the Black community as part of an interracial coalition working within the political system. This approach is consistent with the NABF's practice of organizing within the African American community first, yet using Black women's history and experiences as a springboard for coalition building.

"Blacks have a history of being in the forefront of support for human rights legislation," begins Eichelberger. "The Missing Link" provides an intersectional analysis in its blueprint for mobilizing the African American community for the ERA, and outlines a broad vision of cross-racial coalition activism rooted in the historical experience of the Black freedom struggle. Quoting a public opinion poll that had placed support for the ERA at 62 percent among whites and 74 percent for nonwhites, Eichelberger first lists, then rejects, the assumptions held by the minority who did not support the ERA. The ERA would, in the eyes of its opponents, disrupt gender roles in the Black community—negatively affecting homemakers and defeminizing Black women—and force Black women to compete for employment with Black men, while only benefitting white women. Eichelberger rejects these assumptions with well-rehearsed arguments used in previous debates about feminism and equality, by pointing out Black women's historical experience of labor force participation, lack of satisfaction with traditional gender roles even among white women, and the growing number of single Black women as heads of households. In fact, the ERA could bring Black women one step closer to gaining the rights outlined in the Black Woman's Bill of Rights. The raised specter of competition between Black women and men in the labor force, Eichelberger notes, is rooted in traditional gender roles expectations and contradicted by numbers that consistently show Black women as underemployed or with higher unemployment rates as compared to Black men and white women. In the end, the author claims, "any injustice the White woman suffers, the Black woman, because of racism, suffers even more."[18] If sexism and racism are both intertwined and cumulative, the argument goes, ratifying the ERA could improve the lives of half the race, and by extension, the lives of their families and communities, an argument inspired by Black economic nationalism, which the NABF had repeatedly expressed, in various forms, throughout its life.

In fact, Eichelberger continues in the next section, African Americans do not have any interest in opposing the ERA, which, in her view, could have an impact similar to previous constitutional amendments and federal laws that have protected the rights of minorities: "our history as Blacks and as women shows that we will never gain full rights by using the band-aid approach of allowing individual states to decide if/when we are to have rights."[19] The real opposition to the ERA, Eichelberger argues, comes from "ultraright conservatives" like the Ku Klux Klan, the John Birch Society, Daughters of the American Revolution, and Phyllis Schlafly's STOP ERA. Eichelberger shares the widely spread misconception, at the time, about anti-ERA efforts being funded by white supremacist organizations. Yet her argument that the Southern states of the Old Confederacy (Alabama, Arkansas, Florida, Georgia, Louisiana, Mississippi, North Carolina, South Carolina, and Virginia) feature prominently among non-ERA states gives credence to the connection between sexism and racism. "These oppressive forces," Eichelberger claims, "have a *vested* interest in perpetuating racism and sexism [emphasis in original], for as long as Blacks and women remain at the bottom of the economic ladder and economically insecure, White male workers can feel superior to others worse off than they, the capitalistic system can continue to thrive."[20] In her analysis, divisions by gender and race can only benefit a capitalist system predicated on exploitation.

Yet, in order to build the coalition between women and men, whites and Blacks, Eichelberger has to refute the alarmist rumors circulated by ERA opponents such as Phyllis Schlafly about its possible consequences, including the destruction of family life; loss of women's legal protections; the imminent arrival of a degendered society with unisex bathrooms,

THE MISSING LINK TO PASSAGE OF THE

EQUAL RIGHTS AMENDMENT

Position Paper of the National Alliance of Black Feminists
written by Brenda Daniels-Eichelberger, Executive Director, November 25, 1980

FIGURE 9. Front cover of position paper titled "The Missing Link to Passage of the Equal Rights Amendment" by Brenda Daniels-Eichelberger, calling for multiracial coalitions led by Black women and men to pass the Equal Rights Amendment, Chicago, Illinois, November 25, 1980. The bottom of the page shows the NABF's motto, "Where feminism is a dimension of humanism," and its logo, alongside the Black Women's Center address and phone number. Chicago History Museum, ICHi-183261.

FIGURE 10. Former NABF activists meet in downtown Chicago in April 2022. From left to right: Helen Whigham, C. A. Lofton, and Beryl Fitzpatrick. Photograph by Ileana Nachescu.

women enrolled in active combat, and legalized same-sex marriage; and the erosion of states' rights. Rightfully calling them myths in this position paper, Eichelberger rejects them one by one, this time appealing to both a Black and white audience, by pointing out that the amendment would protect and enhance women's benefits, including in the military, where, the author notes, women already work and earn significantly more than they would as civilian employees; that the ERA would not mandate unisex bathrooms, same-sex marriage, or end alimony and child support for women. Finally, she points out, if the ERA would destroy any states' rights, only one such right would be affected: "the right to discriminate against half the population."[21]

As the battle for ratification continues at the state level, Eichelberger's coalition strategy centers on the role played by African Americans in these efforts. Several nonratified states, she notes, have large African American populations. Illinois itself had the third largest Black population in the country and the Southern nonratified states counted more than half of all Black citizens. Mobilizing African Americans was the missing link to the passage of the ERA, as part of an interracial coalition: "As Blacks, we are the missing link to the ERA passage chain. And as strong multiracial coalitions, we hold the key which securely *locks* the chain [emphasis in original]."[22]

Eichelberger concludes by recommending various practical strategies for her many audiences: Black people could educate their communities, boycott the nonratified states, and lobby and build coalitions, warning that coalition work is more necessary than ever: "To refuse to form coalitions with sincere whites because of reverse racism on our part is a 'luxury' we just can't afford. Moreover, since these coalitions frequently bring together people who support progressive measures in general, the relationships we establish with them during ERA ratification efforts can help us pass other legislation which will be vital to us in the future."[23] Articulating a position very similar to Johnson Reagon's, Eichelberger insists on the vital necessity of coalitions. While naming Black people's desire for separatist "reverse racism" might appear as a strangely conservative word choice, Eichelberger was speaking as an organizer who had experienced both racism and sexism, and whose desperation at the prospect of losing the ERA battle amplified the urgency of her call. The coalition she envisions could prove crucial for survival ("vital") in contexts both present and future.

For white people, Eichelberger's demands were just as urgent: "Whites first need to confront and acknowledge their own racism. . . . Aware of the blatancies of racism, white human rights activists frequently are not aware of the *subtleties* of racism which they themselves project [emphasis in original]." Eichelberger advises whites eager to form cross-racial coalitions to confront their own attitudes and what today would be called microaggressions. She recommends that white feminists "seek out and include" Black women in their public-facing events, share resources ranging from material to moral support, as well as legal expertise, with Black organizations, and help Black people combat racism.[24] Eichelberger's vision of coalition is redistributive and goes beyond the task at hand (passing the ERA) to build comradeship in the anti-racist struggle.

"The Missing Link" presents a political analysis based on interdisciplinary research, combining statistics, historical facts, political science, and cultural criticism. Like other writings authored by NABF activists, it is a piece of Black feminist scholarship that outlines in detail a broad vision of coalition-organizing under a feminist rallying cause. Unfortunately, the NABF was confronting other difficulties, fighting for its own survival and the preservation of the Black Women's Center at a time of changed economic circumstances.

The End of an Organization

The NABF achieved national recognition by 1980; however, its finances failed to match its cultural capital. Throughout the NABF's long life, rarely did the balance of its bank account add up to more than one or two hundred dollars at the end of any given month; more often than not, the balance was negative, or under ten dollars. The NABF's finances were kept afloat by a delicate equilibrium between the relatively low rent for the Women's Center; membership fees; "loans" and pledges from the leadership; and other incidental sources of income, such as forum tickets, speaker honorariums, and Alternative School fees. The NABF still had to be creative in finding all sorts of financial opportunities beyond yearly membership income. Yet, at the end of the decade and the beginning of the 1980s, the gradual increase in rent for the Women's Center and dwindling membership created a series of financial crises that the NABF leadership fought in an inventive and resolute way.

Historians have placed the end of the NABF at the beginning of the 1980s, although their chronology has lacked specificity. Becky Thompson states about the NBFO, the NABF's predecessor, that "chapters in major cities remained together for years, including one [in] Chicago that survived until 1981."[25] Benita Roth claims, "By the beginning of the 1980s, the NABF had more or less stopped activities,"[26] while Kimberly Springer places the end of the NABF between 1980 and 1981.[27] However, while the NABF indeed lost the space of the Women's Center by 1982 because of increased rents and decreased membership, and thus had to reduce its activism, the organization's leadership continued to try to work on behalf of Black women by submitting grant proposals to the state of Illinois. These grant proposals, drafted by the NABF leadership in 1981 and 1982, document the breadth of the NABF's organizing vision and its commitment to serving poor Black women. Officially, the NABF ended in 1983, when the leadership did not submit a yearly report, and was thus dissolved as a nonprofit by the state of Illinois, although the loss of the Black Women's Center in 1982 was a decisive blow to the struggling organization.

The Black Women's Center at 202 South State Street was the NABF's largest operating expense. Its central position had very tangible advantages, as anyone could easily find it, walk in, join a consciousness-raising group, use its services, and become part of a Black women's organization. Yet, if originally Eichelberger and other leaders had hoped that membership fees could cover the Center's rent and operating expenses, the NABF, despite being nationally known, never had enough dues-paying members to easily meet these costs. While the NABF served a large number of Black women in Chicago, the number of fully paid members varied from year to year: almost one hundred in 1976, approximately sixty from 1977 to 1978, bouncing back to one hundred and fifty the following year. These numbers are based on receipts for yearly membership fees that the NABF kept in its archive.[28] Membership fees, however, covered only a fraction of the NABF's needs, as the leadership put it in a letter from March 1979: "The $15 membership annually does not begin to pay our expenses."[29] The letter asked members to pledge $2.50 a month in order to cover overhead costs, a sum that, if added to the yearly fee, raised the NABF membership cost to $45 dollars per annum,[30] thus placing the NABF's membership completely out of the reach of poor Black women. In August that same year, the women were encouraged to send their pledges in advance.[31] The letter breaks down the NABF's monthly expenses: $160 for rent and utilities, $23 for the answering service, $40 for the telephone service, $40 for postage, and $20 for office supplies.[32]

Both regular members and the NABF leadership did their best to keep the organization afloat. Regular members sometimes made donations to the NABF; more often, the leadership, Eichelberger especially, "loaned" the organization money that they never expected to see again. As a result of these contributions, the Center, a central feminist space operated by Black women, stayed open for more than six years (January 1976–November 1982), a feat matched by few other feminist organizations of that time. While the fleeting groups, organizations, and caucuses of the women's liberation movement did their best to institutionalize at the beginning of the 1980s, the NABF did not need to do that. It was, and had been from its very inception, an institution.

The organizers encountered one rare windfall in 1980, when Eichelberger delivered assertiveness training seminars to the US Environmental Protection Agency, and the fees for twelve three-hour sessions amounted to $1,950, a sum that was donated in its entirety to the NABF and lifted its finances for a few months.[33] The organization's bank statements show that each expense and deposit was carefully double-checked, as each line bears one or even two handwritten check marks, indicating that perhaps more than one person had examined them.[34] Yet the NABF's income could not match the rent increase, and the organization had to use other strategies, as Eichelberger recalls: "What we did initially, when the rent went up abruptly, there was another organization that we invited to move into the space that we had, so that we could share the expenses."[35] By 1981, the NABF was sharing the space at 202 South State Street with another organization, Women in Community Services;[36] their next location was at 53 W. Jackson room 924,[37] but soon they lost that space as well.

In response to the difficulties related to keeping the Center open, the NABF decided to tap into another funding source—state grants for cultural organizations. The NABF started designing cultural projects that were rooted in the experiences of African American women. In 1981, the NABF applied for a grant of $750 from the Illinois Council for the Arts in order to sponsor a cabaret show titled "'Tain't Nobody's Bizz-Ness If I Do," about the lives of Bessie Smith and Billie Holiday, with local artists Sulanya Conway (performing as Bessie Smith) and Rita Warford (performing as Billie Holiday), accompanied by Gloria Morgan.[38] Although this grant was successful, the funds could only delay for a short time the NABF's loss of its central location.

The loss of the Black Women's Center further limited the NABF's ability to attract new members. Eichelberger recalls about the early 1980s:

> Gradually the rent increased . . . then we got to the point when were no longer on State Street. So then we would just meet at someone's house, and that included my house, or somebody else's house. Of course, it was ideal when it was not in anybody's house, because that meant that anybody could just drop in. [At our Women's Center] People would just drop in who were already downtown, or were going downtown, they would just stop by. You could always drop in, that was the advantage of that. If you were meeting at somebody's house, then you had to know in advance whose house, and the address of the person's house, and the time of the meeting. But there were other organizations doing that, they would meet at somebody's house, or at some public place, and we did meet occasionally at a community center that would allow us to meet there.[39]

In spite of this loss, a small group of women, including Eichelberger, Nelson, and C. A. Lofton, continued their fundraising efforts, applying for grants made available by local and state institutions for cultural events. Two of these applications, although unsuccessful, show the depth and breadth of the NABF's organizing vision, rooted in the culture and experiences of Chicago African American women, and focusing on the needs of poor Black women.

In order to submit the applications, the NABF created a new legal structure in 1980, which continued its activism. Women's Organization for Minority Affairs and Needs (W. O. M. A. N.), the nonprofit and tax exempt subsidiary of the NABF, was incorporated in November that same year.[40] The 1981 report lists Eichelberger as president, Sandra Daniels (Eichelberger's sister) as secretary, and Janie Nelson as treasurer, and its activities as offering assertiveness training seminars, speaking out publicly on issues such as ERA and reproductive justice, conducting orientation and CR sessions, and writing position papers.[41] Through W. O. M. A. N., Eichelberger and other members of the NABF's leadership applied for a grant from the Chicago Council on Fine Arts for a project intended to run from June to August 1982. The application describes the event's purpose as "documenting the fact that Black women have a unique culture; highlighting the fact that this cultural heritage—though different—is rich and should be preserved; and demonstrating, through artistic presentation, that the present culture of Black women should be promoted." The grant proposal notes that at the time of the application, W. O. M. A. N. was already sponsoring creative writing and Black folklore workshops led by the poet C. A. Lofton at St. Dorothy's Roman Catholic Elementary School. The grant proposed a two-month long series of summer workshops enrolling forty "female young adults" from the Oaklawn-Douglas area, an underserved, predominantly African American Chicago neighborhood. The proposal envisioned internships for the students, who would attend seminars taught by local artists and writers and participate in off-campus activities, such as gallery visits and literature readings by local authors.[42] Although the grant presented a coherent vision for bringing a Black-centered artistic and literary education to underserved women students, this proposal appears to have been unsuccessful.

In 1981, Eichelberger submitted another major grant proposal to the Illinois Humanities Council, for a Black Women's Arts and Culture Festival for the following year. Featuring local African American women artists and writers, the festival would consist in a series of seminars, poetry readings, gallery visits, and performances spread over three months. Initially, it seemed that some officials from the Illinois Humanities Council were interested and supportive; a host of artists and community organizations wrote letters in support of the application, which requested $8,000 from the Council's Arts and Humanities Fund. However, it seems that the application was denied in the end, as there are no records documenting that the proposed cultural festival took place.[43]

In 1981, Eichelberger and the few remaining NABF members again applied for funding, this time hoping to organize a Child Care Conference. The project intended to create a framework that would allow poor Black women to design the conference themselves by working together to select experts, childcare professionals, and legislators. Rather than a top-down approach attempting to teach poor African American women about their needs, this grant application set up a structure backed by financial support in the form of individual stipends for the participants, who were expected to work together, identify their own needs, and take leadership on issues that affected their daily lives. Another goal of the conference was to create a position paper on childcare and a resource directory for 1982–1983, thus allowing the NABF, now without a public space, to continue to provide referrals to women who needed them, this time via a dedicated phone line. In addition, the NABF planned to connect parents with legislators such as Congresswoman Cardiss Collins and State Representatives Susan Catania, Monica Faith Stewart, and Carol Moseley Braun, who could introduce bills related to childcare at the local, state, and national level,[44] thus building on the long-term connections that the NABF had developed with Black women politicians over many years. While the detailed grant proposal demonstrates the NABF's commitment to empowering Black women and its existing community roots that were likely to make the project successful, it does not appear that the conference took place.

Without a central location, the services the NABF could offer its constituents were dramatically reduced. The NABF end-of-year report for 1982 lists the organization's activities as offering counseling and referral services regarding employment, childcare, and emergency housing. All NABF documents from 1982 bear Brenda Eichelberger's home address.[45] In 1983, the NABF did not file its annual report,[46] thus losing its tax-exempt status and being dissolved as a nonprofit organization by the State of Illinois. The letter, mailed to Eichelberger's home address, bears handwritten notes in the margins that testify that perhaps the organization's Executive Director was not ready to give up yet: "application for reinstatement $25+filing annual report."[47] In August 1983, in response to an inquiry by Eichelberger, a Reinstatement Officer from the Corporations Department of the Illinois Office of the Secretary of State wrote a letter detailing the conditions under which the NABF could be reincorporated. In addition to the reinstatement application, the letter outlined that the NABF needed to submit a report for the year 1983.[48]

About two years later, on November 29, 1985, Archie Motley, curator of Archives and Manuscripts at the Chicago Historical Society, wrote to Brenda Eichelberger to acknowledge the receipt of the organization's archive, expressing his gratitude for the donation and offering to send duplicates to other repositories. This gesture marks the end of the NABF as an activist organization; its archive, carefully preserved by prestigious institutions around Chicago, became an assembly of primary sources.

Beyond the ERA

Although the NABF ended in 1983, individual members continued their feminist work in their careers and everyday lives. C. A. Lofton says,

> When that [the ERA] didn't pass, a lot of people got disillusioned, but that was not the only quest that we were moving for. I think it was more internal, raising yourself up. That's what it did for a lot of people. When their consciousness got raised, they took that and moved on. Brought it to their church, brought it to their school, wherever they bring it. It was just, where do we go from here. The vision was limited by some people who thought the end goal was the ERA, when others of us felt that the end goal was raising the consciousness and acting on that for the rest of your life.[49]

Like other members, Lofton insists that neither the failure of the ERA nor the end of the organization signified an end to the NABF's influence of its members' lives. On the contrary, the raised consciousness and lessons about Black women irreversibly changed members' lives, as former members worked as community organizers, built successful careers, and took the lessons learned during their NABF years in new directions.

Acting on a consciousness irreversibly changed by her participation in the movement, C. A. Lofton continued her organizing work as an activist for NARAL and AFSCME (American Federation of State, County, and Municipal Employees), fighting against discrimination based on gender and sexual identity within the Federation. She held a position with the union until she retired. Beryl Fitzpatrick, another former member who continued to work as a community organizer after the NABF, joined the Byllye Avery's National Black Women's Health Project and worked for Planned Parenthood. Fitzpatrick is currently the Director of Communications and Compliance at Community HealthNet in Gary, Indiana, a network of health providers serving indigent populations.[50] She has also been active with the National Alliance against Racist and Political Repression, a national organization that originated in Chicago in 1973.[51]

Other former members continued their activism part time, in addition to their careers. Eichelberger continued to work for the Chicago school district,[52] but her reputation as an organizer and writer was well established. She continued to be a guest speaker at feminist meetings, such as the one held at the Mountain Moving feminist coffeeshop in Evanston. In the 1980s, as the AIDS crisis hit the city of Chicago, she organized a group of activists who went to hospitals to provide support to African American AIDS patients.[53] She moved to Washington, DC, after a while, in order to be closer to her mother and sister.

Other NABF members contributed to Black women's intellectual history through their academic and legal work. Based on her experience in the NABF, Janie Nelson completed her dissertation, "Attitude-Behavior Consistency among Black Feminist and Traditional Black Women," at Kent

State University in 1981.[54] After obtaining her degree, Nelson continued to work in the Chicago public school system, and later on opened her own business, the Academy for Tutoring and Counseling, which she ran until 1995. She credits her insights acquired during the NABF years for empowering her to open her own business.[55] Sharon Wells, who was working as a librarian when she joined the organization, received her law degree from the John Marshall School of Law in Chicago in 1980, and for twenty years held the position of Administrative Law Judge, writing more case documents than any other Administrative Law Judge ever appointed by the Labor Relations Board.[56] Monica Stewart, the first Black woman to be elected as Illinois State Representative in 1981, worked on the Rape Study Commission, and in 1982 sponsored a measure providing for increased penalties in cases of gang rape. After a visit to South Africa, she served as Director of the Illinois Office of Trade and Investment in that country, providing consulting services for both private and public institutions.[57]

Former NABF organizers continued to reimagine the concept of sisterhood in their intellectual and activist labor. Beti Ellerson completed her doctorate in African Studies at Howard University, and in 1996–1997, as a Rockefeller Humanities Fellow, produced a documentary titled *Sisters of the Screen: African Women in the Cinema* (2002). The documentary combines video interviews with African women filmmakers and footage from their works, placing them in a dialogue about sisterhood and cultural authenticity. Based on her documentary research, Ellerson later published a book, *Sisters of the Screen: Women of Africa on Film, Video and Television* (Africa World Press Inc., 2000). While the author dubs her book "a 'conversation' among women in the cinema," in her preface she states that the book creates her own "projection of a sisterhood": while her interviewees were aware of each other's works, they were reluctant to perceive themselves as having much in common. Rather, the author adds, "the phrase 'sisters of the screen' elicits a kindred spirit among women where the screen is their ultimate point of convergence."[58] Ellerson continued her project by founding and directing the Center for Study and Research on African Women in Cinema, whose website, titled "African Women in Cinema," is updated regularly.[59]

Both the concept of sisterhood and the NABF's commitment to Black women's health influenced Gayle Porter's professional trajectory. She completed her doctorate in clinical psychology at the University of Chicago and became the first African American woman to occupy a full-time faculty position at Johns Hopkins University's Mental Health and Psychiatry Department. In the late 1970s, Porter met Dr. Marylin Gaston on a televised panel focused on the experiences of middle-aged Black women. Together,

Porter and Gaston wrote *Prime Time: The African American Woman's Complete Guide to Midlife Health and Wellness* (2003). *Essence* listed the book as a bestseller; it received enthusiastic endorsements from *Ebony*, poet Nikki Giovanni, Byllye Avery (the founder of the National Black Women's Health Project), and other public health professionals.

The self-help manual begins by stressing the commonality of experience between authors and readers and pointing out the marginalization experienced by middle-aged Black women: "As African American women in the middle years, we are often part of all women, all Blacks or Black women of all ages, but rarely is there a space for us."[60] While celebrating the improvements in Black women's lives in the post-Civil Rights era, the authors point out lingering disparities in illness and mortality rates for Caucasian and African American women. Their explanation privileges a personal rather than systemic explanation: "we don't make ourselves our number one priority, and we live unhealthy lifestyles."[61] *Prime Time* teaches readers to prioritize their own needs, change their habits, and practice a philosophy of wellness by creating a support system, a "sister circle"[62] led by trained community members. While initially the sister circles were designed for women of color, in 2011, the authors expanded the program to include women from all backgrounds, and by 2013, more than two thousand women had completed the program. Asked whether the Prime Time Sister Circles were in any way similar to the consciousness-raising groups of the women's liberation movement, Porter replied: "Without question, they are meant to be consciousness-raising groups that translate into actions, just like our other consciousness-raising groups were. Their purpose is to activate. We are there not only to provide women with information but with empowerment to change. We see it as a movement, as a health movement."[63] Porter and Gaston's work, like an echo reverberating over many years, carries the NABF's philosophy of sisterhood and consciousness-raising into the new millennium.[64]

When remembering the years of their work with the NABF, all the former members interviewed for this project regret the organization's demise: "It was such a positive organization!" recalls Elnora Washington, who retired after a long career as a public school teacher in Gary, Indiana. Others, such as Helen Whigham, who continued her career working in finance, think that the NABF was ahead of its time:

> It was a good organization. Again, we talked about positive childcare. We talked about criminal justice. Like I said, we were way ahead of our time. It's just too bad that we didn't go further. We didn't stay together. It saddens me because it was really . . . Like I said again, we were trailblazers

> and we were ahead of our time. I guess sometimes I often wonder why . . . why we haven't gotten back together and tried to do it again.[65]

Over the years, Whigham has learned to appreciate even more the groundbreaking insights and activisms that occurred under the NABF's umbrella. She sees the possibility of getting together with former members again, as the decades that have passed since her activist work have only cemented her belief in the value of Black feminism. Indeed, for many former NABF activists, the time they spent working for the NABF represents a crucial crossroads in their lives, one in which they developed their life philosophy and that influenced their careers long after the organization formally ended. Beryl Fitzpatrick remembers:

> I know it was significant for me. I feel like I'm again learning as my mother said, "I never stop learning unless you're putting dirt on me." I subscribe to that ideology. The Alliance of Black Feminists was such a critical point in my life because it allowed for me to expand my world of not only Black women, but to appreciate and learn true sisterhood. . . . There was a phrase that we used to say, "our women keep our skies from falling." Just being able to understand that in its entirety. That was such an important part of my experience with the Alliance of Black Feminists. I applaud that time, I embrace that time and I love all the people that I met during that time.[66]

This sense of a widening of horizons, of learning about other women's lives, shows that the NABF was a catalyst for not only for personal liberation and community building, but for a lifelong commitment to the lessons learned during that time.

Conclusion

The NABF emerged at a time when it seemed that the gains of the Civil Rights movement and of women's liberation could change dramatically, for the better, Black women's lives. Yet within the nine years of its existence (1974–1983), Black women witnessed the return to conservative politics and a growing separation between the middle and working classes, which particularly affected communities already vulnerable, such as poor Black women. Aware of the complexity of their position, always ready to theorize and build activism from their own experiences, the NABF both empowered individual Black women to create trailblazing careers in their fields and created collective mechanisms to offer services to poor women, support incarcerated Black women, and educate the local community through forums and outreach events.

The beginning of the 1980s, and especially the post-ERA years, witnessed the institutionalization of many women's liberation activist groups, although a large number were short-lived or simply disappeared. Lack of resources caused the NABF's untimely end, although its main organizers were ready to fight for Black women in new, more conservative circumstances. Many former members perceived the NABF as being ahead of its time, and indeed, unlike other women's groups, the NABF did not need to institutionalize at the beginning of the 1980s. It had been a national institution all along.

Conclusion
Toward a History of the Black Women's Liberation Movement

In her application to the 1979 Institute on Women's History held at Sarah Lawrence College, Brenda Eichelberger writes about the uses of women's history in the NABF's work:

> I feel that our organization can improve the use of women's history in our programs by recording oral history, visual history, genealogical survey, and discography on women in general and Black women in particular. I also feel we can use women's history in our programs by doing research and writing on the topics of women for archives and for dissemination of information. In addition, we plan to publish a Black woman's calendar annually beginning 1980.[1]

Like other Black feminists of her time, Eichelberger saw history as imbuing every facet of NABF organizing, from Black women's history mobilized in support of feminism as a political project in NABF publications to the history of the women's movement taught at orientation sessions, community forums, and Alternative School courses. She saw documenting the NABF's work as a project that ran concurrent to her many others, and recorded and archived sources—whether aural, visual, or written—thus documenting every facet of the organization. As the excerpt above shows, she planned to write Black women's history herself and collectively create a calendar that would further solidify the connection between past and present in Black women's lives.

For the NABF, and Eichelberger especially, archiving signified a political and intellectual act sustained over almost a decade and a determined resistance to erasure. *The National Alliance of Black Feminists: A History* mines the organization's extraordinarily rich archives to document the NABF's history in depth. Aided by the vivid recollections of former members, these archival sources permit a granular level of analysis that explores the daily life and interactions, both personal and political, public and private, of Midwestern Black feminists, and situates these interactions in the context of Black women's history and the 1970s feminist movement. In addition to traditional primary sources, such as organizational documents and oral history interviews, I have read grant applications and analyzed recordings of both public-facing and private consciousness-raising sessions in order to document the NABF's political vision, with its roots in the experiences of Black women, as well as the organizers' efforts to transform that vision into reality, at the local and national level. The criterion of success versus failure is not the most illuminating, given the enormous forces Black feminists were battling: overall lack of resources, racism within the women's movement and sexism in their own communities, lesbian baiting, respectability politics, and accusations of undermining the Black freedom struggle, in addition to the factionalism and tensions naturally occurring within a political movement that aimed to transform both society and individuals at the same time.

The NABF's long life between 1974 and 1983, at the height of the women's liberation movement, positions it as a nexus that connects Black feminist organizing temporally, from the mid- and late 1970s through the early 1980s and intellectually, from the activist writings of the Black women's liberation movement to academic Black feminism. Given its geographical position and the spread of its chapters and affiliates, the NABF further connects Black feminism on the East Coast with the West Coast. These connecting threads of Black feminism, in their turn, reveal continuities—spatial, temporal, and intellectual—that consolidate the history of a national Black women's liberation movement, simultaneous with, yet independent from, the predominantly white women's liberation movement unfolding in towns and cities around the country throughout the 1970s and early 1980s. A history of Black women's conferences throughout the 1970s will undoubtedly not only further consolidate the geographic spread of Black feminist organizations (whether they embraced the feminist label or not), but also illuminate their determined efforts to build a movement together.

The 1970s are remembered as the decade of the turn toward conservativism, of the reversal of the Civil Rights movement's wins, and of emergent conservative activism among white women. The history of the NABF helps us understand the 1970s as the time of an expanding national Black feminist movement that resisted at every step of the way the erosion of the Civil Rights movement's gains and fought hard for the passing of the Equal Rights Amendment. The NABF's comprehensive activism on behalf of

Black women engaged issues ranging from antirape to antiviolence against women, and from reproductive rights to prison activism. The intellectual effervescence of the Black feminist spaces of that era prepared the ground for academic Black feminism.

Historians have repeatedly noticed Black women's apparent lack of interest in the women's liberation movement, especially given their support for feminist values overall at the beginning of the 1970s. It is worth remembering that the predominantly white women's liberation movement, with certain exceptions, did not make race one of its central axes of analysis, although it borrowed symbols, ideas, and organizing strategies from Black Power. The NABF's history shows that, despite these alienating factors, Black women were very much interested in building a feminist movement of their own, within independent organizations of Black women or women of color, working in coalitions with other women of color groups and predominantly white women's organizations. As NABF history demonstrates, many Black women responded enthusiastically whenever they saw their sisters identifying as feminists on television, when they learned about intersectional consciousness-raising, or when they encountered Black feminist readings or speakers. While Black women were active in a variety of social movements during the 1970s, many critical of the women's liberation movement, a significant number of Black women openly identified as feminist, or, even when they rejected the label, worked hard for gender justice, which they saw as part of racial liberation.

The NABF's history also helps illuminate 1970s Chicago as a hub for Black feminist activism. Chicago is known for Black Power activism and its brutal state repression; as the site of a vibrant women's movement, beginning in the late 1970s, with the Chicago Women's Liberation Union, in addition to other organizations; as an urban space with an energetic (predominantly white) LGBT political community; and as a center for multicultural union organizing. While histories of Black feminism have mostly focused on large coastal cities, the NABF demonstrates the presence of Black feminist groups and organizations throughout the Midwest. Chicago itself, home to one of the largest African American communities in the country and one of the most segregated cities in the nation, was the center of a vital Black feminist movement that was regional in reach and national in ambition. In their local activism, the NABF brought a Black feminist perspective to their collaborations with local agencies concerned with Black people's images, rape victim assistance, and violence against women, including sexual harassment in schools. The "Meeting of the Minds" conference brought to the city Black women from around the country. The NABF galvanized its members' energies to pursue trailblazing careers in law, public health, and politics, and many others who continued to serve Black women and poor communities of color in their work or activism, thus continuing to infuse a Black feminist philosophy into various domains of the city's public life.

The history of the NABF helps us better understand the unique features of 1970s Black feminist organizing, starting with the emphasis on intersectional consciousness-raising. The NABF excelled at theorizing this process for both Black women and men and at using it to generate both feminist theory and activism. They also embraced consciousness-raising's less political offspring, assertiveness training, which they adapted from an intersectional perspective. Black humanist feminism, a unique philosophy developed by the NABF, anchored a larger project of liberation for all, based on the recognition of Black women's humanity. The demand for Black women's rights, central to Black humanist feminism, anticipates by decades the discourse of women's rights as human rights and grounds the NABF's intersectional analysis and organizing for the Equal Rights Amendment. The NABF's coalition work, the other defining manifestation of Black humanist feminism, was continuous throughout the organization's life. The NABF worked together with Black men, local agencies, other groups of women of color, and white feminists, despite experiences of marginalization, censorship, and erasure in their collaborations with their white sisters.

The NABF's history challenges researchers to reconsider received categories of feminist historiography to describe the complex picture of the NABF's political and theoretical work and its place in the women's liberation movement in the 1970s. The categories developed by white women for feminist theory, such as radical, liberal, Marxist, ecofeminism, psychoanalytic and postmodern, while lumping "women of color" all together, thereby erasing differences in their theoretical approaches,[2] do not do justice to 1970s Black feminism. A Black feminist theoretical vocabulary of the 1970s and 1980s includes, alongside womanism and identity politics, Black humanist feminism and radical humanism (Robin D. G. Kelley's term for the Combahee River Collective's philosophy), politico-ethical coalitions, and others that need to be excavated from the archives.

The national Black feminist movement in the 1970s occurred simultaneously with, yet independently from, the predominantly white women's liberation movement. Historians have noted the whitewashing of women's liberation history, yet it is worth noting that this process started early, at the time of the movement, with the censorship of Black feminist voices critical of racism in the movement. Although there were exceptions such as socialist and lesbian feminist organizations and publications, which often promoted an anti-racist politics and supported Black feminists, feminist publishing rarely centered the works of Black women, and the institutionalization of women's studies mirrored this process. As images of the women's liberation movement still ground common public understandings of feminism, the censorship and erasure of Black women's voices create an inaccurate image that continues to erase 1970s feminism's relevance for younger generations.

The history of the NABF enriches the field of African American women's history by uncovering the work of prodigious Black feminist activists and intellectuals, such as Brenda Eichelberger, Gayle Porter, Beti Ellerson, Janie Nelson, and C. A. Lofton. It documents the efforts that Black women invested in raising the feminist consciousness of the Black community in Chicago, as well as their partial success. This monograph further documents Black women's commitment to the struggle for the passing of the Equal Rights Amendment, currently seen as a predominantly white feminist endeavor. Through their commitment to fighting for reproductive rights, against rape and domestic violence, and critiques of patriarchal family arrangements, Black women active in the NABF proved willing to challenge the norms of respectability politics. However, their willingness to publicly support lesbians only went this far, as Black feminists contributed to the secondary marginalization of Black lesbians.

The NABF's history contributes to the history of Chicago politics by documenting the work of a group of Black women who disrupted the continuity of a gentrified area in downtown Chicago by reclaiming it for Black women, who could walk into the Black Women's Center at any time to use its resources, socialize, study, or participate in meetings. Black feminism in the 1970s and early 1980s was ubiquitous in the local press, on the radio and local television stations, and at marches, rallies, and public events organized by various progressive social movements, where NABF organizers were often leaders. The NABF was present in Black communities, where they organized community forums; at cultural events, where they organized debates on Black women's experiences and representations; and at local and regional universities, where they lectured and participated in conferences. In addition, many of the Black women who attended NABF meetings became judges, politicians, educators, administrators, and labor organizers, further infusing Chicago life with a Black feminist sensibility. Furthermore, the NABF's archives document Chicago as the site of a Black lesbian community. Chicago's Black lesbians sometimes joined racially mixed, although predominantly white, lesbian communities, but also socialized on their own and sometimes became active politically in the Black feminist movement.

The NABF's history helps us better understand the institutionalization of women's studies in Chicago and elsewhere. Despite their recurrent attempts to get a footing in academe, NABF intellectuals were present only as temporary lecturers or guest speakers. The NABF openly supported a Black feminist education in colleges and through their Alternative School. Yet women's studies, in Chicago as elsewhere, institutionalized by centering a white subject. The arrival of women of color feminism on campuses in the 1980s has been narrated as both a corrective and challenge to this presupposed unity of the women's studies subject. Yet, Black feminism's presence on university campuses in the Midwest dates back to the 1970s, with the NABF's speaking engagements, courses taught by Eichelberger, and the NABF's support for academic courses by and about Black women. Academic Black feminism in the 1980s had been nourished by these efforts, in addition to the intellectual activism of 1970s Black feminists. As for women's and gender studies, it is conceivable that a different version of feminism could have institutionalized, one that placed the experiences of racialized women at its center. Vanguard politics, which Black feminists articulated in various theoretical iterations, could have guaranteed women's studies as an intersectional field from its very inception, allowing more identities as experiential nexuses, even at the cost of decentering white women as the norm of feminism. Yet, this is not how history unfolded. The NABF's history lesson is that 1970s white feminism was simply one stream of feminism among many, dominant because of its access to resources and sites of discursive power, which institutionalized in academe and was able to whitewash the movement's history.

At a time when attacks on critical race theory and identity politics have become a daily occurrence, when the Dobbs decision is putting lifesaving medical care out of the reach of poor women of color, when new educational standards in states such as Texas and Florida attempt to erase both the history of slavery and the teaching of gender identity, it is more important than ever to preserve, circulate, and critically engage with Black feminism's recent history. Starting in the mid-1970s, a community of Black feminists in a large Midwestern city met for nine years to raise each other's consciousness, theorize their experiences, read Black women's writings, and imagine a world that would celebrate their humanity. The NABF's intellectual and political work, nearly forgotten today, highlights the theoretical and activist diversity of the Black women's liberation movement, with its achievements and limitations, resistance against erasure, and resilience in front of enormous obstacles. To answer Eichelberger's question quoted in the introduction, in the 1970s the Black feminist movement was alive and well, vibrant and generative. Half a century later, its lessons remain urgent and vital.

Black Woman's Bill of Rights

Historically Black women from all walks of life have suffered from the negative effects of racism and sexism. Such sufferings have heightened our awareness of the plight of others in their multifold oppressions. Accordingly, wherever possible, we have rallied to the cause of oppressed people. However, we now feel the need to organize around our own priorities as Black women against both racism and sexism. Our organizing principle is feminism which we view as a dimension of humanism. We are pro Black women, yet anti no one. Therefore, we are willing to work with any person or group of persons dedicated to the establishment of a more humane world. In such a world certain rights are basic to the development of all people. As Black women in a hostile world we therefore feel compelled to establish the following Bill of Rights.

i. ACCURATE MEDIA PORTRAYAL. The RIGHT to non-racist, non-sexist media image in films, television, radio, newspapers, magazines, books, literature, advertising, and other areas of the mass media—to media coverage proportionate to her number in the population
ii. QUALITY HEALTH CARE. The RIGHT to access to knowledge of and control of her own body—to quality health care free of sexism, racism, and classism—to supportive services for the individual and her family in cases of the "battered" wife, "runaway" wife, "abusive" mother, "suicidal" woman, or any other woman in crisis—to research and development without exploitation into the high incidence of suicide, coronaries, breast cancer mortality, hypertension, and other major maladies afflicting the Black woman—to freedom from unwarranted

hysterectomies, mastectomies, and unnecessary surgery—to freedom from medically administered physiologically damaging drugs, devices, and similar agents—to the expansion of public and private health insurance to provide for women's special needs—to the establishment and implementation of informed consent as the right of every patient

iii. QUALITY EDUCATION. The RIGHT to quality, continuing education without sex and race bias—to comprehensive, accurate compilation of historical data on the Black woman—to access to knowledge of her own history (herstory)—to the development of sexist-free, racist-free language and the usage thereof

iv. ECONOMIC/CONSUMER DEVELOPMENT. The RIGHT to equal employment opportunity, meaningful work, just compensation, and equitable promotion in all occupational categories—to an adequate standard of living—to comprehensive consumer protection under the law—to equitable laws governing social security, insurance, pension, retirement, and inheritance—to non-race coded credit in her own name—to equal access to full participation in the entrepreneurial system—to a wider range of goods and services accommodating all body dimensions, skin tones, and hair textures—to fair taxation free of marital status discrimination

v. PURSUIT OF STABLE HOME LIFE. The RIGHT to promote and establish a home life comprised of the sole individual, herself and her mate, the nuclear family, the extended family, the single-parent family, or any other family unit most viable for her and her loved ones—to laws denoting and connoting **equal** partnership in marriage including the sharing of child rearing by **both** parents and the sharing of household tasks—to adequate housing in any area in which she and her family choose to live—to rent and buy housing in the absence of race, sex, and marital status bias either implicit or explicit—to equitable laws allowing for the economic independence of the displaced homemaker—to access to professional individual, marriage, and family counseling regardless of socioeconomic status

vi. POLITICAL ADVANCEMENT. The RIGHT to political representation proportionate to her number in the population—to unionize for increased maternity/paternity benefits, increased rights of the household worker, and overall improvement of working conditions—to lobby for better living standards—to organize for equal rights under the law—to promote and establish a free forum for her ideas

vii. CIVIL/CRIMINAL JUSTICE. The RIGHT to equal protection under the law for her life, limb, and property—to increased preventive measures to secure her protection from sexual abuse—to adequate legal representation without socioeconomic class restrictions—to justice in the courts, penal institutions, and work release programs free of discrimination based on race, sex, and socio-economic status—to appropriate assistance to victims and witnesses of crimes—to decriminalization of laws against private, sexual, consensual behavior among adults

viii. CULTURAL PARTICIPATION. The RIGHT to full and equal participation and access to egalitarian subsidy in the arts and in sports and recreational activities—to full participation in the ceremonies and hierarchy of organized religion—to the promotion of customs, mores, and lifestyles free of race, sex, age, and marital status bias

ix. QUALITY CHILD CARE. The RIGHT to comprehensive, educational, parent-involved convenient child care facilities inclusive of program development for the recognition, treatment, and prevention of child abuse—to non-sex role stereotypic childrearing—to equitable child custody awards—to progressive legislation to secure adequate child support payments—to supportive services to facilitate child development—to the inclusion of child care as a tax deductible expense—to the promotion of broader-based laws encouraging Blacks to adopt Black children, especially the child who is older, "socially" maladjusted, mentally/physically handicapped, or of mixed racial parentage

x. INDIVIDUAL FREEDOM. The RIGHT to privacy of health, educational, employment, tax, credit, and other consumer records—to freedom from unwarranted search and seizure—to freedom from police harassment, government spying, illegal wire-tapping, and governmental intervention of her mail—to total freedom to express her sexuality in private with any consenting adult of her choosing

(This version was taken from an NABF brochure, 1976, National Alliance of Black Feminists Collection, Special Collections and University Archives, University of Illinois at Chicago, 2. Note that similar brochures are also stored at the Eichelberger Papers, 1974–1981, Chicago History Museum, and at the Eichelberger NABF Papers, 1974–1997, Harsh Collection.)

Notes

Introduction

1. For this monograph, I have conducted research at the following archival sites: Brenda Eichelberger / National Alliance of Black Feminists Papers, 1974–1997, Vivian G. Harsh Research Collection of Afro-American History and Literature, Chicago Public Library; Brenda Eichelberger Papers, 1974–1981, Chicago History Museum Research Center; and National Black Feminist Organization collection, Special Collections and University Archives, University of Illinois at Chicago (NBFO Archives, UIC).

2. Kimberle Crenshaw, "Demarginalizing the Intersection of Race and Sex," 67.

3. Kimberly Springer, *Living for the Revolution*, 75; Benita Roth, *Separate Roads to Feminism*, 9; Duchess Harris, *Black Feminist Politics from Kennedy to Obama* (New York: Palgrave Macmillan, 2011).

4. Dayo F. Gore, Jeanne Theoharis, and Komozi Woodard, *Want to Start a Revolution? Radical Women in the Black Freedom Struggle* (New York: New York University Press, 2009); Ashley D. Farmer, *Remaking Black Power*; Premilla Nadasen, *Welfare Warriors: The Welfare Rights Movement in the United States* (New York: Routledge, 2005). Crystal M. Moten, *Continually Working. Black Women, Community Intellectualism, and Economic Justice in Postwar Milwaukee* (Washington, D.C.: Smithsonian National Museum of American History, 2023).

5. Reiland Rabaka, *Black Women's Liberation Movement Music.*

6. Roth, *Separate Roads to Feminism*, 24.

7. Perhaps to solidify this status, the 2007 NWSA Annual Convention was titled "40 Years Since Combahee."

8. Winifred Breines, *The Trouble Between Us*, 7–9. Histories of the women's movement centered on the experiences of white women were published from

the movement's early years and continued into the twentieth century. The chronological list below, most likely not exhaustive, includes both scholarly books and memoirs by former participants, although sometimes, former participants became scholars who wrote academic books on the movement's history. See Judith Hole and Ellen Levine (eds.), *Rebirth of Feminism*; Maren Lockwood Carden, *The New Feminist Movement* (New York: Russell Sage Foundation, 1974); Jo Freeman, *The Politics of Women's Liberation*; Robin Morgan, *Going Too Far*; Barbara Sinclair, *The Women's Movement*; Alice Echols, *Daring to Be Bad*; Flora Davis, *Moving the Mountain*; Barbara Ryan, *Feminism and the Women's Movement*; Susan Brownmiller, *In Our Time*; Ruth Rosen, *The World Split Open*; Myra Marx Ferree and Beth B. Hess, *Controversy and Coalition: The New Feminist Movement Across Three Decades of Change*, 3rd ed. (New York: Routledge, 2000); Judith Ezekiel, *Feminism in the Heartland*; Sarah Evans, *Tidal Wave*; Stephanie Gilmore, *Groundswell*; and Victoria Hesford, *Feeling Women's Liberation*. Compared to earlier works, Evans, Gilmore, Ryan, and Hesford offer more detailed accounts of feminists of color present in the movement and of white feminists grappling with race, yet their narratives center white women's experiences.

9. Leila J. Rupp and Verta Taylor, *Survival in the Doldrums*.

10. Farmer, *Remaking Black Power*, 6–7. See also Ula Taylor, *The Veiled Garvey*, and Dayo F. Gore, *Radicalism at the Crossroads*; and Sherie M. Randolph, *Florynce "Flo" Kennedy*.

11. Springer, *Living for the Revolution*, 10; see also 39–67. Other attempts to grapple with the chronology of the women's movement are gathered in the collection by Nancy A. Hewitt (ed.), *No Permanent Waves*.

12. In some cases, like at Merritt College in Oakland, California, it was Black student activists demanding a Black Studies department and a Black leadership at the college that catalyzed the emergence of the Black Power movement. See Donna Jean Murch, *Living for the City*. In the case of Black feminism, collections such as *But Some of Us Are Brave* and *Still Brave* evidence the flourishing of the field since the 1980s. See Akasha Gloria Hull, Patricia Bell-Scott, and Barbara Smith, *All the Women Are White, All the Blacks Are Men, but Some of Us Are Brave: Black Women's Studies* (Old Westbury, NY: Feminist Press, 1982); and Stanlie M. James, Frances Smith Foster, and Beverly Guy-Sheftall, *Still Brave*. Women's Studies as a discipline changed to embrace intersectionality as a central concept. See Nneka D. Dennie, "The State and Future of Black Women's Studies."

13. Farah Jasmine Griffin, "Conflict and Chorus: Reconsidering Toni Cade's *The Black Woman: An Anthology*," in *Is It Nation Time? Essays in Black Power and Black Nationalism*, edited by Eddie S. Glaude (Chicago: University of Chicago Press, 2002), 22; Brittney Cooper, *Beyond Respectability*, 32–34.

14. Stephanie Gilmore, *Feminist Coalitions*; Anne M. Valk, *Radical Sisters*; Jennifer Nelson, *Women of Color and the Reproductive Rights Movement*; Christina Greene, *Free Joan Little*, 237.

15. Liza Taylor, "Coalition from the Inside Out: Women of Color Feminism and Politico-Ethical Coalition Politics," *New Political Science* 40, no. 1 (2018): 9–36.

16. Michelle Murphy, *Seizing the Means of Reproduction*; Ellen Herman, *The Romance of American Psychology*.

17. Cellestine Ware, *Woman Power*.

18. Barbara Winslow, *Revolutionary Feminists*.

19. Brenda Eichelberger, oral history interview with the author, Silver Spring, MD, August 3, 2013.

20. Brenda Eichelberger, "Biographical Sketch," in "Black Feminism—A New Directive: Consciousness Raising Guidelines for Black Men and Women," Conference Paper submitted to the Association of Black Psychologists' Seventh Annual Convention, August 26–28, 1974, Nashville, Tennessee, UIC, Box 1, Folder 1.

21. Enobong Branch, *Opportunity Denied*, 27.

22. Teresa Amott and Julie Matthaei, *Race, Gender and Work*, 79.

23. Keeanga-Yamahtta Taylor, *From #BlackLivesMatter to Black Liberation*, 80–88; William H. Chafe, *The Unfinished Journey: America since World War II*, 442; Cathy J. Cohen, *The Boundaries of Blackness*, 66.

24. Barbara Sinclair Deckard, *The Women's Movement: Political, Socioeconomic, and Psychological Issues*, 3rd edition (New York: Harper & Row, 1983), 326.

25. Deckard, *Women's Movement*, 355.

26. Donald T. Critchlow, *Phyllis Schlafly and Grassroots Conservatism: A Woman's Crusade* (Princeton, NJ: Princeton University Press, 2005), 26.

27. Jeffrey Escoffier, "Fabulous Politics," 98.

28. Thomas Borstelman, *The 1970s*, 7–8.

29. Robert Cook, *Sweet Land of Liberty? The African American Struggle for Civil Rights in the Twentieth Century* (New York: Longman, 1998), 280.

30. Ibid., 27.

31. Peniel E. Joseph, "Introduction: Toward a Historiography of the Black Power Movement," in *The Black Power Movement*, edited by Peniel E. Joseph (New York: Routledge Taylor and Francis Group, 2006).

32. Rhonda Williams, *Concrete Demands: The Search for Black Power in the 20th Century* (NY: Routledge, 205), 24–48.

33. Judson L. Jeffries, ed. *The Black Panther Party in a City Near You*.

34. Jakobi Williams, *From the Bullet to the Ballot*.

35. David Treuer, *The Heartbeat of Wounded Knee*, 296–338.

36. Jeffrey O. G. Ogden, "Rainbow Radicalism," 94.

37. Eric Porter, "Affirming and Disaffirming Actions," 64.

38. Kathleen Conzen et al., "The Invention of Ethnicity," *Journal of American Ethnic History* 2, no. (1992), 29–30.

39. Keeanga-Yamahtta Taylor, *From #BlackLivesMatter to Black Liberation*, 52.

40. Justin Gomer, *White Balance*, 2.

41. Borstelman, *The 1970s*, 3.

42. Donna Murch, "Toward a Black Working-Class History of the Long 1980s."

43. Gomer, *White Balance*, 64.

44. Nancy Fraser, "Feminism, Capitalism, and the Cunning of History," 283–87.

45. Cooper, *Beyond Respectability*, 26.

46. Mia Bay et al., *Toward an Intellectual History of Black Women*, 2.

47. Franca Iacovetta, Katrina Srigley, and Stacey Zembrzycki, "Introduction," in *Beyond Women's Words*, 8.

48. Claudia Sadowski-Smith, *The New Neoliberal Whiteness*, 3–4.

49. Voichita (Ileana) Nachescu, "Unclassifiable Outsiders," 208, 189–200.

50. Edouard Glissant, "For Opacity," in *Poetics of Relation*, translated by Betsy Wing (University of Michigan Press, 997), 89.

Chapter 1. The Growing Dynamo

1. Brenda Eichelberger, Letter to Margaret Sloan, May 11, 1974. University of Illinois at Chicago, National Black Feminist Organization Papers (hereafter NBFO Papers, UIC), Box 1, Folder 3.

2. "Chicago Area Black Feminists," n.d., NBFO Papers, UIC, Folder 3.

3. "Diane Nash, 1938—," *Civil Rights Digital Library*, accessed on August 19, 2024, https://crdl.usg.edu/people/nash_diane_1938.

4. Miriam Lynnell Harris, *From Kennedy to Combahee*, 105–6.

5. "Vernita Gray," *The Chicago LGBT Hall of Fame*, accessed on August 19, 2024, https://chicagolgbthalloffame.org/gray-vernita/.

6. Benita Roth, *Separate Roads to Feminism*, 106; Kimberly Springer, *Living for the Revolution*, 50.

7. Roth, *Separate Roads to Feminism*, 91.

8. Deborah Gray White, *Too Heavy a Load*, 242.

9. National Black Feminist Organization, "Statement of Purpose," n.d., in National Black Feminist Organization Collection, File 12.

10. National Black Feminist Organization Chicago Chapter (hereafter NBFO Chicago), "Minutes of the First Meeting," NBFO Papers, UIC, Folder 1–2.

11. NBFO Chicago, "Minutes of the Second Meeting: National Black Feminist Organization Chicago Chapter," NBFO Papers, UIC, Folder 2; NBFO Chicago, "Minutes of the Third Meeting: National Black Feminist Organization Chicago Chapter," NBFO Papers, UIC, Folder 2; NBFO Chicago, "Minutes of the Fourth Meeting: National Black Feminist Organization Chicago Chapter," NBFO Papers, UIC, Folder 2; NBFO Chicago, "Minutes of the Fifth Meeting: National Black Feminist Organization Chicago Chapter," NBFO Papers, UIC, Folder 2.

12. NBFO Chicago, "Minutes of the Fifth Meeting."

13. NBFO Chicago, "Minutes from the Steering Committee: July 30, 1974," NBFO Papers, UIC, Folder 2.

14. NBFO Chicago, "By Laws," NBFO Papers, UIC, Folder 6.

15. Letter from Brenda Eichelberger to Sandra Hollins Flowers, August 21, 1971, NBFO Papers, UIC, folder 1–3.

16. Judith Hole and Ellen Levine (eds.), *Rebirth of Feminism*, 126.

17. Vivian Gornick, "Consciousness," 291.

18. Ronnie Lichman, "Sisterhood and the Small Group," reprinted from *WIN magazine*, n.d., Women's Liberation Papers, Sophia Smith College Archives, Box 20, Folder 12.

19. Mary Lou Thomson, "Feminism—Growth and Challenge," 219.

20. Marge Piercy and Jane Freeman, "Getting Together."

21. Irene Peslikis, "Consciousness-Raising."

22. NBFO Chicago, "Minutes of the Third Meeting."

23. Ileana Nachescu, "Intersectional Consciousness Raising, Black Women Political Intellectuals, and the National Alliance of Black Feminists," 205.

24. Lee Rainwater and William L. Yancey, *The Moynihan Report and the Politics of Controversy*, 75.

25. Nikol Alexander Floyd, *Re-Imagining Black Women*, 8.

26. Brenda Eichelberger, "Black Feminism," 2.

27. Ibid., 12.

28. Ibid., 16.

29. Ibid., 6.

30. Marge Piercy and Jane Freeman, "Getting Together."

31. Eichelberger, "Black Feminism," 8.

32. "Supplemental Guidelines for Black Women," n.d., Eichelberger NABF 1974–1997, Harsh Collection, Box 4, File "Consciousness-Raising."

33. Small groups for (usually white) men were also part of the movement. In these groups, men were encouraged to critically examine gender roles and their process of socialization into masculinity.

34. Eichelberger, "Black Feminism," 12.

35. Ibid., 13.

36. Ibid., 18.

37. Toni Cade Bambara, *The Black Woman*.

38. Tia Cross, Freada Klein, Barbara Smith, and Beverly Smith, "Face-to-Face, Day-to-Day," 52–56.

39. Carol Kleiman, "When Black Women Rap, the Talk Sure Is Different," *Chicago Tribune*, June 1, 1975, 13, in Eichelberger Papers, 1974–1981, Chicago History Museum, Box 2, File 14.

40. Gayle Porter, oral history interview by author, September 5, 2013.

41. Letter from Brenda Eichelberger to Jeanette Galters, August 30, 1974, NBFO Papers, UIC, Folder 9.

42. Letter from Brenda Eichelberger to Adelina Cook, September 1, 1974, NBFO Papers, UIC, Folder 3.

43. Brenda Eichelberger, Letter to Kim Krushop, February 5, 1975, NBFO Papers, UIC, Folder 1–13.

44. Brenda Eichelberger, Letter to Alfred E. Cain, editor of *Living Together*, 20 August 1974, NBFO Papers, UIC, Folder 3.

45. National Black Feminist Organization Chicago Chapter, *Newsletter*, vol. 1, no. 2 (Dec. 1974), NBFO Papers, UIC, Folder 1–13.

46. Brenda Eichelberger, Letter to Sandra Hollins Flowers, November 5, 1974, NBFO Papers, UIC, Folder 1–3.

47. *Chicago Tribune*, October 28, 1974, NBFO Papers, UIC, Folder 1–12.

48. "Black Women Assail TV Show as 'Demeaning,'" *The Atlanta Journal*, Friday, October 4, 1974, and "TV Sexism, Racism, Hit by Feminists," *Atlanta Daily World*, Sunday, October 6, 1974, NBFO Papers, UIC, Folder 1.

49. Kimberly Springer, "*Good Times* for Florida and Black Feminism."

50. Barbara H. Eible, Co-coordinator of workshops, Letter to Brenda Eichelberger, October 1974, NBFO Papers, UIC, Folder 5.

51. Rose Levinson, Letter to Brenda Eichelberger, September 20, 1974, NBFO Papers, UIC, Folder 11.

52. Brenda Eichelberger, Letter to Jane Galvin-Lewis, February 10, 1975, NBFO Papers, UIC, Folder 1–13.

53. National Black Feminist Organization Chicago Chapter, *Newsletter*, vol. 2, no. 1 (Jan. 1975), NBFO Papers, UIC, Folder 1–13 (hereafter NBFO Chicago *Newsletter* [Jan. 1975].)

54. Sinclair Deckard, *The Women's Movement*, 351.

55. Brenda Eichelberger, Letter to Iva Caruthers, February 13, 1975, NBFO Papers, UIC, Folder 1–13.

56. Brenda Eichelberger, Letter to Lillie Alexis, February 6, 1975, NBFO Papers, UIC, Folder 1–13.

57. NBFO Chicago *Newsletter* (Jan. 1975), 4.

58. Cade Bambara, *The Black Woman*.

59. NBFO Chicago Chapter, *Newsletter*, vol. 2, no. 4 (Apr. 1975), Eichelberger Papers, 1974–1981, Chicago History Museum, Box 17, Folder 6, p. 8 (hereafter NBFO Chicago *Newsletter* [Apr. 1975]).

60. NBFO Chicago *Newsletter* (Apr. 1975), 8.

61. Participants included Carol Adams of Still Doing Time; Linda Anderson from the American Library Association, Library Service to the Disadvantaged; Maisha Bennett from the Chicago Chapter of the National Association of Black Psychologists; Arnita Boswell, representing the League of Black Women; Jean Fairman of Women in New Directions; Clara Grant, National Association of University Women; Sheila Griffie of Women's, Inc.; Judy Hagans, from the Socialist Workers Party; Crystal Hudson, from the Bureau of the Census; Marilyn Isabel of the Chicago Women's Prison Project; Mamie Moore of the Day Care Crisis Council of the Chicago Area; Lavondia Neely, from Women in New Directions; Janine Raymond from the Illinois Women's Political Caucus;

Charlotte Walker, representing the National Alliance Against Racist and Political Repression; and Nezzie Willis of the Chicago Welfare Rights Organization.

62. NBFO Chicago *Newsletter* (Apr. 1975), 2.

63. Brenda Eichelberger, Letter addressed "Dear Brother," March 24, 1975, Eichelberger Papers, 1974–1981, Chicago History Museum, Box 17, Folder 7.

64. Springer, *Living for the Revolution*, 135.

65. Brenda Eichelberger, follow-up phone conversation with the author, March 19, 2015.

66. NBFO Chicago *Newsletter* (Apr. 1975), 7.

67. Among the discussants were Douglas Andrews, president of the Garfield Park Chamber of Commerce; James Battles, from the Socialist Workers Party; Larry Bullock, president of Mid-South Services, Inc.; Robert Devine, Rabbi, House of Israel Hebrew Culture Center; Charles Harris, editor of Chicago Metro News; Robert Henley, Jr., from the Chicago Urban League; Don Johnson, from the December Fourth Committee; Joseph Long, insurance manager at Prudential Insurance; Evan Gregory Moore, psychiatrist; Andrew Pulley, from the Student Coalition Against Racism; Howard Safford, president of the Afro-American Patrolmen's League, who had collaborated with the NBFO before in their community antirape meetings; Ibn Sharrief, Islamic historian; Hamilton Talbert Jr., from the Fourth Ward Republican Organization; and Edward Williams, of Wilfox International.

68. NBFO Chicago *Newsletter* (Apr. 1975), 3.

69. "Minutes of the Fourth Meeting."

70. Brenda Eichelberger, Letter to Dr. Herman Roberts, n.d., NBFO Papers, UIC, Box 1, Folder 1–3.

71. The myth of Black women's sexual availability, rooted in the experience of chattel slavery, continued through Reconstruction and the Jim Crow years, and still influences the way Black women talk about sexuality today. Work by Darlene Clark Hine and Tricia Rose bookend a long list of references; see Hine, "Rape and the Inner Lives of Black Women in the Midwest," and Rose, *Longing to Tell*.

72. Dawn Rae Flood, *Rape in Chicago*, 15. See also Danielle L. McGuire, *At the Dark End of the Street*.

73. Flood, *Rape in Chicago*, 18.

74. Ibid., 143.

75. Ibid., 140.

76. In response, the National Black Nurses' Association, founded in 1971, planned to address "concerns regarding the growing inequalities in health care for African Americans and the lack of a voice from black nurses on their issues." See Flood, *Rape in Chicago*, 142.

77. National Black Feminist Organization Chicago Chapter, *Newsletter*, vol. 1, no. 1 (Nov. 1974), NBFO Papers, UIC, Folder 1–12 (hereafter NBFO Chicago *Newsletter* (Nov. 1974).

78. Brenda Eichelberger, Letter to Dr. Herman Roberts, n.d., NBFO Papers, UIC, folder 1–2.

79. Letter from Brenda Eichelberger to Renault Robinson, November 4, 1974, NBFO Papers, UIC, Folder 1–2.

80. NBFO Calendar of Events, November 1974, NBFO Papers, UIC, Folder 1.

81. NBFO Chicago *Newsletter* (Jan. 1975).

82. NBFO Chicago *Newsletter* (Apr. 1975), 6.

83. McGuire, *Dark End of the Street*, 215.

84. NBFO Chicago *Newsletter* (Apr. 1975), 6.

85. Christina Greene, *Free Joan Little*.

86. Christina Greene, *Our Separate Ways*, 225–26.

87. NBFO Chicago *Newsletter* (Jan. 1975), 5. Also in NBFO Chicago *Newsletter* (Apr. 1975), 9.

88. NBFO Chicago *Newsletter* (Apr. 1975), 9.

89. NBFO Chicago *Newsletter* (Jan. 1975), 5.

90. NBFO Chicago *Newsletter* (Nov. 1974).

91. NBFO Chicago *Newsletter* (Jan. 1975).

92. NBFO Chicago *Newsletter* (Apr. 1975), 9.

93. Edelin later published a memoir about this experience, *Broken Justice: A True Story of Race, Sex, and Revenge in a Boston Courtroom*.

94. Woolfolk, Tondalola Therese, Registration Form, 1974 (dated in the upper right corner), Eichelberger Papers, 1974–1981, Chicago History Museum, Box 2, Folder 11.

95. Brenda Eichelberger, Letter to Jane Galvin-Lewis, July 10, 1975, Eichelberger Papers, 1974–1981, Chicago History Museum, Box 24, Folder NBFO 1974–1975.

96. Brenda Eichelberger, Letter to Jane Galvin-Lewis, July 1, 1975, Eichelberger Papers, 1974–1981, Chicago History Museum, Box 24, Folder NBFO 1974–1975.

97. NBFO Chicago *Newsletter* (Jan. 1975).

98. Phyllis A. Wallace, *Black Women in the Labor Force*, 59.

99. Sandra Hollin Flowers, Letter to Brenda Eichelberger, August 15, 1974, NBFO Papers, UIC, Folder 1–3.

100. National Black Feminist Organization, Letter addressed "Dear Sister," NBFO Papers, UIC, Folder 1–4.

101. Brenda Eichelberger, letter to Jane Galvin-Lewis, September 1, 1974, NBFO Papers, UIC, Folder 1–3.

102. NBFO Chicago *Newsletter* (Apr. 1975), 9.

103. Roth, *Separate Roads*, 114.

104. Brenda Eichelberger, Letter to Galvin-Lewis, July 10, 1975.

105. Brenda Eichelberger, Letter to Jane Galvin-Lewis, July 10, 1975.

106. Brenda Eichelberger, Letter to Riley B. Davis, Jr., September 10, 1975, Eichelberger Papers, 1974–1981, Chicago History Museum, Box 24, Folder NBFO 1974–1975.

107. M. Gordon, letter to "Sisters," June 5, 1975, Eichelberger Papers, 1974–1981, Chicago History Museum, Box 2, Folder 19-G.

108. Dorothy Roquemore, Letter to the N. B. F. A. [*sic*], June 6, 1975, Eichelberger Papers, 1974–1981, Chicago History Museum, Box 2, Folder 29-R.

109. Cynthia Wilson, Letter to Dear Ms.(s), June 7, 1975, Eichelberger Papers, 1974–1981, Chicago History Museum, Box 2, Folder 32-W.

110. Regina Arderia Lowery, Letter to Chicago Black Feminists, July 10, 1975, Eichelberger Papers, 1974–1981, Chicago History Museum, Box 2, Folder 24-L.

111. Sharon Johnson, Letter to Dear NBFO, June 10, 1975, Eichelberger Papers, 1974–1981, Chicago History Museum, Box 2, Folder 22-J.

112. Juanita Hill, Letter to NBFO, May 29, 1975, Eichelberger Papers, 1974–1981, Chicago History Museum, Box 2, Folder 20-H.

113. Barbara McCants, Letter to NBFO, June 24, 1975, Eichelberger Papers, 1974–1981, Chicago History Museum, Box 2, Folder 25-M.

114. Diane Momon, Letter to Dear Ms. Eichelberger, January 7, 1974, Eichelberger Papers, 1974–1981, Chicago History Museum, Box 2, Folder 25-M.

115. Loraine Anderson, Letter to Dear Brenda, June 2, 1975, Eichelberger Papers, 1974–1981, Chicago History Museum, Box 2, Folder 12-A.

116. Diana L. Pughsley, Letter to NBFO, received on October 9, 1975, Eichelberger Papers, 1974–1981, Chicago History Museum, Box 2, Folder 27.

117. Velma Jean Powell, Letter addressed "To Whom It May Concern," June 16, 1975, Eichelberger Papers, 1974–1981, Chicago History Museum, Box 2, Folder 27.

118. Few other organizations used both Black and feminist in their name. The Black Feminist Alliance, which was founded in New York City as a spinoff of the SNCC, changed its name to Third World Women's Alliance in 1970.

Chapter 2. The Theory and Practice of Black Humanist Feminism

1. Tommie Shelby, "Two Conceptions of Black Nationalism," 665.

2. Ibid., 667.

3. E. Frances White, "Africa on My Mind," 73.

4. Eddie S. Glaude Jr., "Introduction: Black Power Revisited," in *Is It Nation Time? Contemporary Essays on Black Power and Black Nationalism*, edited by Eddie S. Glaude Jr. (Chicago: University of Chicago Press, 2002), 1.

5. Ogbar, *Black Power*, 2.

6. Ashley Farmer, *Remaking Black Power*, 159–92. Springer, *Living for the Revolution*, 47–49.

7. Stokely Carmichael and Charles V. Hamilton, *Black Power*, 37–38.

8. NABF brochure, 1976, National Alliance of Black Feminists Collection, Special Collections and University Archives, University of Illinois at Chicago (hereafter NABF Collection).

9. In Black Power organizations, activists created new models of revolutionary Black womanhood and, by asserting the primacy of women in political organizing, challenged patriarchal ideas. Robyn Spencer and Mary Phillips insist that Black women's leadership in Black Power organizations allowed them to navigate what were ultimately patriarchal environments while being somewhat successful in steering their gender ideology toward a more inclusive vision of justice. See Robyn C. Spencer, *The Revolution Has Come*; and Mary Phillips, "The Power of the First-Person Narrative." Tracye Matthews and Angela LeBlanc-Ernest have contributed revisionist histories of the Black Panther Party (BPP), examining the various competing gender ideologies it promoted and documenting the major role women played in the Party throughout its existence. Tracye Matthews, "No One Ever Asks What a Man's Role in the Revolution Is"; Angela D. LeBlanc-Ernest, "'The Most Qualified Person to Handle the Job': Black Panther Party Women, 1966–1982," 305–27. Within the Nation of Islam, as Ula Taylor convincingly shows, Black women found protection and community, and "worked within a patriarchal structure, yielding where they could, resisting where they had to." See Ula Yvette Taylor, *The Promise of Patriarchy*, 183. See also Sylvia Chan-Malik, *Being Muslim*.

10. Farmer, *Remaking Black Power*, 4.

11. Stephen M. Ward, "The Third World Women's Alliance"; Sherie M. Randolph, *Florynce "Flo" Kennedy*.

12. Quoted in Matthews, "No One Ever Asks What a Man's Role in the Revolution Is," 275.

13. Brenda Eichelberger, "Voices on Black Feminism," *Quest*, 26.

14. Komozi Woodard, *A Nation within A Nation*.

15. These political demands go back to Depression era "don't shop where you can't work" campaigns, where African American women boycotted white businesses operating in Black neighborhoods that refused to hire Black employees. See Lizabeth Cohen, *A Consumers' Republic*, 41–54.

16. NABF brochure, 1976.

17. Quoted in Matthews, "No One Ever Asks What a Man's Role in the Revolution Is," 276.

18. NABF brochure, 1976.

19. Lee Rainwater and William L. Yancey, *The Moynihan Report and the Politics of Controversy*.

20. Keeanga-Yamahtta Taylor, *How We Get Free: Black Feminism and the Combahee River Collective* (Chicago: Haymarket Books; 2017).

21. Patricia Romney, *We Were There*, 179.

22. Jessica Grogan, *Encountering America*, x.

23. Ellen Herman, *The Romance of American Psychology*, 273.

24. Ibid., 9.

25. Herman, 291–292.

26. The National Organization for Women, "Statement of Purpose."

27. Pamela Allen, "Free Space," in *Radical Feminism*, edited by Anne Koedt, Ellen Levine, and Anita Rapone (New York: Quadrangle / The New York Times Book Co., 1973), 278.

28. Cellestine Ware, *Woman Power*, 110.

29. Brenda Eichelberger, "Black Women and the Feminist Movement," 6.

30. Juan M. Floyd-Thomas, *The Origins of Black Humanism in America*, 5.

31. Aimé Césaire, *Discourse on Colonialism*, 56.

32. Léopold Segar Senghor, "L'humanisme noir," quoted in Michel Fabre, Randall Cherry, and Jonathan P. Eburne, "René, Louis and Léopold," 927. See also Reiland Rabaka, *The Negritude Movement*, 228–43.

33. Erich Fromm, "Introduction," ix.

34. Léopold Senghor, "Socialism Is a Humanism," 53.

35. George Lichtheim, Review of *Socialist Humanism*.

36. NABF, "Articles of Incorporation" n.d., Eichelberger NABF Papers, 1974–1997, Harsh Collection, Box 2, Folder 1.

37. NABF, "The Black Woman's Bill of Rights."

38. Liza Taylor, *Feminism in Coalition*, 71.

39. Lynn Hunt, *Inventing Human Rights*, 21.

40. Letter from Brenda Eichelberger to Dear Mert (Myrtlene Clark), February 12, 1976, Eichelberger Papers, 1974–1981, Chicago History Museum, Box 2, Folder 35-C.

41. Brittney Cooper, *Beyond Respectability*, 26.

42. Carol Kleiman, "When Black Women Rap, the Talk Sure Is Different," *Chicago Tribune*, June 1, 1975, 13, Eichelberger Papers, 1974–1981, Chicago History Museum, Box 2, File 14.

43. "Paid Membership List: Chicago Chapter National Black Feminist Organization," June 30, 1975, Eichelberger NABF Papers, 1974–1997, Harsh Collection, Box 1, Folder 12.

44. Jacqueline Moore, "3 Women's Groups Common Goals: Aid Black Women," in *Chicago Defender*, Saturday, June 26, 1976, 12, Eichelberger NABF Papers, 1974 1997, Harsh Collection, Box 1, Folder 8.

45. National Alliance of Black Feminists (NABF), "Minutes," August 30, 1976 and September 13, 1976, Eichelberger Papers, 1974–1981, Chicago History Museum, Box 16, Folder 36.

46. NABF brochure, 1976, 2.

47. Demanding rights for African Americans through a Declaration of Rights had of course more distant predecessors, going back to Marcus Garvey's "Declaration of the Rights of Negro People," created August 1920 at the UNIA International Convention of the Negro Peoples of the World. See Gray White, *Too Heavy a Load*, 112.

48. Brenda Eichelberger, follow-up phone interview by author, March 19, 2015.

49. Renita Alexander, Letter to Dear sisters, July 1, 1976, Eichelberger Papers, 1974–1981, Chicago History Museum, Box 2, Folder 33-A.

50. Tiyo Salah and David Jones, Letter, June 18, 1976, Eichelberger Papers, 1974–1981, Chicago History Museum, Box 2, Folder 51-S.

51. National Alliance of Black Feminists, Letter to Margaret Anderson, July 29, 1976, Eichelberger Papers, 1974–1981, Chicago History Museum, Box 2, Folder 33.

52. National Alliance of Black Feminists, "For Immediate Release," May 17, 1976, Eichelberger NABF Papers, 1974–1997, Harsh Collection, Box 1, Folder 7 Press Releases.

53. NABF Memorandum to Honorary Members, May 9, 1976, Eichelberger Papers, 1974–1981, Chicago History Museum, Box 16, Folder 20.

54. Executive Director, President, Recording Secretary, and Corresponding Secretary, and the Board Functions, Eichelberger Papers, 1974–1981, Chicago History Museum, box 16, folder 22.

55. NABF, Letter to Dear member, June 25, 1975, Eichelberger Papers, 1974–1981, Chicago History Museum, Box 16, Folder 15.

56. NABF Committees and Their Function, n.d., Eichelberger Papers, 1974–1981, Chicago History Museum, Box 16, Folder 16 Committee Outline.

57. NABF Committee Outline, n.d., Eichelberger Papers, 1974–1981, Chicago History Museum, Box 16, Folder 22.

58. Helen Whigham, phone interview by author, September 21, 2015.

59. "Reverend Willie T. Barrow."

60. "International Civil Rights Walk of Fame: Addie L Wyatt."

61. For more information about Ethel Payne, see James McGrath Morris, *Eye on the Struggle*.

62. National Alliance of Black Feminists, "Press Release," May 23, 1976, Eichelberger NABF Papers, 1974–1997, Harsh Collection, Box 1, Folder 7 (Press Releases).

63. "The membership of the organization's governing body," n.d., Eichelberger NABF Papers, Harsh Collection., Box 1, Folder 11 (Minutes, NABF Meetings [1974?-1981?]).

64. "NABF Board Members," n.d., Eichelberger NABF Papers, 1974–1997, Harsh Collection, Box 1, Folder NABF Board Members.

65. NABF brochure, 1976.

66. Letter to Dear Sister, n.d., Eichelberger Papers, 1974–1981, Chicago History Museum, Box 3, Folder Membership Letters.

67. Nancy Lewers, Letter to Brenda Eichelberger, March 28, 1977, Eichelberger Papers, 1974–1981, Chicago History Museum.

68. Rosemary Bray, Letter to Dear Brenda, December 14, 1976, Eichelberger Papers, 1974–1981, Chicago History Museum, Box 2, Folder 34-B.

69. Hannah Frisch, Letter, December 6, 1976, Eichelberger Papers, 1974–1981, Chicago History Museum, Box 2, Folder 38-F.

70. Stephanie Guilloud and William Cordery, "Fundraising Is Not a Dirty Word," 107.

71. Ibid.

72. The archives preserve signed notes by Eichelberger certifying the number of hours completed by community action workers. See Brenda Eichelberger, To Whom It May Concern, May 4, 1978, Eichelberger NABF Papers, 1974–1997, Harsh Collection, Box 3, Folder 3. https://www.iacaanet.org/about-iacaa.

73. Springer, *Living for the Revolution*, 127–28.

74. Barbara J. Williams, n.d., Eichelberger Papers, 1974–1981, Chicago History Museum, Box 16, folder 22.

75. Marta White, n.d., Eichelberger Papers, 1974–1981, Chicago History Museum, Box 16, Folder 22.

76. Barbara J. Williams, n.d., Eichelberger Papers, 1974–1981, Chicago History Museum, Box 16, folder 22.

77. Brenda Eichelberger, Letter to Cindy Jaquith, November 11, 1976, Eichelberger NABF Papers, 1974–1997, Harsh Collection, Box 3, Folder 1.

78. The Socialist Workers Party, "A Transitional Program for Black Liberation," 108.

79. Eichelberger, "Black Women and the Feminist Movement," in *Women Organizing: A Socialist Feminist Bulletin* 3, no. 7 (1979): 2–8.

80. Eichelberger, "Black Women and the Feminist Movement," 7.

81. Janie Nelson, oral history interview with the author, Chicago, Illinois, April 12, 2013.

82. NABF, June 1979 Membership Letter, Eichelberger Papers, 1974–1981, Chicago History Museum, Box 4, Folder Membership Letters.

83. Michelle Hall, Letter to Dear Sisters, February 8, 1979, CHM, Box 3, Folder 33.

84. C. A. Lofton, follow-up interview, Chicago, Illinois, June 16, 2019.

85. Ibid.

86. NABF, July/August 1979 Membership Letter, Eichelberger Papers, 1974–1981, Chicago History Museum, Box 4, Folder Membership Letters, 6.

87. NABF Chapter Formation Guidelines, Eichelberger NABF Papers, 1974–1997, Harsh Collection, Box 1, Folder 24, 1.

88. National Black Feminist Organization, "A Meeting of the Minds" conference flyer, NBFO Archives, UIC, Folder 1.

89. "ERA Meeting and Prison Conditions," April 23, 1977, Cassette, Eichelberger Papers, 1974–1981, Chicago History Museum, Box 14.

90. Brenda Eichelberger, Letter to Rose Marie Burwell, March 30, 1977, Eichelberger Papers, 1974–1981, Chicago History Museum, Box 24, Folder Correspondence Speaking.

91. Chicago NBFO *Newsletter*, vol. 2, no. 4 (Apr. 1975), Eichelberger NABF Papers, 1974–1997, Harsh Collection, Box 17, Folder 6.

92. Flyer, "Clear Cassandra Peten," Eichelberger Papers, 1974–1981, Chicago History Museum, Box 5, Folder Special Events, Activities, Projects, Coalitions.

93. Meeting of the Chicago Coalition, Cassandra Peten Defense Committee, September 25, 1978 and October 9, 1978, Eichelberger Papers, 1974–1981, Chicago History Museum, Box 16, Folder 7 NABF Group Actions.

94. NABF, Calendar of Events: November 1978, Eichelberger Papers, 1974–1981, Chicago History Museum, Box 4, Folder Calendars of Events.

95. Prison Culture, "No Selves to Defend No. 5."

96. Cassandra Peten, Membership Application Form, Eichelberger Papers, 1974–1981, Chicago History Museum, Box 1, Folder 9.

Chapter 3. 202 South State Street

1. National Alliance of Black Feminists, "Press Release," May 23, 1976, Eichelberger NABF Papers, 1974–1997, Harsh Collection, Box 1, Folder 7 (Press Releases).

2. Brenda Eichelberger, follow-up phone conversation with the author, March 19, 2015.

3. Katherine McKittrick, *Demonic Grounds*, xviii-xix.

4. Gayle Porter, phone interview by author, September 5, 2013.

5. Chicago Women's Liberation Herstory Project, "Feminism Curriculum and Archive."

6. Estelle Carol, "The Chicago Women's Graphics Collective," 104–5.

7. Judith Gardiner, "Rethinking Collectivity."

8. Rima Lunin Schultz and Adele Hast, *Women Building Chicago 1790–1990*, lix.

9. Mujeres Latinas en Acción: Empowering Latinas and Their Families, "¿Quiénes Somos? / Who We Are," accessed October 21, 2024, https://mujereslatinasenaccion.org/whowearequiensomos.

10. Leonard G. Ramirez, *Chicanas of 18th Street*.

11. Anne Enke, *Finding the Movement*, 7.

12. Jeanne Theoharis and Komozi Woodard, *Freedom North*, 3.

13. Roger Biles, "Race and Housing in Chicago," 31–38.

14. Natalie Y. Moore, *The South Side*, 113.

15. Jon Rice, "The World of the Illinois Panthers," 43.

16. Chicago Urban League, *Where Blacks Live*, 5–7.

17. Chicago Historical Society, "The Loop."

18. Gregory D. Squires, *Capital and Communities in Black and White*, 104.

19. Although the Chicago NAACP fought for an end to employment discrimination in the Loop and other Chicago neighborhoods, businesses adamantly fought against government interference and blocked the passage of fair employment codes until 1961. See Christopher Robert Reed, *The Chicago NAACP and the Rise of Black Professional Leadership, 1910–1966*, 178.

20. National Black Feminist Organization Chicago Chapter (hereafter NBFO Chicago), *Newsletter*, vol. 1, no. 1, Nov. 1974, NBFO Archives, UIC, Folder 1–12.

21. Ian Rocksborough-Smith, "Margaret T. J. Burroughs and Black Public History in Cold War Chicago," 26–42.

22. Davarian Baldwin, *Chicago's New Negroes: Modernity, the Great Migration, and Black Urban Life* (Durham: University of North Carolina Press, 2009), 23.

23. Anne Meis Knupfer, *The Chicago Black Renaissance and Women's Activism.*

24. Erik S. McDuffie, "Chicago, Garveyism, and the History of the Diasporic Midwest."

25. Mariame Kaba and Essence McDowell, *Lifting as They Climbed.*

26. NBFO Chicago, *Newsletter*, vol. 1, no. 2, Dec. 1974, NBFO Archives, UIC, Folder 1–13.

27. Brenda Eichelberger, follow-up phone conversation with the author, March 19, 2015.

28. C. A. Lofton, follow-up phone interview by author, July 30, 2023.

29. Elnora Washington, interview by the author, Gary, IN, June 29, 2015.

30. NABF, July/August 1979 Membership Letter, Eichelberger Papers, 1974–1981, Chicago History Museum, Box 4, Folder Membership Letters, 4.

31. Elnora Washington, interview by the author, Gary, IN, June 29, 2015.

32. Interview with Laverne Love Bennett by the author, Chicago, July 1, 2015.

33. Former member, follow-up conversation with the author.

34. Cathy Cohen, *The Boundaries of Blackness*, 27.

35. Marlon M. Bailey and Rashad Shabazz, "Editorial," 318.

36. Susan Stryker, *Transgender History*, 130–32.

37. Finn Enke, "Collective Memory and the Transfeminist 1970s," 13.

38. Beryl Fitzpatrick, phone interview by author, February 28, 2016.

39. Nancy Fraser, "Rethinking the Public Sphere," 67.

40. Michael C. Dawson, "A Black Counterpublic?," 211.

41. Catherine Squires, "Rethinking the Black Public Sphere," 458.

42. NABF Retreat/Program/Itinerary: 3/23/79–3/25/79, Eichelberger Papers, 1974–1981, Chicago History Museum, Box 5, Folder Retreat.

43. NABF, April 1979 Membership Letter, Eichelberger Papers, 1974–1981, Chicago History Museum, Box 4, Folder Membership Letters.

44. NABF, Calendar of Events: June 1979, Eichelberger Papers, 1974–1981, Chicago History Museum, Box 4, Folder Membership Letters.

45. NABF Women's Party flyer, May 19, 1979, Eichelberger Papers, 1974–1981, Chicago History Museum, Box 16, Folder 8.

46. NABF, April 1979 Membership Letter, Eichelberger Papers, 1974–1981, Chicago History Museum, Box 4, Folder Membership Letters.

47. NABF, January 1979 Membership Letter, Eichelberger Papers, 1974–1981, Chicago History Museum, Box 4, Folder Calendar of Events.

48. NABF, September 1979 Membership Letter, Eichelberger Papers, 1974–1981, Chicago History Museum, Box 4, Folder Membership Letters.

49. NABF, Board Meeting of November 12, 1978, Eichelberger Papers, 1974–1981, Chicago History Museum, Box 16, Folder 9 Board Meetings.

50. NABF, Calendar of Events: November 1978, Eichelberger Papers, 1974–1981, Chicago History Museum, Box 4, Folder Calendars of Events.

51. NABF, January 1979 Membership Letter, Eichelberger Papers, 1974–1981, Chicago History Museum, Box 4, Folder Calendars of Events.

52. NABF, Calendar of Events: June 1979, Eichelberger Papers, 1974–1981, Chicago History Museum, Box 4, Folder Calendars of Events.

53. Eichelberger, "New Myths for Old."

54. Ibid., 11.

55. Ibid., 13.

56. NABF, Calendar of Events: December 1978, Eichelberger Papers, 1974–1981, Chicago History Museum, Box 4, Folder Membership Letters.

57. NABF, "Historical Sketch," n.d., Eichelberger NABF Papers, 1974–1997, Harsh Collection, Box 1, Folder 2.

58. C. A. Lofton, interview by author, Chicago, Illinois, January 14, 2016.

59. "'Colored Girls' Rumble at Kuumba," *Chicago Defender*, Wednesday, January 25, 1978.

60. Kimberly Springer, "Black Feminists Respond to Black Power," 114.

61. NABF, "Speakers/Writers and Their Topics," Eichelberger NABF Papers, 1974–1997, Harsh Collection, Box 1, Folder 16.

62. NABF, Calendar of Events: May 1976, Eichelberger Papers, 1974–1981, Chicago History Museum, Box 4, Folder Calendars of Events.

63. NABF, Calendar of Events: June 1976, Eichelberger Papers, 1974–1981, Chicago History Museum, Box 4, Folder Calendars of Events.

64. Glenn Deutsch, Letter to Brenda Eichelberger, Feb. 21, 1977, Eichelberger Papers, 1974–1981, Chicago History Museum, Box 3, Folder 4.

65. Nancy Lewers, Letter to Brenda Eichelberger, March 28, 1977, Eichelberger Papers, 1974–1981, Chicago History Museum, Box 3, Folder 10.

66. C. A. Lofton, interview by author, Chicago, Illinois, January 14, 2016.

67. Stephanie Guilloud and William Cordery, "Fundraising Is Not a Dirty Word," 110–11.

68. Jeffrey Ogbar points out that a central Black Power organization, the Black Panther Party, was the first major Black organization to publicly endorse the women's and gay liberation movements. See Jeffrey Ogbar, *Black Power*, 105. In a similar vein, Kathleen Cleaver argues that accusations of misogyny simply deflect the radical critique of society formulated by the BPP. See Kathleen Cleaver and George Katsiaficas, *Liberation, Imagination, and the Black Panther Party*, 124.

69. Ashley Farmer, *Remaking Black Power*, 4–5.

70. "National Alliance of Black Feminists Forum Program," Eichelberger Papers, 1974–1981, Chicago History Museum, Box 4, Folder 1976 Forums.

71. NABF, "For Immediate Release: Black Woman / Man Relationship Forum, Part II," Eichelberger Papers, 1974–1981, Chicago History Museum, Box 4, Folder 1976 Forums.

72. NABF, "Black Woman / Man Relationships Forum," Eichelberger Papers, 1974–1981, Chicago History Museum, Box 4, Folder 1976 Forums.

73. Black Woman / Man Relationship Forum, n.d. Eichelberger Papers, 1974–1981, Chicago History Museum, Box 14, Plastic Box 1. This is the source for all quotes taken from the forum.

74. "Thomas N. Todd."

75. Brenda Eichelberger, follow-up phone conversation with the author, March 19, 2015.

76. Brenda Eichelberger, "Black Women and the Feminist Movement," 5.

77. Brenda Eichelberger, "Voices on Black Feminism" (Spring 1977).

78. Ibid., 17.

79. Ibid., 20.

80. Ibid., 23.

81. Erica Townsend-Bell, "Writing the Way to Feminism," 18.

82. Eichelberger, "Voices on Black Feminism," 18.

83. Ibid., 21.

84. Ibid., 26.

85. Ibid., 24.

86. Eichelberger, "Voices on Black Feminism," 28.

87. Quest, *Building Feminist Theory*.

88. Barrie Thorne, "Review of Building Feminist Theory."

89. Zillah Eisenstein, *Capitalist Patriarchy and the Case for Socialist Feminism*.

90. Brenda Eichelberger, "Voices on Black Feminism," in *The Women Say, the Men Say*, 225–31.

91. Gloria Bowles, "Review of Textbooks in Women's Studies."

92. Barbara Smith, "A Press of Our Own Kitchen Table," 11–12.

93. Patricia Frampton, Letter to "Dear Ladies Sisters," November 9, 1976, Eichelberger Papers, 1974–1981, Chicago History Museum, Box 2, Folder 38-F.

94. Delores Watson, Letter, June 27, 1976, in Eichelberger Papers, 1974–1981, Chicago History Museum, Box 2, Folder 55.

95. Cynthia Lawrence Wallace, Letter to the National Alliance of Black Feminists, November 19, 1976, Eichelberger Papers, 1974–1981, Chicago History Museum, Box 2, Folder 55-W.

96. Wanda Edwards, Letter to Dear Sisters, October 26, 1976, Eichelberger Papers, 1974–1981, Chicago History Museum, Box 2, Folder 37-E.

97. Mary Wiggs, Letter to NABF, December 10, 1076, Eichelberger Papers, 1974–1981, Chicago History Museum, Box 2, Folder 55-W.

98. Senora M. Amos, Letter to "Dear sisters," October 26, 1976, Eichelberger Papers, 1974–1981, Chicago History Museum, Box 2, Folder 33-A.

99. Lynette Cherie Spurlock Morris, Letter to the National Alliance of Black Feminist [*sic*], received November 16, 1976, Eichelberger Papers, 1974–1981, Chicago History Museum, Box 2, Folder 51-S.

100. Glenda Pierson, Letter, November 8, 1976, Eichelberger Papers, 1974–1981, Chicago History Museum, Box 2, Folder 48.

101. Sandra Black, Letter addressed 'To whom it may concern," November 11, 1976, Eichelberger Papers, 1974–1981, Chicago History Museum, Box 2, Folder 34.

102. Audrey J. Hutton, Letter to Brenda Eichelberger, September 14, 1979, in Eichelberger Papers, 1974–1981, Chicago History Museum, Box 3, Folder 33.

103. White, *Too Heavy a Load*, 247.

104. NABF, Letter to Dear Sister, n.d., Eichelberger Papers, 1974–1981, Chicago History Museum, Box 3, Folder Membership Letters.

Chapter 4. Mapping the Black Feminist Movement

1. Brenda Eichelberger, "Voices on Black Feminism," *Quest* (Spring 1977), 28.

2. Benita Roth, *Separate Roads*, 76–129.

3. NABF, Calendar of Events: December 1977, Eichelberger Papers, 1974–1981, Chicago History Museum, Box 4, Folder Calendars of Events, 1.

4. Brenda Eichelberger, Letter to Cardiss Collins, August 12, 1977, Eichelberger Papers, 1974–1981, Chicago History Museum, Box 3, Folder C 3.

5. Brenda Eichelberger, Letter to Angela Davis, August 15, 1977, Eichelberger Papers, 1974–1981, Chicago History Museum, Box 3, Folder C 3.

6. Brenda Eichelberger, Letter to Ntozake Shange, August 12, 1977, Eichelberger Papers, 1974–1981, Chicago History Museum, Box 16, Folder 29.

7. Brenda Eichelberger, Letter to Toni Morrison, September 11, 1977, Eichelberger Papers, 1974–1981, Chicago History Museum, Box 16, Folder 31.

8. Brenda Eichelberger, Letter to Carolyn Rodgers, September 7, 1977, Eichelberger Papers, 1974–1981, Chicago History Museum, Box 3, Folder R 18.

9. Brenda Eichelberger, Letter to Aileen Hernandez, August 15, 1977, Eichelberger Papers, 1974–1981, Chicago History Museum, Box 3, Folder 19.

10. Brenda Eichelberger, letter to Aileen Hernandez, September 26, 1977, Eichelberger Papers, 1974–1981, Chicago History Museum, Box 3, Folder 19.

11. Brenda Eichelberger, letter to M. A. Terry, August 31, 1977, Eichelberger Papers, 1974–1981, Chicago History Museum, Box 3, Folder 19.

12. Open House Chicago, "West Chicago Hotel City Center (Midland Club/Hotel)," accessed August 23, 2024, https://openhousechicago.org/sites/site/w-chicago-hotel-city-center-midland-club-hotel.

13. NABF, "A Meeting of the Minds" conference flyer, NBFO Archives, UIC, Folder 1.

14. The National Alliance of Black Feminists, "Black Women's Conference October 21–23, 1977: Conference Schedule" in Eichelberger Papers, 1974–1981, Chicago History Museum, Box 4, Folder 1977 Conference, 1–4.

15. Basic Rules of Procedure, n.d., Eichelberger Papers, 1974–1981, Chicago History Museum, Box 16, Folder 38 Conference Resolutions.

16. NABF, "A Meeting of the Minds" Conference Flyer.

17. *Chicago Metro News*, "Black Feminists Conf. [hic!] Set for Weekend at Midland Hotel," Saturday, October 22, 1977, Eichelberger NABF Papers, 1974–1997, Harsh Collection, Box 1, Folder 8.

18. *Chicago Metro News*, "Black Feminists Conf."

19. Ray Moseley, "Writers Assail TV, Film Images of Black Women," *Chicago Tribune*, Saturday, October 22, 1977, 10, Eichelberger NABF Papers, 1974–1997, Harsh Collection, Box 1, Folder 8.

20. NABF Lifestyles, Tape Recording, Eichelberger Papers, 1974–1981, Chicago History Museum, Box 14, Folder 1.

21. NABF Lifestyles, Tape Recording, Eichelberger Papers, 1974–1981, Chicago History Museum, Box 14, Folder 1.

22. NABF Lifestyles, Tape Recording, Eichelberger Papers, 1974–1981, Chicago History Museum, Box 14, Folder 1.

23. "Resolutions Adopted during the National Black Woman Conference," NBFO Archives, UIC, Box 1, Folder 1, 7.

24. Willie Mae Reid, "200 Women Attend Black Feminist Conference," in *The Militant*, November 11, 1977, Eichelberger Papers, 1974–1981, Chicago History Museum, Box 16, Folder 41.

25. "Resolutions Adopted," 16.

26. "Resolutions Adopted," 7.

27. Monica Faith Stewart, "Black Women's Conference," in *Women's News . . . For a Change*, October 1977, Eichelberger Papers, 1974–1981, Chicago History Museum, Box 16, Folder 41.

28. National Black Feminist Organization, "A Meeting of the Minds" conference flyer, NBFO Archives, UIC, Box 1, Folder 1.

29. Betty Washington, "'Double Whammy' on Black Women," *Chicago Daily News*, October 19, 1977, Eichelberger NABF Papers, 1974–1997, Harsh Collection, Box 1, Folder 8.

30. Brenda Eichelberger, "Black Women and the Feminist Movement," 7.

31. Doreen J. Mattingly and Jessica L. Nare, "A Rainbow of Women," 97. See also Laura L. Lovett, Rachel Jessica Daniel, Kelly N. Giles (eds.), *It's Our Movement Now: Black Women's Politics and the 1977 National Women's Conference*. 1st ed. (University Press of Florida, 2023).

32. U.S. Department of State, The President's Interagency's Council on Women, "National Plan for Action: Texas 1977."

33. Raffle ticket, Eichelberger Papers, 1974–1981, Chicago History Museum, Box 11, Folder Special Activities.

34. NABF, Board Meeting of July 15, 1978, Eichelberger Papers, 1974–1981, Chicago History Museum, Box 16, Folder 9 Board Meetings.

35. Helen Whigham, phone interview by author, September 21, 2015.

36. Sharron Kornegay, "Group Aims to Link Feminism, Blacks," in *Chicago Sun-Times*, Saturday, Oct. 22, 1977, Eichelberger NABF Papers, 1974–1997, Harsh Collection, Box 1, Folder 8.

37. Lorraine Anderson, "Feminists Are Also Humanists," in *Witness*, (Wilmington, OH), May 23, 1975, Eichelberger NABF Papers, 1974–1997, Harsh Collection, Box 1, Folder 8.

38. Lorraine Branham, "Black Women Say White Women Insensitive to Their Needs; Seek to Form Local Chapter of NABF," *Philadelphia Tribune*, Tuesday, June 15, 1976, Eichelberger NABF Papers, 1974–1997, Harsh Collection, Box 1, Folder 8.

39. NABF, Calendar of Events: June 1976, Eichelberger Papers, 1974–1981, Chicago History Museum, Box 4, Folder Calendars of Events, 1.

40. NABF, Calendar of Events: January 1977, Eichelberger Papers, 1974–1981, Chicago History Museum, Box 4, Folder Calendars of Events, 2.

41. NABF, Calendar of Events: July 1976, Eichelberger Papers, 1974–1981, Chicago History Museum, Box 4, Folder Calendars of Events, 1.

42. NABF, June 1979 Membership Letter, Eichelberger Papers, 1974–1981, Chicago History Museum, Box 4, Folder Membership Letters.

43. NABF, Calendar of Events: November 1978, Eichelberger Papers, 1974–1981, Chicago History Museum, Box 4, Folder Calendars of Events, 1.

44. NABF, July / August 1979 Membership Letter, Eichelberger Papers, 1974–1981, Chicago History Museum, Box 4, Folder Membership Letters.

45. NABF, June 1979 Membership Letter, Eichelberger Papers, 1974–1981, Chicago History Museum, Box 4, Folder Membership Letters.

46. NABF, July / August 1979 Membership Letter, Eichelberger Papers, 1974–1981, Chicago History Museum, Box 4, Folder Membership Letters.

47. Beverley Bryan, Stella Dadzie, and Suzanne Scafe, "Chain Reactions: Black Women Organizing," 21. See also Beverley Bryan, Stella Dadzie, and Suzanne Scafe, *The Heart of the Race*.

48. Bryan, Dadzie, and Scafe, "Chain Reactions," 3–13.

49. Marlene T. Boggle, "Brixton Black Women's Centre," 133.

50. Nydia A. Swaby, "Disparate in Voice, Sympathetic in Direction," 15.

51. Brixton Black Women's Group, "Black Women Organizing," 84.

52. Ibid., 86.

53. Swaby, "Disparate in Voice," 18.

54. Nicole M. Jackson, *The Politics of Care*, 198–99.

55. Organization of Women of African and Asian Descent 8/18/79, Tape Recording, Eichelberger Papers, 1974–1981, Chicago History Museum, Box 14, Folder 3.

56. Oganization of Women of African and Asian Descent 8/18/79, Tape Recording, Eichelberger Papers, 1974–1981, Chicago History Museum, Box 14, Box 3.

57. Bryan, Dadzie, and Scafe, "Chain Reactions," 13.

58. Ibid., 25.

59. Swaby, "Disparate in Voice," 20.

60. NABF, September 1979 Membership Letter, Eichelberger Papers, 1974–1981, Chicago History Museum, Box 4, Folder Membership Letters.

61. Janie Nelson, follow-up conversation, July 1, 2015, Chicago, IL.
62. Barbara Smith, "A Press of Our Own: Kitchen Table," 11–12.
63. Barbara Smith, *Ain't Gonna Let Nobody Turn Me Around*, 92.
64. Kimberly Springer, *Living for the Revolution*, 56–61.
65. Robin D. G. Kelley, *Freedom Dreams*, 138.
66. Patricia Romney, *We Were There*.
67. Linda Burnham, interview by Christina Greene, quoted in Greene, *Free Joan Little*, 174.

Chapter 5. The NABF, Coalition Politics, and Colorblind Feminism in the Late 1970s

Epigraph: Bernice Johnson Reagon, "Coalition Politics: Turning the Century," 356–57.
1. Liza Taylor, *Feminism in Coalition*, 119.
2. Reagon, "Coalition Politics," 346–47.
3. Taylor, *Feminism in Coalition*, 81.
4. See Jaime Harker and Cecilia Konchar Farr (eds.), *This Book Is an Action: Feminist Print Culture and Activist Aesthetics* (Urbana: University of Illinois Press, 2015).
5. Chicago Council on Crimes Against Women, Statement of Purpose, n.d., Eichelberger Papers, 1974–1981, Chicago History Museum, Box 22, Folder CCAW.
6. Chicago Council on Crimes Against Women, "Legislative Suggestions Regarding Sexual Abuse of Students," Eichelberger NABF Papers, 1974–1997, Harsh Collection, Box 2, Folder 10 By-Laws/misc. Chicago Council on Crimes Against Women [n.d.].
7. Chicago Council on Crimes Against Women, "Minutes of June 3, 1978, Board Meeting," Eichelberger NABF Papers, 1974–1997, Harsh Collection, Box 2, Folder 10 By-Laws/misc. Chicago Council on Crimes Against Women [n.d.].
8. NABF, July / August 1979 Membership Letter and September 1979 Membership Letter, Eichelberger Papers, 1974–1981, Chicago History Museum, Box 4, Folder Membership Letters.
9. NABF, Calendar of Events: September 1979, Eichelberger Papers, 1974–1981, Chicago History Museum, Box 4, Folder Calendars of Events.
10. "Take Back the Night" flyer, Eichelberger Papers, 1974–1981, Chicago History Museum, Box 2, Folder 14.
11. Brenda Eichelberger, Letter to Carol Moseley Braun, September 10, 1980, Eichelberger NABF Papers, 1974–1997, Harsh Collection, Box 3, Folder 5 Correspondence (1980).
12. Jennifer Nelson, *Women of Color and the Reproductive Rights Movement*, 57.

13. NABF, September 1979 Membership Letter, Eichelberger Papers, 1974-1981, Chicago History Museum, Box 4, Folder Membership Letters.

14. NABF, "Press Release," Eichelberger Papers, 1974–1981, Chicago History Museum, Box 16, Folder 3.

15. Brenda Eichelberger, Letter to Barbara Omolade, April 30, 1979, Eichelberger Papers, 1974–1981, Chicago History Museum, Box 20, Folder 19.

16. NABF, July / August 1979 Membership Letter, Eichelberger Papers, 1974–1981, Chicago History Museum, Box 4, Folder Membership Letters.

17. See "Guide to the Barbara Omolade Papers," Sarah Lawrence College, accessed August 27, 2024, https://www.sarahlawrence.edu/archives/collections/finding-aids/b/barbara-omolade-papers1.html.

18. Barbara Winkler, "A Comparative History of Four Women's Studies Programs," 235.

19. See Judith Kegan Gardiner, "Rethinking Collectivity," 191–201.

20. From 1971–1972, the WSC taught as many as 1400 students in 60 courses. See Elizabeth Lapovski-Kennedy, "Dreams of Social Justice."

21. Barbara Shircliffe, *The History of a Student-Run Women's Studies Program, 1971–1985*, 201.

22. Ibid., 200.

23. Kum Kum Bhavnani, "Women's Studies and Its Interconnections with 'Race,' Ethnicity, and Sexuality," 31.

24. Clark A. Pomerleau, *Califia Women*.

25. Angela D. LeBlanc-Ernest, "The Most Qualified Person to Handle the Job," 317.

26. Barbara Williams Jackson, *The Interrelatedness of Black Self-Concept*.

27. John Russell Rickford, *We Are an African People*; Ericka Huggins and Angela D LeBlanc-Ernest, "Revolutionary Women, Revolutionary Education," 161–84.

28. NABF Press Release, 13 February 1979, Eichelberger Papers, 1974–1981, Chicago History Museum, Box 11, Folder Press Releases.

29. NABF, Late Spring 1979 Registration Form, Eichelberger Papers, 1974–1981, Chicago History Museum, Box 11, Folder AT Registration Forms Late Spring 1979.

30. NABF, "Are You Passive, Aggressive, Or Assertive? Take Our Course to Find Out!," Eichelberger Papers, 1974–1981, Chicago History Museum, Box 11, Folder 1980 AT Flyer Summer 1979.

31. Ibid.

32. "The Black Woman," in NABF Alternative School Program, 9, NBFO Archives, UIC, Box 1, Folder 1.

33. "Female Sexuality," in NABF Alternative School Program, NBFO Archives, UIC, National Alliance of Black Feminists Collection, 6. Also Springer, Living for the Revolution 104.

34. "Human Sexuality," in NABF Alternative School Program, 8.

35. Patricia Jacubowski-Spector, "Facilitating the Growth of Women through Assertiveness Training."

36. Elan Cummings with Blanche Adams et al., *Woman, Assert Yourself*, 27.
37. Robert Alberti and Michael Emmons, *Your Perfect Right*.
38. *Time*, May 19, 1975.
39. Yvonne Hardaway and Karen LaPointe, *Facilitating Assertive Training Groups*.
40. Carolyn Zerbe Enns, "Self-Esteem Groups."
41. Ileana Nachescu, "The Kind of World We Wanted to Be In," 192–224.
42. NABF Press Release, n.d., Eichelberger Papers, 1974–1981, Chicago History Museum, Box 11, Folder Press Releases Re Classes.
43. NABF, Calendar of Events: February 1979, Eichelberger Papers, 1974–1981, Chicago History Museum, Box 4, Folder Calendars of Events.
44. NABF, Calendar of Events: June 1979, Eichelberger Papers, 1974–1981, Chicago History Museum, Box 4, Folder Calendars of Events.
45. "Philosophy of NABF," in NABF Alternative School Program, 20.
46. Kimberly Springer makes a similar argument. See Kimberly Springer, "Black Feminists Respond to Black Power Masculinism."
47. "Characterological Lifechart of People We All Know," Eichelberger Papers, 1974–1981, Chicago History Museum, Box 4, Folder Assertion Training Handouts.
48. NABF Alternative School Program, Box 1, Folder 1.
49. Stanlee Phelps and Nancy Austin, *The Assertive Woman*, 92.
50. Springer, "Black Feminists Respond to Black Power," 104.
51. NABF, Calendar of Events: May 1976, Eichelberger Papers, 1974–1981, Chicago History Museum, Box 4, Folder Calendars of Events, 2.
52. Cummings, Adams, et al., *Woman, Assert Yourself*; Susan M. Osborne and Gloria G. Harris, *Assertive Training for Women*; Phelps and Austin, *The Assertive Woman*; Lynn Z. Bloom, Karen Coburn, and Joan Perlman, *The New Assertive Woman*; and Donald Cheek, *Assertive Black . . . Puzzled White*.
53. Cheek, *Assertive Black*, 77.
54. Patricia Jacubowski-Spector, "Facilitating the Growth of Women through Assertiveness Training," 75–86.
55. NABF, Calendar of Events: May 1976, Eichelberger Papers, 1974–1981, Chicago History Museum, Box 4, Folder Calendars of Events, 2.
56. Cheek, *Assertive Black*, 91.
57. Janie Nelson, "Attitude-Behavior Consistency Among Black Feminist and Traditional Black Women," 1.
58. The dissertation distinguished between "attitude," the set of beliefs held by a certain woman, and "behavior," namely, the way she put these beliefs into practice. Thus, the research, in addition to measuring attitude through self-reported questionnaires, also attempted to quantify the behavior of the women involved, through participant observation of groups of ten women from each organization.
59. Nelson, "Attitude-Behavior Consistency," 54.
60. Ibid., 53.
61. Ibid., 56.

62. NABF, Assertion Session Evaluation, Eichelberger Papers, 1974–1981, Chicago History Museum, Box 25, Folder Assertion Training for Women.

63. The germinal collection edited by Toni Cade Bambara, *The Black Woman: An Anthology*, did not have a successor until the 1980s. In the meantime, white feminists published a plethora of collections, and some of the ones listed below include an insignificant number of works by women of color. See Robin Morgan (ed.), *Sisterhood Is Powerful*; Mary Lou Thomson (ed.), *Voices of the New Feminism*; Joanne Cook, Charlotte Bunch-Weeks, and Robin Morgan (eds.), *The New Women*; Vivian Gornick and Barbara K. Moran (eds.), *Woman in Sexist Society*; and Anne Koedt, Ellen Levine, and Anita Rapone (eds.), *Radical Feminism* (New York: Quadrangle/The New York Times Book Company, 1973). Single-authored books published only in the first few years of the movement might include Shulamith Firestone, *The Dialectic of Sex*; Kate Millett, *Sexual Politics*; Jill Johnston, *Lesbian Nation*; Jo Freeman, *The Politics of Women's Liberation*; Susan Brownmiller, *Against Our Will*; and many, many others. According to Agatha Beins, the number of feminist periodicals increased from 25 in 1969 to 85 the following year and more than 550 by 1974. See Agatha Beins, *Liberation in Print*. It is unclear, however, how many of these periodicals systematically published works by women of color.

64. Ileana Nachescu, "Censoring Anglogynophobia."

65. Brenda Eichelberger, "Anglogynophobia!," 5.

66. Eichelberger, "Anglogynophobia!," 4.

67. Ibid.

68. Gayle Porter, phone interview by author, September 5, 2013.

69. Audre Lorde, "The Great American Disease," 18–19.

70. Eichelberger, "Anglogynophobia!"

71. Ibid., 6.

72. Brenda Eichelberger, "Black Feminist Forum: Anglogynophobia!," Eichelberger NABF Papers, 1974–1997, Harsh Collection, Box 5, Folder 10.

73. Toni Morrison, "What the Black Woman Thinks about Women's Lib," 15.

74. Ibid., 16.

75. Ibid., 65.

76. Margaret Simmons, "Racism and Feminism," 398.

77. Brenda Eichelberger, follow-up phone interview with the author, March 19, 2015.

78. Brenda Eichelberger, Letter to Elaine Goldberg, June 26, 1978, Eichelberger NABF Papers, 1974–1997, Harsh Collection, Box 3, Folder 3.

79. Elaine Goldberg, Letter to Brenda Eichelberger, August 24, 1978, Eichelberger NABF Papers, 1974–1997, Harsh Collection, Box 3, Folder 3.

80. Christina Greene, *Free Joan Little*, 194.

Chapter 6. Between Public Silence and Private Support

Epigraph: Barbara Smith, "Building Black Women's Studies," in *Ain't Gonna Let Nobody Turn Me Around*, 124–25.

1. Betty Rowland, Letter, 31 May 1975, Eichelberger Papers, 1974–1981, Chicago History Museum, Box 2, Folder 17.
2. Marie Cain (gay name Ronnie), Letter, n.d. (from Olala, Florida), Eichelberger Papers, 1974–1981, Chicago History Museum, Box 2, Folder 3.
3. Kimberly Springer, *Living for the Revolution*, 135.
4. Catherine Squires, "Rethinking the Black Public Sphere," 458.
5. Evelyn Brooks Higginbotham, *Righteous Discontent*, 196.
6. Lorraine Branham, "Black Women Say White Women Insensitive to Their Needs; Seek to Form Local Chapter of NABF."
7. Patricia Hill Collins, *Black Sexual Politics*, 110.
8. Alexis DeVeaux, *Warrior Poet*, 56.
9. E. James West, "I See Enough Queers Walking the Streets in This City," 286.
10. Thaddeus Russell, "The Color of Discipline," 117. See also Lisa B. Thomson, *Beyond the Black Lady*.
11. Trimiko Melancon, *Unbought and Unbossed*, 82–83.
12. Daniel Geary, *Beyond Civil Rights*, 150–51.
13. West, "I See Enough Queers," 292.
14. Quoted in Melancon, *Unbought and Unbossed*, 38.
15. Melancon, *Unbought and Unbossed*, 42.
16. Elnora Washington, interview by the author, Gary, Indiana, June 29, 2015.
17. Helen Whigham, phone interview by author, September 21, 2015.
18. Thomson, *Beyond the Black Lady*.
19. Timothy Stewart-Winter, *Queer Clout*, 124.
20. Janie Nelson, follow-up phone interview by author, June 11, 2019.
21. David Allyn, *Make Love Not War*.
22. Jane Gerhard, *Desiring Revolution*, 87.
23. Ibid., 99.
24. Ruth Rosen, *The World Split Open*, 164.
25. Elizabeth Lapovski-Kennedy and Madeline Davis, *Boots of Leather, Slippers of Gold*.
26. Rosen, *The World Split Open*, 172.
27. Ibid., 166.
28. Ibid., 174.
29. Stephanie Gilmore, *Groundswell*, 66.
30. Ibid., 89.
31. Stewart-Winter, *Queer Clout*, 136.
32. Ibid., 124–31.

33. Ibid., 142.

34. DeVeaux, *Warrior Poet*, 56–57.

35. Brenda Eichelberger, Letter to Michael Weissman, Sexuality Committee Chairman, November 11, 1976, Eichelberger NABF Papers, 1974–1997, Harsh Collection, Box 3, Folder 2.

36. "Human Sexuality," in NABF Alternative School Program, NBFO Archives, UIC, 8.

37. "Female Sexuality," in NABF Alternative School Program, NBFO Archives, UIC, Box 1, Folder 1, 6. Also see Springer, *Living for the Revolution*, 104.

38. "Resolutions Adopted during the National Black Woman Conference," p. 7, NBFO Archives, UIC, Box 1, Folder 1.

39. Cathy Cohen, *The Boundaries of Blackness*, 73–75.

40. Springer, *Living for the Revolution*, 130–31.

41. Barbara Smith, "A Press of Our Own," 11–12.

42. Other members of Jemima, according to Donna Allegra's recollections, were Linda Brown, Robin Christian, Yvonne Flowers (aka Maua), Sapphire, Georgia Brooks, Irare Sabasu, Candace Boyce, and Chirlayne McCray. Donna Allegra, "Remarks for the Harlem Book Fair Gay and Lesbian Panel," July 21, 2001, p. 1–2. In Donna Allegra Papers, Sc MG 792, Box 1, Folder 1.

43. Patricia Romney, *We Were There*, 76. See also Tiana U. Wilson, "The Making of Triple Jeopardy," in *WSQ: Women's Studies Quarterly* 51:1&2 (Spring / Summer 2023), 205–6.

44. Springer, *Living for the Revolution*, 131.

45. Ibid., 130.

46. "Black Lesbianism: 3/19/78," Eichelberger Papers, 1974–1981, Chicago History Museum, Harsh Collection, Cassette, Box 14.

47. Homosexuality was listed as a mental disorder in the Diagnostics and Statistics Manual II (DSMII) in 1968. In 1973, a majority of the members of the American Psychiatric Association voted to remove homosexuality from the DSM. See Neel Burton, "When Homosexuality Stopped Being a Mental Disorder," *Psychology Today*, June 24, 2024, https://www.psychologytoday.com/us/blog/hide-and-seek/201509/when-homosexuality-stopped-being-amental-disorder.

48. "Black Lesbians," Eichelberger Papers, 1974–1981, Chicago History Museum, Box 14. All excerpts transcribed by author.

49. Helen Whigham, phone interview by author, September 21, 2015.

50. Gayle Porter, phone interview by author, September 5, 2013.

51. Beryl Fitzpatrick, phone interview by author, February 28, 2016.

52. Gayle Porter, phone interview by author, September 5, 2013.

53. Janie Nelson, follow-up phone interview by author, June 11, 2019.

54. Helen Whigham, phone interview by author, September 21, 2015.

55. The Black Women's Expo is a Chicago-based annual exposition for Black women. Advertised as celebrating "strength, success, and sisterhood," the Black Women's Expo combines networking, advertising for small businesses,

seminars, and cultural events. This yearly event, now in its twenty-ninth iteration, also provided booths for Black women-owned businesses to advertise and sell their products. See BWeNEXT: The Black Women's Expo, https://bwenext.com/, accessed August 29, 2024.

56. Helen Whigham, follow-up phone conversation by author, January 7, 2024.

57. Smith, *Ain't Gonna Let Nobody Turn Me Around*, 176.

Chapter 7. Beyond the Equal Rights Amendments

Epigraph: National Alliance of Black Feminists (NABF), "The Missing Link to Passage of the Equal Rights Amendment: Position Paper of the National Alliance of Black Feminists," by Brenda Daniels-Eichelberger, Executive Director, November 25, 1980; Eichelberger Papers, 1974–1981, Chicago History Museum, Box 1, Folder Writings, 11.

1. Shirley Eversley and Michelle HabellPallan, "Introduction: The 1970s," *WSQ* 43:3&4 (Fall/Winter 2015): 19.

2. Donald T. Critchlow, *Phyllis Schlafly and Grassroots Conservatism: A Woman's Crusade* (Princeton: Princeton University Press, 2005), 216.

3. Maryann Barasko, *Governing NOW: Grassroots Activism in the National Organization for Women* (Ithaca, NY: Cornell University Press, 2004), 4.

4. Brenda Eichelberger, follow-up phone conversation with author, March 19, 2015.

5. Liza Taylor, *Feminism in Coalition*, 71.

6. Phyllis Schlafly, "What's Wrong with 'Equal Rights' for Women?"

7. Critchlow, *Phyllis Schlafly and Grassroots Conservatism*, 218.

8. Ibid., 220.

9. Jane J. Mansbridge, *Why We Lost the ERA*, 174.

10. Critchlow, *Phyllis Schlafly and Grassroots Conservatism*, 221–22.

11. NABF, Calendar of Events: May 1976, Eichelberger Papers, 1974–1981, Chicago History Museum, Box 4, Folder Calendars of Events.

12. Sharon Scoby, Letter to Dear Friend, April 20, 1977, Eichelberger Papers, 1974–1981, Chicago History Museum, Box 3, Folder 19.

13. Brenda Eichelberger, "Black Women and the Feminist Movement," 5.

14. Critchlow, *Phyllis Schlafly and Grassroots Conservatism*, 266.

15. William H. Chafe, *The Unfinished Journey*, 455.

16. Ibid., 457.

17. NABF, "The Missing Link to Passage of the Equal Rights Amendment: Position Paper of the National Alliance of Black Feminists," by Brenda Daniels-Eichelberger, Executive Director, November 25, 1980; Eichelberger Papers, 1974–1981, Chicago History Museum, Box 1, Folder Writings, 15.

18. NABF, "The Missing Link," 5.

19. Ibid., 7.

20. Ibid., 8.

21. Ibid., 11.

22. NABF, "The Missing Link," 14.
23. Ibid., 12.
24. Ibid., 13.
25. Becky Thompson, "Multiracial Feminism," 42.
26. Benita Roth, *Separate Roads to Feminism*, 120.
27. Kimberly Springer, *Living for the Revolution*, 142.
28. NABF Yearly Membership Fees, Eichelberger Papers, 1974–1981, Chicago History Museum, Box 1, File 1–12.
29. NABF, March 1979 Membership Letter, Eichelberger Papers, 1974–1981, Chicago History Museum, Box 4, Folder Membership Letters.
30. NABF, June 1979 Membership Letter, Eichelberger Papers, 1974–1981, Chicago History Museum, Box 4, Folder Membership Letters.
31. NABF, July / August 1979 Membership Letter, Eichelberger Papers, 1974–1981, Chicago History Museum, Box 4, Folder Membership Letters.
32. NABF, Letter to Dear Member, October 1979, Eichelberger Papers, 1974–1981, Chicago History Museum, Box 4, Folder Membership Letters.
33. Brenda Eichelberger, Letter to Beverley Smith, May 23, 1980, Eichelberger Papers, 1974–1981, Chicago History Museum, Box 3, Folder 70.
34. NABF Bank Statements, Eichelberger Papers, 1974–1981, Chicago History Museum, Box 18, Folder Expense Records.
35. Eichelberger, follow-up phone conversation, March 19, 2015.
36. NABF, "Child Care Conference Proposal," n.d., Eichelberger NABF Papers, 1974–1997, Harsh Collection, Box 2, Folder 13 Grant Proposals, 5.
37. LaSalle National Bank Statement, 11/30/1981, Eichelberger Papers, 1974–1981, Chicago History Museum, Box 18, Folder Expense Records.
38. "Application for a Chairman's Grant," n.d., Eichelberger NABF Papers, 1974–1997, Harsh Collection, Box 2, Folder 13 Grant Proposals.
39. Brenda Eichelberger, follow-up phone conversation, March 19, 2015.
40. Internal Revenue Service, Department of the Treasury, Letter to Dear Applicant, November 19, 1980, Eichelberger NABF Papers, 1974–1997, Harsh Collection, Box 1, Folder 9 Tax/Financial Records 1980–83.
41. W. O. M. A. N., Annual Report 1981, Eichelberger NABF Papers, 1974–1997, Harsh Collection, Box 1, Folder 10 Annual Reports [1981–1983].
42. W. O. M. A. N., Grant Application, Chicago Council on Fine Arts, Eichelberger NABF Papers, 1974–1997, Harsh Collection, Box 2, Folder 13 Grant Proposals.
43. Letter from Carol Fryer to Brenda Eichelberger, August 12, 1981; Margaret Ticker, Letter addressed "To Whom It May Concern," August 11, 1981; Letter to Cynthia Miles from Linda M. Bright, Director of the Children's Theater, August 13, 1981; South Side Community Arts Center, Letter to Cynthia Miles, August 12, 1981; Eichelberger Papers, 1974–1981, Chicago History Museum, Box 11, Folder Illinois Arts Council Application.
44. NABF, "Child Care Conference Proposal," n.d., Eichelberger NABF Papers, 1974–1997, Harsh Collection, Box 2, Folder 13 Grant Proposals, 5.

45. W. O. M. A. N., Annual Report 1982, Eichelberger NABF Papers, 1974–1997, Harsh Collection, Box 1, Folder 10 Annual Reports [1981–1983].

46. Office of the Secretary of State, Letter to W. O. M. A. N., September 1, 1983, Eichelberger NABF Papers, 1974–1997, Harsh Collection, Box 1, Folder 10 Annual Reports [1981–1983].

47. State of Illinois, Office of the Secretary of State, "Certificate of Dissolution of Domestic Corporation," August 2, 1983, Eichelberger NABF Papers, 1974–1997, Harsh Collection, Box 1, Folder 10 Annual Reports [1981–1983].

48. Edward Zink, Letter to Brenda Eichelberger, Eichelberger NABF Papers, 1974–1997, Harsh Collection, Folder Correspondence 1983, 3/7.

49. C. A. Lofton, interview by author, Chicago, Illinois, January 14, 2016.

50. Beryl Fitzpatrick, phone interview by author, February 28, 2016.

51. National Alliance against Racist and Political Repression, "About Us," accessed September 1, 2024, https://naarpr.org/about.

52. Roth, *Separate Roads to Feminism*, 228.

53. Eichelberger herself did not mention this feminist work in her interviews with me. They are pieced together from the archives and from interviews. C. A. Lofton, follow-up interview by author, June 2019.

54. Janie Nelson, "Attitude-Behavior Consistency among Black Feminist and Traditional Black Women," 1.

55. Janie Nelson, oral history interview with the author, Chicago, Illinois, April 12, 2013.

56. "Sharon Wells."

57. History Makers, "The Honorable Monica Stewart."

58. Beti Ellerson, *Sisters of the Screen*, xviii.

59. Beti Ellerson, "African Women in Cinema Blog."

60. Gayle Porter and Marilyn K. Gaston, *Prime Time*, 3.

61. Ibid., 6.

62. Ibid., 7.

63. Gayle Porter, phone interview by author, September 5, 2013.

64. More on Dr. Porter's activity and trailblazing career is documented online on her website, accessed September 1, 2024, https://www.gastonandporter.org/dr-gayle-porter.

65. Helen Whigham, phone interview by author, September 21, 2015.

66. Beryl Fitzpatrick, oral history interview by author, Gary, Indiana, June 21, 2019.

Conclusion

1. Brenda Eichelberger, "Institute on Women's History July 12–27, 1979 Application," April 24, 1979, 2, Barbara Omolade Collection, Folder Summer Institute in Women's History for Leaders of Women's Organizations Applications-Completed, Sarah Lawrence College Archive, Bronxville, NY.

2. Rosemary Tong, *Feminist Thought*.

Bibliography

Alberti, Robert, and Michael Emmons. *Your Perfect Right*. New York: Impact, 1974.

Alexander-Floyd, Nikol. *Re-Imagining Black Women: A Critique of Post-Feminist and Post-Racial Melodrama in Culture and Politics*. New York: New York University Press, 2021.

Allen, Pamela. *Free Space: A Perspective on the Small Group in Women's Liberation*. 2nd edition, revised. New York: Times Change Press, 1970.

Allyn, David. *Make Love Not War: The Sexual Revolution: An Unfettered History*. New York: Routledge, 2001.

Amott, Teresa, and Julie Matthaei. *Race, Gender and Work: A Multicultural Anthology*. Boston: South End Press, 1996.

Austin, Algernon. *Achieving Blackness: Race, Black Nationalism, and Afrocentrism in the Twentieth Century*. New York: New York University Press, 2006.

Bailey, Marlon M., and Rashad Shabazz. "Editorial: Gender and Sexual Geographies of Blackness: Anti-Black Heterotopias (part 1)." *Gender, Place and Culture: A Journal of Feminist Geography* 21, no. 3 (2014): 316–21. https://doi.org/10.1080/0966369X.2013.781305.

Bambara, Toni Cade. *The Black Woman: An Anthology*. New York: Mentor, 1970.

Barasko, Maryann. *Governing NOW: Grassroots Activism in the National Organization for Women*. Ithaca, NY: Cornell University Press, 2004.

Bay, Mia, et al., eds. *Toward an Intellectual History of Black Women*. Chapel Hill: University of North Carolina Press, 2015.

Beins, Agatha. *Liberation in Print: Feminist Periodicals and Social Movement Identity*. Athens: University of Georgia Press, 2017.

Bhavnani, Kum Kum. "Women's Studies and Its Interconnections with 'Race,' Ethnicity, and Sexuality." In *Introducing Women's Studies*, edited by V. Robinson and D. Richardson, 27–53. Washington Square: New York University Press, 1997.

Biles, Roger. "Race and Housing in Chicago." *Journal of the Illinois State Historical Society (1998–)* 94, no. 1 (2001): 31–38.

Bloom, Lynn Z., Karen Coburn, and Joan Perlman. *The New Assertive Woman.* New York: Dell Publishing, 1975.

Boggle, Marlene T. "Brixton Black Women's Centre: Organizing on Child Sexual Abuse." *Feminist Review* 28 (1988): 132–35.

Borstelman, Thomas. *The 1970s: A New Global History from Civil Rights to Economic Inequality.* Princeton, NJ: Princeton University Press, 2012.

Bowles, Gloria. "Review of Textbooks in Women's Studies." *Women's Studies International Forum* 15, no. 1 (1982): 109–12.

Branch, Enobong. *Opportunity Denied: Limiting Black Women to Devalued Work.* 1st edition. Piscataway, NJ: Rutgers University Press, 2011.

Branham, Lorraine. "Black Women Say White Women Insensitive to Their Needs; Seek to Form Local Chapter of NABF." *Philadelphia Tribune*, June 15, 1976.

Breines, Winifred. *The Trouble Between Us: An Uneasy History of White and Black Women in the Feminist Movement.* New York: Oxford University Press, 2006.

Brixton Black Women's Group. "Black Women Organizing." *Feminist Review* 17 (Autumn 1984): 84–89.

Broussard, Albert S. "Race and Oral History." In *The Oxford Handbook of Oral History*, edited by Donald A. Ritchie, 186–201. Oxford: Oxford University Press, 2012.

Brownmiller, Susan. *Against Our Will: Men, Women, and Rape.* New York: Bantam Books, 1975.

———. *In Our Time: Memoir of a Revolution.* New York: Dial Press, 1999.

Bryan, Beverley, Stella Dadzie, and Suzanne Scafe. "Chain Reactions: Black Women Organizing." *Race & Class* XXVII, no. 1 (1985): 1–28.

———. *The Heart of the Race: Black Women's Lives in Britain.* London: Virago, 1985.

Carden, Maren Lockwood. *The New Feminist Movement.* New York: Russell Sage Foundation, 1974.

Carmichael, Stokely, and Charles V. Hamilton. *Black Power: The Politics of Liberation in America.* New York: Random House, 1967.

Carol, Estelle. "The Chicago Women's Graphics Collective: A Memoir." *Feminist Studies* 44, no. 1 (2018): 104–24.

Césaire, Aimé. *Discourse on Colonialism.* Translated by Joan Pinkham. New York: Monthly Review Press, 1972.

Chafe, William H. *The Unfinished Journey: America since World War II.* New York: Oxford University Press, 1986.

Chan-Malik, Sylvia. *Being Muslim: A Cultural History of Women of Color in American Islam.* New York: New York University Press, 2018.

Cheek, Donald. *Assertive Black . . . Puzzled White: A Black Perspective on Assertive Behavior.* San Luis Obispo, CA: Impact Publishers, 1976.

Chicago Historical Society. "The Loop." Encyclopedia of Chicago. Accessed August 7, 2024. http://www.encyclopedia.chicagohistory.org/pages/764.html.

Chicago Urban League (publisher). *Where Blacks Live: Race and Residence in Chicago in the 1970s* by Roger Fox and Deborah Haines. Chicago: Chicago Urban League and the Illinois Department of Research, 1978.

Chicago Women's Liberation Union Herstory Project. "Feminism Curriculum and Archive." https://www.cwluherstory.org/.

Cleaver, Kathleen, and George Katsiaficas, eds. *Liberation, Imagination, and the Black Panther Party: A New Look at the Panthers and Their Legacy*. New York: Routledge, 2001.

Cohen, Cathy J. *The Boundaries of Blackness: AIDS and the Breakdown of Black Politics*. Chicago: University of Chicago Press, 1999.

Cohen, Lizabeth. *A Consumers' Republic: The Politics of Mass Consumption in Postwar America*. New York: Vintage Books, 2004.

Collins, Patricia Hill. *Black Feminist Thought: Knowledge, Consciousness, and the Politics of Empowerment*. New York: Routledge, 2015.

———. *Black Sexual Politics: African Americans, Gender, and the New Racism*. New York: Routledge, 2004.

Conzen, Kathleen, et al. "The Invention of Ethnicity: A Perspective from the U.S.A." *Journal of American Ethnic History* 12, no. 1 (1992): 3–41.

Cook, Joanne, Charlotte Bunch-Weeks, and Robin Morgan, eds. *The New Women*. Greenwich, CT: Fawcett Premier, 1970.

Cook, Robert. *Sweet Land of Liberty? The African American Struggle for Civil Rights in the Twentieth Century*. New York: Longman, 1998.

Cooper, Brittney C. *Beyond Respectability: The Intellectual Thought of Race Women*. Urbana: University of Illinois Press, 2017.

Crenshaw, Kimberle. "Demarginalizing the Intersection of Race and Sex: A Black Feminist Critique of Antidiscrimination Doctrine, Feminist Theory and Antiracist Politics." *University of Chicago Legal Forum* 1989, no. 1: 139–67.

Cross, Tia, Freada Klein, Barbara Smith, and Beverly Smith. "Face-to-Face, Day-to-Day: Racism CR." In *But Some of Us Are Brave: Black Women's Studies*, edited by Gloria T. Hull et al., 52–56. Old Westbury, NY: The Feminist Press, 1982.

Cummings, Elan, with Blanche Adams et al. *Woman, Assert Yourself: An Instructive Handbook about Assertiveness Training for Women*. Produced by Seattle–King County NOW. New York: Harper & Row, 1974.

Dalwin, Bavarian. *Chicago's New Negroes: Modernity, the Great Migration, and Black Urban Life*. Durham: University of North Carolina Press, 2009.

Davidson, James West, and Mark Little. *After the Fact: The Art of Historical Detection*. New York: Knopf, 1981.

Davis, Flora. *Moving the Mountain: The Women's Movement in America since 1960*. New York: Simon & Schuster, 1991.

Dawson, Michael C. "A Black Counterpublic? Economic Earthquakes, Racial Agenda(s), and Black Politics." In *The Black Public Sphere: A Public Culture Book*, edited by The Black Public Sphere Collective, 195–223. Chicago: University of Chicago Press, 1995.

Dennie, Nneka D. "The State and Future of Black Women's Studies: The Black Women's Studies Association and the National Women's Studies Association in Conversation." *Feminist Studies* 47, no. 1 (2021): 230–37.

DeVeaux, Alexis. *Warrior Poet: A Biography of Audre Lorde*. New York: Norton, 2004.

Echols, Alice. *Daring to Be Bad: Radical Feminism in America 1967–1975*. Minneapolis: University of Minnesota Press, 1989.

Edelin, Kenneth C. *Broken Justice: A True Story of Race, Sex, and Revenge in a Boston Courtroom*. Sarasota, FL: PondView Press, 2007.

Eichelberger, Brenda. "Anglogynophobia!" *Women's News . . . for a Change* 1, no. 7 (Nov. 1977).

——. "Anglogynophobia!" *Women's News . . . for a Change* 1, no. 10 (Feb. 1978).

——. "Black Feminism: A New Directive: Consciousness Raising Guidelines for Black Men and Women." Paper presented at the Association of Black Psychologists Seventh Annual Convention, August 26–28, 1974, Nashville, Tennessee. NBFO Papers, UIC, Box 1, Folder 1.

——. (Brenda Daniels-Eichelberger). "Black Women and the Feminist Movement." In *Women Organizing: A Socialist Feminist Bulletin*, no. 3 (1979).

——. "New Myths for Old—Black Macho and the Myth of the Superwoman." In *Moving On: Monthly Magazine of the New American Movement* 3, no. 6. (Aug.–Sept. 1979).

——. "Voices on Black Feminism." *Quest* 3, no. 4 (Spring 1977): 16–28.

——. "Voices on Black Feminism." In *The Women Say, the Men Say: Women's Liberation and Men's Consciousness*, edited by Evelyn Shapiro and Barry Shapiro, 225–31. New York: Dell Publishing, 1979.

Eisenstein, Zillah, ed. *Capitalist Patriarchy and the Case for Socialist Feminism*. New York: Monthly Review Press, 1979.

Ellerson, Beti. "African Women in Cinema Blog." African Women in Cinema Blog. Accessed August 7, 2024. http://africanwomenincinema.blogspot.com/.

——. *Sisters of the Screen: Women of Africa on Film, Video, and Television*. Trenton, NJ: Africa World Press, Inc., 2002.

Enke, Anne. *Finding the Movement: Sexuality, Contested Space, and Feminist Activism*. Durham, NC: Duke University Press, 2008.

Enke, Finn. "Collective Memory and the Transfeminist 1970s: Toward a Less Plausible History." *TSQ: Transgender Studies Quarterly* 5, no. 1 (Feb 2018): 9–29.

Enns, Carolyn Zerbe. "Self-Esteem Groups: A Synthesis of Consciousness-Raising and Assertiveness Training." *Journal of Counseling and Development* 71 (Sept.–Oct. 1992): 7–13.

Escoffier, Jeffrey. "Fabulous Politics: Gay, Lesbian, and Queer Movements, 1969–1999." In *The World That the Sixties Made: Politics and Culture in Recent America*, edited by Van Gosse and Richard Moser, 191–218. Philadelphia: Temple University Press, 2003.

Evans, Sarah. *Tidal Wave: How Women Changed America at Century's End.* New York: The Free Press, 2003.

Eversley, Shirley, and Michelle Habell-Pallan. "Introduction: The 1970s." *WSQ* 43, no. 3–4 (Fall/Winter 2015).

Ezekiel, Judith. *Feminism in the Heartland.* Columbus: Ohio State University Press, 2002.

Fabre, Michel, Randall Cherry, and Jonathan P. Eburne. "René, Louis and Léopold: Senghorian Négritude as a Black Humanism." *MFS Modern Fiction Studies* 51, no. 4 (Winter 2005).

Farmer, Ashley D. *Remaking Black Power: How Black Women Transformed an Era.* Chapel Hill: University of North Carolina Press, 2017.

Firestone, Shulamith. *The Dialectic of Sex: The Case for Feminist Revolution.* New York: Bantam Books, 1970.

Flood, Dawn Rae. *Rape in Chicago: Race, Myth, and the Courts.* Urbana: University of Illinois Press, 2018.

Floyd-Thomas, Juan M. *The Origins of Black Humanism in America: Reverend Ethelred Brown and the Unitarian Church.* New York: Palgrave Macmillan, 2008.

Fraser, Nancy. "Feminism, Capitalism, and the Cunning of History," in *Fortunes of Feminism: From State-Managed Capitalism to Neoliberal Crisis.* 2nd edition. 283–308. London: Verso, 2020.

——. "Rethinking the Public Sphere: A Contribution to the Critique of Actually Existing Democracy." *Social Text* 25–26 (1990): 56–80.

Freeman, Jo. *The Politics of Women's Liberation.* New York: Longman, 1975.

Friedan, Betty. *The Feminine Mystique.* New York: Dell Publishing, 1963.

Fromm, Erich. "Introduction." In *Socialist Humanism: An International Symposium*, edited by Erich Fromm, vii–xiii. New York: Anchor Books, 1966.

Gardiner, Judith Kegan. "Rethinking Collectivity: Chicago Feminism, Athenian Democracy, and the Consumer University." In *Women's Studies on Its Own: A Next Wave Reader in Institutional Change*, edited by Robyn Wiegman, 191–201. Durham, NC: Duke University Press, 2002.

Garvey, Marcus. "Declaration of the Rights of Negro People." Speech delivered at the United Negro Improvement Association's (UNIA) International Convention of the Negro Peoples of the World. New York, August 1920.

Geary, Daniel. *Beyond Civil Rights: The Moynihan Report and Its Legacy.* 1st edition. Philadelphia: University of Pennsylvania Press, 2015.

Gerhard, Jane. *Desiring Revolution: Second-Wave Feminism and the Rewriting of the American Sexual Thought, 1920 to 1982.* New York: Columbia University Press, 2001.

Gilley, Jennifer. "Feminist Publishing / Publishing Feminism: Experimentation in Second Wave Book Publishing." In *This Book Is an Action: Feminist Print Culture and Activist Aesthetics*, edited by Jaime Harker and Cecilia Konchar Farr, 23–45. Urbana: University of Illinois Press, 2015.

Gilmore, Stephanie. *Feminist Coalitions: Historical Perspectives on Second-Wave Feminism in the United States*. Urbana: University of Illinois Press, 2008.

———. *Groundswell: Grassroots Feminist Activism in Postwar America*. New York: Routledge, 2013.

Glissant, Edouard. "For Opacity." In *Poetics of Relation*. Translated by Betsy Wing. Ann Arbor: University of Michigan Press, 1997.

Gomer, Justin. *White Balance: How Hollywood Shaped Colorblind Ideology and Undermined Civil Rights*. Chapel Hill: University of North Carolina Press, 2020.

Gore, Dayo F. *Radicalism at the Crossroads: African American Women Activists in the Cold War*. New York: New York University Press, 2011.

Gornick, Vivian. "Consciousness." In *Radical Feminism: A Documentary Reader*, edited by Barbara Crow, 287–300. New York: New York University Press, 2000.

Gornick, Vivian, and Barbara K. Moran, eds. *Woman in Sexist Society: Studies in Power and Powerlessness*. New York: Basic Books, 1971.

Greene, Christina. *Free Joan Little: The Politics of Race, Sexual Violence, and Imprisonment*. Chapel Hill: University of North Carolina Press, 2022.

———. *Our Separate Ways: Women and the Black Freedom Movement in Durham, North Carolina*. Chapel Hill: University of North Carolina Press, 2005.

Grogan, Jessica. *Encountering America: Humanistic Psychology, Sixties Culture, and the Shaping of the Modern Self*. New York: Harper Perennial, 2013.

Guilloud, Stephanie, and William Cordery. "Fundraising Is Not a Dirty Word: Community Based Economic Struggles for the Long Haul." In *Colonize This! Young Women of Color on Today's Feminism*, edited by Daisy Hernandez and Bushra Rehman, 107–12. New York: Seal Press, 2002.

Haraway, Donna. "Situated Knowledges: The Science Question in Feminism and the Privilege of Partial Perspective." *Feminist Studies* 14, no. 3 (1988): 575–99. https://doi.org/10.2307/3178066.

Hardaway, Yvonne, and Karen LaPointe. *Facilitating Assertive Training Groups: A Manual*. Carbondale: Counseling Center at Southern Illinois University, 1974.

Harris, Miriam Lynnell. "From Kennedy to Combahee." PhD dissertation. Graduate School of the University of Minnesota, May 1997.

Herman, Ellen. *The Romance of American Psychology: Political Culture in the Age of Experts*. Berkeley: University of California Press, 1995.

Hesford, Victoria. *Feeling Women's Liberation*. Durham, NC: Duke University Press, 2013.

Hewitt, Nancy A., ed. *No Permanent Waves: Recasting Histories of U.S. Feminism*. New Brunswick, NJ: Rutgers University Press, 2010.

Higginbotham, Evelyn Brooks. *Righteous Discontent: The Women's Movement in the Black Baptist Church, 1880–1920*. Cambridge, MA: Harvard University Press, 1993.

Hine, Darlene Clark. "Rape and the Inner Lives of Black Women in the Midwest: Reflections on a Culture of Dissemblance." In *Words of Fire: Anthology of African American Feminist Thought*, edited by Beverly Guy Sheftall, 380–89. New York: The New Press, 1992.

History Makers. "The Honorable Monica Stewart." Accessed August 7, 2024. https://www.thehistorymakers.org/biography/honorable-monica-stewart.

Hole, Judith, and Ellen Levine, eds. *Rebirth of Feminism*. New York: Quandrangle Books, 1971.

hooks, bell. *Ain't I a Woman? Black Women and Feminism*. Boston: South End Press, 1981.

Huggins, Ericka, and Angela D. LeBlanc-Ernest. "Revolutionary Women, Revolutionary Education: The Black Panther Party's Oakland Community School." In *Want to Start a Revolution?*, edited by Dayo F. Gore, Jeanne Theoharis, and Komozi Woodard, 161–84. New York: New York University Press, 2020.

Hunt, Lynn. *Inventing Human Rights: A History*. New York: Norton, 2007.

Iacovetta, Franca, Katrina Srigley, and Stacey Zembrzycki. "Introduction." In *Beyond Women's Words: Feminism and the Practices of Oral History in the Twenty-First Century*, edited by Katrina Srigley, Stacey Zembrzycki, and Franca Iacovetta, 1–24. New York: Routledge, 2018.

"International Civil Rights Walk of Fame: Addie L Wyatt." Nps.gov, Martin Luther King National Historical Site. Accessed August 7, 2024. http://www.nps.gov/features/malu/feat0002/wof/Addie_Wyatt.htm.

Jackson, Barbara Williams. "The Interrelatedness of Black Self-Concept, Consciousness-Raising, and Black Education." PhD dissertation. Syracuse University, 1975. Microfilm on file at Schomburg Center for Research in Black Culture, New York Public Library.

Jackson, Nicole M. "The Politics of Care: Black Community Activism in England and the United States, 1975–1985." PhD dissertation. Ohio State University, 2012.

Jacubowski-Spector, Patricia. "Facilitating the Growth of Women through Assertiveness Training." *The Counseling Psychologist* 4 (1973).

Jacubowski-Spector, Patricia, et al. *Assertive Training for Women: A Stimulus Film*. Washington, DC: American Personnel and Guidance Association, 1974.

James, Stanlie M., Frances Smith Foster, and Beverly Guy-Sheftall. *Still Brave: The Evolution of Black Women's Studies*. New York: Feminist Press, 2009.

Jeffries, Judson L., ed. *The Black Panther Party in a City Near You*. Athens: University of Georgia Press, 2018.

Johnston, Jill. *Lesbian Nation: The Feminist Solution*. New York: Simon and Schuster, 1973.

Jones, Alethia, Virginia Eubanks, and Barbara Smith, eds. *Ain't Gonna Let Nobody Turn Me Around: Forty Years of Movement Building with Barbara Smith*. Albany: State University of New York Press, 2014.

Kaba, Mariame, and Essence McDowell. *Lifting as They Climbed: Mapping a History of Black Women on Chicago's South Side. A Self-Guided Tour*. Chicago: Chicago Black Women Tour, 2017.

Kelley, Robin D. G. *Freedom Dreams: The Black Radical Imagination*. Boston: Beacon Press, 2002.

Klein, Ethel. *Gender Politics: From Consciousness to Mass Politics*. Cambridge, MA: Harvard University Press, 1984.

Knupfer, Anne Meis. *The Chicago Black Renaissance and Women's Activism*. Chicago: University of Illinois Press, 2006.

Lapovski-Kennedy, Elizabeth, and Madeline Davis. *Boots of Leather, Slippers of Gold: The History of a Lesbian Community*. New York: Routledge, 1993.

———. "Dreams of Social Justice: Building Women's Studies at the State University of New York at Buffalo." In *The Politics of Women's Studies: Testimonies from Thirty Founding Mothers*, edited by Florence Howe, 242–63. New York: The Feminist Press, 2000.

LeBlanc-Ernest, Angela D. "'The Most Qualified Person to Handle the Job': Black Panther Party Women, 1966–1982." In *The Black Panther Party Reconsidered*, edited by Charles E. Jones, 305–34. Baltimore: Black Classic Press, 1998.

Liberation Now! Writings from the Women's Liberation Movement. New York: Dell Publishing, 1971.

Lichtheim, George. Review of *Socialist Humanism: An International Symposium*, edited by Erich Fromm. *The New York Review of Books* 5 (Sept. 16, 1965): 14.

Lorde, Audre. "The Great American Disease." *The Black Scholar* 10, no. 8–9 (May 1979).

Lovett, Laura L., Rachel Jessica Daniel, and Kelly N. Giles, eds. *It's Our Movement Now: Black Women's Politics and the 1977 National Women's Conference*. 1st ed. Gainesville: University Press of Florida: 2023.

Mansbridge, Jane J. *Why We Lost the ERA*. Chicago: University of Chicago Press, 1986.

Matthews, Tracye. "'No One Ever Asks What a Man's Role in the Revolution Is': Gender and the Politics of the Black Panther Party, 1966–1971." In *The Black Panther Party Reconsidered*, edited by Charles E. Jones, 267–304. Baltimore: Black Classic Press, 1998.

Mattingly, Doreen J., and Jessica L Nare. "'A Rainbow of Women': Diversity and Unity at the 1977 U. S. International Women's Year Conference." *Journal of Women's History* 26, no. 2 (2014): 88–112.

McDuffie, Erik S. "Chicago, Garveyism, and the History of the Diasporic Midwest." *African and Black Diaspora: An International Journal* 8, no. 2: 129–45. https://doi.org/10.1080/17528631.2015.1027332.

McGuire, Danielle L. *At the Dark End of the Street: Black Women, Rape, and*

Resistance—A New History of the Civil Rights Movement from Rosa Parks to the Rise of Black Power. New York: Alfred A. Knopf, 2011.

McKittrick, Katherine. *Demonic Grounds: Black Women and the Cartographies of Struggle*. Minneapolis: University of Minnesota Press, 2006.

Melancon, Trimiko. *Unbought and Unbossed: Black Women, Sexuality, and Representation*. Philadelphia: Temple University Press, 2014.

Millett, Kate. *Sexual Politics*. New York: Ballantine Books, 1970.

Moore, Natalie Y. *The South Side: A Portrait of Chicago and American Segregation*. New York: St. Martin's Press, 2016.

Moraga, Cherrie, and Gloria Anzaldúa. *This Bridge Called My Back: Writings by Radical Women of Color*. New York: Kitchen Table Press, 1981.

Morgan, Robin. *Going Too Far: The Personal Documents of a Feminist*. 1st ed. New York: Random House, 1977.

———, ed. *Sisterhood Is Powerful: An Anthology of Writings from the Women's Liberation Movement*. New York: Vintage, 1970.

Morris, James McGrath. *Eye on the Struggle: Ethel Payne, the First Lady of the Black Press*. New York: Harper Collins, 2015.

Morrison, Toni. "What the Black Woman Thinks about Women's Lib." *New York Times Magazine*, Aug. 22, 1971.

Moten, Crystal M. *Continually Working: Black Women, Community Intellectualism, and Economic Justice in Postwar Milwaukee*. Washington, D.C.: Smithsonian National Museum of American History, 2023.

Mujeres Latinas en Acción: Empowering Latinas and Their Families. "Mujeres Latinas en Acción: ¿Quiénes Somos? (Who We Are)." Accessed October 15, 2024. https://mujereslatinasenaccion.org/whowearequiensomos/.

Murch, Donna Jean. *Living for the City: Migration, Education, and the Rise of the Black Panther Party in Oakland, California*. Chapel Hill: University of North Carolina Press, 2010.

———. "Toward a Black Working-Class History of the Long 1980s." *The Journal of African American History* 108, no. 3 (2023): 425–46. https://doi.org/10.1086/725887.

Murphy, Michelle. *Seizing the Means of Reproduction: Entanglements of Feminism, Health, and Technoscience*. Durham, NC: Duke University Press, 2012.

Nachescu, Ileana. "Censoring Anglogynophobia: Reconsidering the Disappearance of the National Alliance of Black Feminists." *Feminist Studies* 47, no. 1 (2021): 201–29. https://doi.org/10.15767/feministstudies.47.1.0201.

———. "Intersectional Consciousness Raising, Black Women Political Intellectuals, and the National Alliance of Black Feminists." In *"Lifting as We Climb": Black Women Intellectuals in Modern U.S. History*, edited by Hettie V. Williams, 205–25. Santa Barbara, CA: Praeger, 2017.

———. "'The Kind of World We Wanted to Be In': Protocol Feminism and Participatory Democracy in Intersectional Consciousness-Raising Groups." In *Feeling Democracy: Emotional Politics in the New Millennium*, edited by Sarah Tobias and Arlene Stein. New Brunswick, NJ: Rutgers University Press, 2024.

Nachescu, Voichita [Ileana]. "Unclassifiable Outsiders: Transnational Whiteness, Eastern European Women, and the American Academe." In *Narratives of Marginalized Identities in Higher Education*, edited by Santosh Khadka, Joanna C. Davis-McElligatt, and Keith Dorwick, 189–200. New York: Routledge, 2018.

The National Organization for Women. "Statement of Purpose." Accessed August 12, 2024. https://now.org/about/history/statement-of-purpose.

Nelson, Janie. "Attitude-Behavior Consistency among Black Feminist and Traditional Black Women." PhD dissertation. Kent State University, 1981.

Nelson, Jennifer. *Women of Color and the Reproductive Rights Movement*. New York: New York University Press, 2003.

Ogbar, Jeffrey O. G. *Black Power: Radical Politics and African American Identity*. Updated edition. Baltimore: Johns Hopkins University Press, 2019.

Ogden, Jeffrey O. G. "Rainbow Radicalism: The Rise of Radical Ethnic Nationalism." In *The Black Power Movement: Rethinking the Civil Rights Black Power Era*, edited by Peniel E. Joseph, 193–228. New York: Routledge, 2006.

Osborne, Susan M., and Gloria G. Harris. *Assertive Training for Women*. Springfield, IL: Charles C. Thomas, 1975.

Peslikis, Irene. "Consciousness-Raising: A Dead End?" In *Radical Feminism*, edited by Anne Koedt, Ellen Levine, and Anita Rapone, 282–84. New York: Quadrangle/The New York Times Book Company, 1973.

Phelps, Stanlee, and Nancy Austin. *The Assertive Woman*. San Luis Obispo, CA: Impact Publishers, 1975.

Phillips, Mary. "The Power of the First-Person Narrative: Ericka Huggins and the Black Panther Party." *Women's Studies Quarterly* 43, no. 3–4 (2015): 33–51. https://doi.org/10.1353/wsq.2015.0060.

Piercy, Marge, and Jane Freeman. "Getting Together: How to Start a Consciousness-Raising Group." Cape Cod Women's Liberation Organization, 1972, published online by WMST-L. Accessed August 12, 2024. https://userpages.umbc.edu/~korenman/wmst/crguide2.html.

Pomerleau, Clark A. *Califia Women: Feminist Education against Sexism, Classism, and Racism*. 1st edition. Austin: University of Texas Press, 2014.

Porter, Eric. "Affirming and Disaffirming Actions: Remaking Race in the 1970s." In *America in the Seventies*, edited by Beth Bailey and David Farber, 50–74. Lawrence: University Press of Kansas, 2004.

Porter, Gayle, and Marilyn K. Gaston. *Prime Time: The African American Woman's Complete Guide to Midlife Health and Wellness*. New York: Ballantine Books, 2003.

Prison Culture. "No Selves to Defend No. 5: Cassandra Peten." *Prison Culture: How the PIC Structures Our World*, Jun 19, 2014. http://www.usprisonculture.com/blog/2014/06/19/no-selves-to-defend-5-cassandra-peten.

Quest. *Building Feminist Theory—Essays from* Quest: A Feminist Quarterly. New York: Longman, Inc., 1981.

Rabaka, Reiland. *Black Women's Liberation Movement Music*. New York: Routledge, 2024.

——. *The Negritude Movement: W. E. B. Du Bois, Leon Damas, Aime Cesaire, Leopold Senghor, Frantz Fanon, and the Evolution of an Insurgent Idea*. Lanham, MD: Lexington Books, 2015.

Rainwater, Lee, and William L. Yancey. *The Moynihan Report and the Politics of Controversy*. Cambridge, MA: M.I.T. Press, 1967.

Ramirez, Leonard G. *Chicanas of 18th Street: Narratives of a Movement from Latino Chicago*. Chicago: University of Illinois Press, 2011.

Randolph, Sherie M. *Florynce "Flo" Kennedy: The Life of a Black Feminist Radical*. Chapel Hill: University of North Carolina Press, 2003.

Reagon, Bernice Johnson. "Coalition Politics: Turning the Century." In *Home Girls: A Black Feminist Anthology*, edited by Barbara Smith, 356–68. New York: Kitchen Table—Women of Color Press, 1983.

Reed, Christopher Robert. *The Chicago NAACP and the Rise of Black Professional Leadership, 1910–1966*. Bloomington: Indiana University Press, 1997.

"Reverend Willie T. Barrow." The History Makers. Accessed August 12, 2024. https://www.thehistorymakers.org/biography/reverend-willie-t-barrow.

Rice, Jon. "The World of the Illinois Panthers." In *Freedom North: Black Freedom Struggles Outside the South, 1940–1980*, 41–64. New York: Palgrave Macmillan US, 2003.

Rich, Adrienne. "Compulsory Heterosexuality and Lesbian Existence." *Signs: Journal of Women in Culture and Society* 5, no. 4 (1980): 631–60. https://doi.org/10.1086/493756.

Rickford, Russell John. *We Are an African People: Independent Education, Black Power, and the Radical Imagination*. New York: Oxford University Press, 2016.

Rocksborough-Smith, Ian. "Margaret T. G. Burroughs and Black Public History in Cold War Chicago." *The Black Scholar* 41, no. 3 (2011): 26–42.

Romney, Patricia. *We Were There: The Third World Women's Alliance and the Second Wave*. New York: The Feminist Press, 2021.

Rose, Tricia. *Longing to Tell: Black Women Talk about Sexuality and Intimacy*. New York: Picador, 2003.

Rosen, Ruth. *The World Split Open: How the Women's Movement Changed America*. New York: Penguin, 2000.

Roth, Benita. *Separate Roads to Feminism: Black, Chicana, and White Feminist Movements in America's Second Wave*. Cambridge: Cambridge University Press, 2003.

Rupp, Leila J., and Verta A. Taylor. *Survival in the Doldrums: The American Women's Rights Movement, 1945 to the 1960s*. New York: Oxford University Press, 1987.

Russell, Thaddeus. "The Color of Discipline: Civil Rights and Black Sexuality." *American Quarterly* 60, no. 1 (2008): 101–28. https://doi.org/10.1353/aq.2008.0000.

Ryan, Barbara. *Feminism and the Women's Movement: Dynamics of Change in Social Movement Ideology and Activism*. 1st ed. London: Routledge, 1992.

Sadowski-Smith, Claudia. *The New Neoliberal Whiteness: Race, Neoliberalism, and the Post-Soviet Migration to the United States*. New York: New York University Press, 2018.

Schlafly, Phyllis. "What's Wrong with 'Equal Rights' for Women? 1972." Iowa State University Archives of Women's Political Communication. Reprinted from *Phyllis Schlafly Report* 5, no. 7 (Feb. 1972). Accessed August 12, 2024. https://awpc.cattcenter.iastate.edu/2016/02/02/whats-wrong-with-equal-rights-for-women-1972.

Schultz, Rima Lunin, and Adele Hast, eds. *Women Building Chicago 1790–1990. A Biographical Dictionary*. Bloomington: Indiana University Press, 2001.

Senghor, Léopold Segar. "L'humanisme noir." *L'etudiant Martiniquais* 1 (March 1935).

Senghor, Léopold. "Socialism Is a Humanism." In *Socialist Humanism: An International Symposium*, edited by Erich Fromm, 53–64. New York: Anchor Books, 1966.

"Sharon Wells: October 24, 1943–July 23, 2013." Doty Nash Funeral Home. Accessed August 12, 2024. http://www.dotynashfuneralhome.com/obituaries/Sharon-Wells/#!/Obituary.

Shelby, Tommie. "Two Conceptions of Black Nationalism: Martin Delany on the Meaning of Black Political Solidarity." *Political Theory* 31, no. 5 (October 2003): 664–92.

Shircliffe, Barbara. "The History of a Student-Run Women's Studies Program, 1971–1985." PhD dissertation. State University at Buffalo, 1996.

Simmons, Margaret. "Racism and Feminism: A Schism in the Sisterhood." *Feminist Studies* 5, no. 2 (Summer 1979): 384–401.

Sinclair, Barbara. *The Women's Movement: Political, Socioeconomic, and Psychological Issues*. New York: Harper & Row, 1979.

Smith, Barbara. "A Press of Our Own Kitchen Table: Women of Color Press." In *Frontiers: A Journal of Women's Studies* 10, no. 3 (1989): 11–13.

——. *Ain't Gonna Let Nobody Turn Me Around*. Albany: State University of New York Press, 2014.

Smith, Barbara, et al. *Home Girls: A Black Feminist Anthology*. New York: Kitchen Table Press, 1982.

Smith, Manuel J. *When I Say No, I Feel Guilty*. New York: Dial Press, 1975.

Socialist Workers Party, "A Transitional Program for Black Liberation." In *Black Separatism and Social Reality: Rhetoric and Reason*, edited by Raymond Hall, 101–9. New York: Pergamon Press, 1977.

Spelman, Elizabeth V. "Theories of Race & Gender/The Erasure of Black Women." *Quest (Washington)* 5, no. 4 (1982): 36–40.

Spencer, Robyn C. *The Revolution Has Come: Black Power, Gender, and the Black Panther Party in Oakland*. Durham, NC: Duke University Press, 2016.

Springer, Kimberly. "Black Feminists Respond to Black Power Masculinism." In *The Black Power Movement: Rethinking the Civil Rights Black Power Era*, edited by Peniel E. Joseph, 105–18. New York: Routledge, 2006.

——. "*Good Times* for Florida and Black Feminism." *Cercles* 8 (2003): 122–35.

———. *Living for the Revolution: Black Feminist Organizations, 1968–1980*. Durham, NC: Duke University Press, 2005.

Squires, Catherine. "Rethinking the Black Public Sphere: An Alternative Vocabulary for Multiple Public Spheres." *Communication Theory* 12, no. 4 (November 2002): 446–68.

Squires, Gregory D. *Capital and Communities in Black and White: The Intersection of Race, Class, and Uneven Development*. Albany: State University of New York Press, 1994.

Stewart-Winter, Timothy. *Queer Clout: Chicago and the Rise of Gay Politics*. Philadelphia: University of Pennsylvania Press, 2016.

Stryker, Susan. *Transgender History: The Roots of Today's Revolution*. New York: Seal Press, 2017.

Swaby, Nydia A. "'Disparate in Voice, Sympathetic in Direction': Gendered Political Blackness and the Politics of Solidarity." *Feminist Review* 108, no. 1 (2014): 11–25. https://doi.org/10.1057/fr.2014.30.

Taylor, Keeanga-Yamahtta. *From #BlackLivesMatter to Black Liberation*. Chicago: Haymarket Books, 2016.

Taylor, Liza. *Feminism in Coalition: Thinking with US Women of Color Feminism*. 1st edition. Durham, NC: Duke University Press, 2022.

Taylor, Ula Yvette. *The Promise of Patriarchy: Women and the Nation of Islam*. Chapel Hill: University of North Carolina Press, 2017.

———. *The Veiled Garvey: The Life & Times of Amy Jacques Garvey*. Chapel Hill: University of North Carolina Press, 2002.

Theoharis, Jeanne, and Komozi Woodard. *Freedom North: Black Freedom Struggles Outside the South, 1940–1980*. 1st ed. New York: Palgrave Macmillan, 2003.

"Thomas N. Todd." The History Makers. Accessed August 13, 2024. https://www.thehistorymakers.org/biography/thomas-n-todd-39.

Thompson, Becky. "Multiracial Feminism: Recasting the Chronology of Second Wave Feminism." *Feminist Studies* 28, no. 2 (2002): 337–60. https://doi.org/10.2307/3178747.

Thomson, Lisa B. *Beyond the Black Lady: Sexuality and the New African American Middle Class*. University of Illinois Press, 2009.

Thomson, Mary Lou. "Feminism—Growth and Challenge." In *Voices of the New Feminism*, edited by Mary Lou Thomson, 219–234. Boston: Beacon Press, 1975.

———, ed. *Voices of the New Feminism*. 2nd ed. Boston: Beacon Press, 1975.

Thorne, Barrie. "Review of Building Feminist Theory. Essays from *Quest: A Feminist Quarterly*." *Signs* 7, no. 3 (Spring 1982): 710.

Tong, Rosemary. *Feminist Thought: A More Comprehensive Introduction*. Boulder, CO: Vest View Press, 2014.

Townsend-Bell, Erica. "Writing the Way to Feminism." *Signs* 38, no. 1 (Autumn 2012): 127–52.

Treuer, David. *The Heartbeat of Wounded Knee: Native America from 1890 to the Present*. New York: Riverhead Books, 2019.

U.S. Department of State, The President's Interagency Council on Women. "National Plan for Action: Texas 1977." Accessed October 15, 2024. https://1997-2001.state.gov/picw/archives/npa.html.

Valk, Anne M. *Radical Sisters: Second-Wave Feminism and Black Liberation in Washington, D.C.* Urbana: University of Illinois Press, 2008.

Wallace, Phyllis A. *Black Women in the Labor Force*. Cambridge, MA: M.I.T. Press, 1980.

Ward, Stephen M. "The Third World Women's Alliance: Black Feminist Radicalism and Black Power Politics." In *The Black Power Movement: Rethinking the Civil Rights-Black Power Era*, edited by Peniel E. Joseph, 131–66. New York: Routledge, 2006.

Ware, Cellestine. *Woman Power: The Movement for Women's Liberation*. New York: Tower Publications, 1970.

West, E. James. "'I See Enough Queers Walking the Streets in This City': Homosexuality and Sexual Geographies in Black Consumer Magazines during the 1970s." *Souls* 18, no. 2–4 (April–December 2016): 283–301.

White, Deborah Gray. *Too Heavy a Load: Black Women in Defense of Themselves, 1894–1994*. 1st ed. New York: W. W. Norton, 1999.

White, E. Frances. "Africa on My Mind: Gender, Counter Discourse, and African American Nationalism." *Journal of Women's History* 2, no. 1 (Spring 1990): 73–97.

Williams, Jakobi. *From the Bullet to the Ballot: The Illinois Chapter of the Black Panther Party and Racial Coalition Politics in Chicago*. Chapel Hill: University of North Carolina Press, 2013.

Wilson, Tiana U. "The Making of *Triple Jeopardy*." *WSQ: Women's Studies Quarterly* 51, no. 1–2 (Spring/Summer 2023): 201–7. https://doi.org/10.1353/wsq.2023.0014.

Winkler, Barbara. "A Comparative History of Four Women's Studies Programs." PhD dissertation. University of Michigan, 1992.

Winslow, Barbara. *Revolutionary Feminists: The Women's Liberation Movement in Seattle*. Durham, NC: Duke University Press, 2023.

Woodard, Komozi. *A Nation within A Nation: Amiri Baraka (LeRoi Jones) and Black Power Politics*. Chapel Hill: University of North Carolina Press, 1999.

Archival Collections

Donna Allegra Papers, Sc MG 792, Schomburg Center for Research in Black Culture, Manuscripts, Archives and Rare Books Division, The New York Public Library, New York, NY.

Chicago Women's History Center, Chicago, IL.

Chicago Women's Liberation Union Collection, Chicago History Museum Research Center, Chicago, IL.

Brenda Eichelberger Papers, 1974–1981. Chicago History Museum Research Center, Chicago, IL. In Explore Chicago Collections, https://explore.chicago

collections.org/marcxml/chicagohistory/31/057cz0n/. (Eichelberger Papers, 1974–1981, Chicago History Museum.)

Brenda Eichelberger / National Alliance of Black Feminists Papers, 1974–1997. Vivian G. Harsh Research Collection of Afro-American History and Literature, Chicago Public Library, Chicago, IL. (Eichelberger NABF Papers, 1974–1997, Harsh Collection.)

Midwest Women's Center Collection, Chicago History Museum Research Center, Chicago, IL.

National Black Feminist Organization Collection, Special Collections and University Archives, University of Illinois at Chicago, Chicago, IL. (NBFO Archives, UIC).

Barbara Omolade Papers, Sarah Lawrence College Archives, Bronxville, NY.

Valley Women's Center Records, Sophia Smith Collection of Women's History, Smith College Libraries, Northampton, MA.

Women's Studies College Records 1971–1987, University at Buffalo Archival and Manuscript Collections, Buffalo, NY.

Rev. Addie and Rev. Claude Wyatt Papers, Vivian G. Harsh Research Collection of Afro-American History and Literature, Chicago Public Library, Chicago, IL.

Oral History Interviews

Baker, Barbara. Oral history interview by author, Chicago, IL, July 1, 2015.

Eichelberger, Brenda. Oral history interview by author, September 4, 2011, Silver Spring, MD.

——. Follow-up conversation, August 31, 2013, Silver Spring, MD.

——. Follow-up phone conversation, March 19, 2015.

Fitzpatrick, Beryl. Oral history interview by author, phone conversation, February 28, 2016.

——. Oral history interview by author, Gary, IN, June 21, 2019.

Lofton, C. A. Interview by author, January 14, 2016, Chicago, IL.

——. Follow-up conversation, June 16, 2019, Chicago, IL.

——. Follow-up conversation, April 2022, Chicago, IL.

——. Follow up-phone interview, July 30, 2023.

Love (formerly Bennett), Laverne. Oral history interview by author, phone conversation, July 1, 2015.

Nelson, Janie. Oral history interview by author, Chicago, IL, April 12, 2013.

——. Follow-up conversation, July 1, Chicago, IL, 2015.

——. Follow-up phone interview by author, June 11, 2019.

Porter, Gayle. Oral history interview by author, phone conversation, September 5, 2013.

Washington, Elnora. Interview by author, Gary, IN, June 29, 2015.

Whigham, Helen. Oral history interview by author, phone conversation, September 21, 2015.

——. Follow-up phone conversation by author, January 7, 2024.

Index

ILEANA NACHESCU is an assistant teaching professor in the Department of Women's, Gender, and Sexuality Studies at Rutgers University.

The University of Illinois Press
is a founding member of the
Association of University Presses.

Composed in 10.5/13 Mercury Text
with Avenir display
by Jim Proefrock
at the University of Illinois Press
Manufactured by Versa Press, Inc.

University of Illinois Press
1325 South Oak Street
Champaign, IL 61820-6903
www.press.uillinois.edu